D1483173

HISTORY OF ART

MODERN ART

JOSEPH BERNARD.   Pomona.

Elie Faure
HISTORY OF ART

MODERN
ART

TRANSLATED FROM THE FRENCH BY WALTER PACH

De Luxe Edition

Garden City Publishing Co., Inc.
GARDEN CITY   NEW YORK

1937
Garden City Publishing Co., Inc.

HISTORY OF ART—
MODERN ART

Printed in the U. S. A.

TO
RENOIR

TABLE OF CONTENTS

Rubens. The Landing of Marie de Medici, detail (*Louvre*).

INTRODUCTION

Margaritas ante porcos

THE French Revolution is the last step in the movement inaugurated by the Renaissance. It is marked by the reformation of social metaphysics and of morality, but in the depths of instinct it is destined, without doubt, to define the individual. It is the violent act which overcomes the last resistance offered by the monarchical system to the investigation which, five centuries earlier, had been outlined by the masons of the French commune and definitely begun by the artists of Italy. The corporations being broken up, the right of association being impaired, and the theoretical equality of social rights and of taxation being won, the social analysis is effected. The philosophic analysis of Kant, which carried to its logical conclusion the effort of Descartes,

of Spinoza, of Bayle, of Montesquieu, of Leibnitz, of
the English sensualists, of Voltaire, of Diderot, and of
Rousseau, as well as the psychological tragedy lived
through by Montaigne, by Cervantes, by Shakespeare,
and by Pascal—all made it necessary. Scientific
analysis will follow in due course, for there is no longer
any political obstacle between the intelligence and the
experience in which, for a century, man will pursue the
absolute. If it leads him only to the relative, the
reason is, perhaps, that he is too eager or that he was
seeking this relative in order to regain mysticism by
liberating his intuition. But no matter. The pos-
sibility of bringing about a new selection, through
social investigation among men and by scientific investigation among facts and ideas, justifies the Revolution.

Men combat it in our own day, in the name of the
aristocratic and religious values which made twenty
centuries of history. Exhausted by their own strength,
these values had turned to dust. The Revolution had
only to breathe upon them. Its errors, its puerilities,
its insufficiencies, its blind hatred for that which it
had to pull down, do not lessen its importance. In
France and outside of France, the individual, unleashed
by it into the full liberty of sensation and research, has
almost risen above his physical surroundings and,
rebounding with all his might into the unexplored
domain of intellectual pride, has given to posterity the
poem of that pride. From Carlyle to Ibsen, from
Stendhal to Emerson, from Schopenhauer to Nietzsche,
a new race of prophets has appeared, summoning men
to follow them or perish. Thus the Revolution, which
had torn men from the old social pantheism already
shaken by the Renaissance, was preparing new rhythms.
For a century everything issues from the Revolution,
even German realism, much nearer, perhaps, to the

forces liberated by the upheaval than are many of the
inorganic doctrines which thrive with difficulty on
the hastily created words which sustain its activity.
The poems of individualism will remake the social
world. When the individual is so strong that he tends
to absorb everything, it is time for him to be absorbed
himself and to merge himself and disappear in the
multitude and the universe.

French painting, for a hundred years, has accomplished the same task. It is still misunderstood,
especially by the French. It is one of the miracles of
history, comparable to the most surprising. It has
produced ten men of genius, more than the great
century of Holland, or of Flanders, or of Spain, as
many as the great centuries of Italy. It appeared
precisely on the morrow of the spread of revolution
over Europe, offering to souls waiting in silence the
power of liberation which the march of the republican
armies brought to the legitimate appetites of the
peoples and to the ideas of their shepherds. It is
thanks to that march that it appeared in France and
not in some other place, as it was thanks to the
struggle of Germany to regain possession of herself from
Napoleon, that the great German music, through
Richard Wagner, closed its heroic cycle. The explosion
of sentiment, so long deferred, employs color as its
expression. Conquered Europe and the Orient, faintly
in view, tumultuously enter the sensuous emotion of
the French. The Romantic dream and classical
realism clash and mingle in France, where Italy and
Germany meet for the third time. And it is here that
the Renaissance of the south and the Renaissance of
the north confront each other to affirm a definitive
accord.

This accord, which French painting consecrates (it
is the eternal destiny of France to balance, in divine

measure, the diffused life of the north and the intelligence of the south) was realized for an hour by Rubens. Through him, the mind of Michael Angelo was linked with the humanity of Rembrandt to define the mission of Europe in its profoundest unity, through the most instinctive, the most spontaneous, the most animalistic, but also the most permanent, work in painting—indifferent to everything except object and movement. Under pain of death the north of Europe had to accept the assimilation of Mediterranean thought, just as Mediterranean thought, in order to survive itself, had to load its arabesque with the tide of direct sensations, of music, of revery, and of mystery brought by the soul of the north. We live by our original innocence; but when movements of ideas are born around us and encircle us little by little, like great waters around an island, if our innocence refuses to extract from them the nourishment which will renew it, a frightful aridity succeeds the bursting forth of fruits which rendered it so savory. That which kills is not learning: it is the failure to feel what one learns. Innocence is immortal to him who is ever seeking. It is reborn of its ashes, and the new presentiment appears only when experience and study have destroyed or confirmed the older presentiment. The north and the south, since the invasions of the barbarians, had influenced each other reciprocally and unceasingly, but never, until Rubens, had the spirit of intellectual prophecy introduced its continuing line into the indistinct torrent of colors and matter in order to force upon the image of the world, through the power of a single man, the form, one and living, of the European mind. It was the decisive step after the mission of Montaigne, the formidable wedding of lyricism and the will recreating an imaginary world upon the ruins of Christian metaphysics which had been undermined by the French pessimist. The theological universe may crumble everywhere. In the soul of the great European, from Montaigne to Schopenhauer, cradled on the moving wave of symphonic painting, uplifted on the great wings of the orchestral poem, supported by the sublime hypothesis of gravitation and transformism, a new myth is reforming itself for the man of the future. Living in the bosom of a world which, very probably, has no other purpose than to interchange uninterruptedly, increasingly, and daily the more complex of the heedless forms of energy and love, the man of the future will not know any other paradise in heaven or on earth than that of overcoming the need to increase and to harmonize his energy and his love within himself. That, at least, is the obscure desire which the heroes of European pessimism have for three hundred years been expressing, unknown to themselves, I admit, in their philosophy, their art, and their science. The modern Prometheus, Don Quixote, believes in the sacredness of his mission. But Cervantes loves this madman far less for the phantoms he pursues in his generosity and his courage, than for the divine power of his illusion.

Why did this movement, which was born in the south, expand in the regions of the north? Italy, through the Venetians, had written the prelude of the great symphonic poem which the north was to carry into the flesh and the bone of Europe through Rubens and Sebastian Bach, which was to be established in its intelligence through Spinoza and Leibnitz, which was to stir its heart through Rembrandt and Beethoven, to extend it into space and time through Newton and Lamarck, to render it subtle by the passionate exchange of souls and sensations through Dostoievsky and the Russian musicians, and finally to be diffused in the will of the élite through the German pessimists and in their sensibility through the French painters—they and others uplifted with lyric intoxication, but supported in their intellectual power by the two centuries of discipline and of method which separate Descartes from Kant.

Only, this effort had exhausted Italy, which, into the bargain, was torn by France and the Empire. Moreover, the discovery of America transported from the southern seas to the ocean the center of gravity of the globe. Finally, the Reformation, wrenching the peoples of the north from the spiritual domination of the Church and from the political tyranny of Spain, had permitted them to explore their own mystery. In fact, there is only one man more in the south, Velasquez, who is a miracle, and in whom one may see, by turns and with equally valid reasons, a mere virtuoso —the greatest of all, it is true—and the rarest mind in painting, the king of silence and of the air. But with the exception of Spain, escaping for another half century the decline of the south on account of her being the first to open the route to the west, the whole life of Europe is concentrated in England, in Flanders, in Holland, or is maintained in France, which is condemned to a kind of spiritual immortality because of her being at the center of all the sea routes and all the ethnic sources which have fashioned the Occident, Italy, Spain, England, Germany, and the Low Countries. When Rubens borrows from Raphael his decisive arabesque, the world feels clearly that its curves will ramble and its lines will be spread out to infinite thinness in the void of abstraction unless there should be supplied to that arabesque, in order to render it fruitful, the cloudy sky of the north, its fat lands, its powerful vegetation, the liquid and changing splendor of its light, the heavy food of its men in whose blood rolled together the juice of meats, revery, beer, the desire for women, moral strength, and mist.

Thus, the powerful man seizes upon the elements of the symphony of the people interrupted by the Renaissance, and raises them slowly from his senses to his brain and fuses them once more in his heart in order, sooner or later, to prepare in the multitudes new reasons for action. In the intelligence of the god, there are no longer isolated forms. The whole poem is in the interpenetration of all the forms of the world, which painting, more than all other languages, expresses with so much force and evidence and in which it precedes, by a long period, the constructions of the biologists and the mathematicians. In each new organism, which a great lyric work is, we shall find henceforth more sensual wealth and more intellectual wealth, and therefore, when the poet dies, more elements given back to life in general, more anguish, more desire, more mystery, more tragic individuals, and more of complex evolution. In the measure that the chorus breaks up into fragments and sinks lower in the multitudes, and swells and mounts in the hero, the solitude of the hero is increased by the indifference or the hostility of the multitudes. But the occult influence of this solitude widens. In the Middle Ages the artist was a workman, lost in the crowd of workmen, loving with the same love as theirs. Later on, under the Renaissance, he was an aristocrat of the mind, moving almost on a par with the aristocrat of birth, later on again, a skilled laborer seized upon by the victorious autocracy; and still later, when the autocracy finally crushes the aristocracy under its own ruins, when workman is separated from workman by the death of the corporations, the artist is lost in the crowd, which is ignorant of his presence or which misunderstands him.

Who shall tell the martyrdom of him who keeps love alive within him and whom love flees or repulses?

There is, with democracy, only one aristocrat, the
artist. That is why it hates him. That is why it
pays divine honors to the slave who is part of it, he
who no longer knows his work, who no longer loves,
who knows the art of complete repose proper to the
cultivated classes, and consents to reign over the other
slaves, a prize-list in his hand. Even when illustrious,
even when hated, even when dragged through the
sieve by the mob of the *salons*, the collectors, and the
critics, even when forcibly introduced into the prison
galleys of the Academies and the Schools, the artist
is alone. David detests the School, the School makes
of him its god. For the bleating herd of David's
pupils, Delacroix, celebrated when twenty years old, is
a wolf. Ingres, who despises Rome and the Institute,
directs the School of Rome and presides over the
Institute. Men oppose the two masters to each other
in the name of theories and systems which both detest.
Baudelaire, Daumier, and Flaubert are dragged before
the magistrates. Daumier, by the way, in whom are
fused the flame of Rembrandt and the force of Michael
Angelo, is only a hired merrymaker. Manet is the
enemy of the people. Zola is driven from the public
journals for defending him. The Impressionists are
hooted because they do not know how to draw;
later on, their drawing is vaunted in order that their
successors may be reviled. The men who pick up a
poor living from the crumbs that fall from their table
declare them incomplete. Men laugh at the construction of Cézanne, who rediscovers construction. Men
mock the color and the bloatedness of Renoir, who
brings back solidity of volume and lyricism of color.
Do they not stand as much alone as Rembrandt dying
of poverty, or Velasquez the valet of the court, or
Watteau, who was picked up consumptive by a charit-
able friend? O painting! sublime art, the highest,

the most subtle, the most sensual, but at the same
time the most intellectual of all, ode, dance, and
music transposed into the objective world, as far from
a common soul as transcendental algebra is from a
primary education; the reader of newspaper novels,
the champion at dominoes, the officeholder, the
chamberlain, and the voter judge you! They give you
prizes, like a fattened ox. O pearl, in which there is
the play of the whole sea and the immense dramatic
sky, and the eternal tragedy of movement and of
color, and the proudest and most mysterious tremors
of the soul, the swine decide your fate! It is well.
Your solitude is so well peopled. You know it. There
is not in the world a sound, a tone, a gesture, a form,
a ray, or a shadow which exists alone. All listen to
one another and answer one another, and enter one
into the other by secret passages; and when, from their
correspondences, from their common reflections, from
their unanimous and joyous direction toward an
invisible focus, harmony is born, it transmits all that
is universal to the solitary man.

A century tending entirely toward scientific research
contributed not a little to the bringing about of a
growing misunderstanding between this solitary man
and the mass, which was more and more incapable of
feeling the language of form. The scientist evicted
the artist, a little more each day, from the place which,
since the Renaissance, he had occupied in the respect
of the men of his time. And men are much more attentive to the humanitarian or practical results obtained
by the seekers than they are to the intrinsic quality
of their work. They erect altars to the latest inventor
of a vaccine or of a stove; they are ignorant of him
who comes to change the equilibrium of souls for a
century or for a thousand years. It is so ordered,
and the myth of Hercules is far better known to the

crowd than the myth of Prometheus. Also, it is
ordered that the crowd shall prefer those who bear
only the stamp of Hercules to the less accessible demi-
urges who propose to us the grandest hypotheses
imagined since the Hindu or Chaldean thinkers, and
who inclose the course of the stars in algebraic formulas or capture life at its sources to conduct it, step
by step, from the primeval clay to the intelligence of
the god. The crowd is ignorant of the fact that these
hypotheses have a formidable power over the practical
direction of science. It is ignorant of the fact that
pure science is only an analytical system destined,
precisely, to verify these hypotheses and to draw
positive results from their activity. It knows even
less that these hypotheses are, fundamentally, of an
æsthetic order, that they yield certitudes to which
pure science does not attain. It does not know that
these hypotheses have this in common with the great
artistic generalizations: that while they bring us the
intoxication of certitude, they are undemonstrable by
experimentation. How then should the crowd understand that, in a way even less known, they also exercise
a magical influence upon the evolution of lyricism,
since the sense of lyricism has been drawing a little
farther away from it every day for five centuries and
has abandoned it completely in the last hundred years?
How should it grasp the fact, for example, that the
realistic art of the end of the last century is only an
echo, almost direct, from scientific materialism; that
Impressionism was born from the necessary encounter
of the most extreme individualism with the most positive conquests of optics, the analysis of the scientists
and the social analysis finally resulting in the separation of man from man as one objective phenomenon is
separated from another? And why should it know this?
Nine times out of ten, the artist himself is ignorant

of it, and that ignorance is of benefit. If he suspects
it, abstraction and system become his guides, and he
ends by confusing the end with the means and dashes
against a wall. The poet is carried to the peak of the
unconscious; he gains consciousness only that he may
better obey the movements of the unknown waves
which cradle him, and that he may widen, through
consciousness itself, the limits of the unconscious. It
is possible that Rembrandt knew Spinoza, even if it
is improbable that he read the *Ethics*, since he did
not know Latin. It is sure that La Tour associated
with Voltaire and read him, that Greuze listened to
Diderot, and that David had read Rousseau. But
it is practically certain that Le Nôtre did not know
the philosophy of Descartes. And as against La Tour,
against Greuze, against David, Le Nôtre was to prove
correct. Thus, without seeking to imitate him, he bore
the greater resemblance to Descartes.

There is no reason why the artist—and perhaps the
most innocent, the least cultivated, especially—should
live outside the currents of instinct which determine
the special direction of the minds of his time. On
the contrary, it would be quite surprising if he did
not consider the universe and destiny from an angle
nearer to the one which guides the thought and the
experiences of the scientists and the philosophers who
are his contemporaries. Solidarity of needs begets
solidarity of ideas and expression. I do not believe
that the scientists themselves, at least in the direction
they give to their research, escape the needs of their
epoch. All our ideas bear the trace of the profound
events which surround us and which touch us, and
the mathematical harmonies themselves, despite their
apparent eternality, are perhaps not much more independent of the moral ground whence they spring than
are the great sensual constructions of the painters or

the musicians. The sensibilities of a given age are all directed toward the same invisible goal; they seize upon the relationships which another age would not seize upon; they erect systems which satisfy the obscurest and the strongest of their desires. It is thus that we should understand the inner, spontaneous, and necessary accord between Phidias and Plato, between Giotto and Dante, between Rembrandt and Spinoza, between Le Nôtre and Descartes, between Auguste Comte and Courbet.

We understand, therefore, how it is that science, acting upon the evolution of men's minds and being influenced by them in return, seems to arrive to-day at conclusions almost antagonistic to those within which certain overeager desires tried to arrest it twenty or thirty years ago. On all sides it is bursting in upon the seemingly exhausted domain of philosophy and of mysticism, and as it penetrates into this domain, it is also acted upon thereby. Intuition is once more in favor, and that was bound to come. What was formerly called Reason—which was, one or two centuries ago, from Descartes to Diderot, an admirable individual instrument for passionate investigation, a kind of living being—had become rationalism, an immobile religion, independent of the senses, emancipated from the heart: a lamp in a sepulcher. Those who little by little created the irreducible antagonism between method and life had not learned to see, on summer evenings after the rain—one of those evenings, green and pure, when colors and forms seem to crystallize in themselves what remains of the daylight—they had not learned to see a bed of geraniums, red as blood, in a geometrical garden whose walls of verdure, carved out by the will, tremble like the surface of water. They do not know the meaning of the Italian arabesque, carrying into life the thunderbolt of its line—which

Rubens, in turn, loaded with all the weight of blood
and matter which it could bear without giving way.
They had never looked at the frieze of the Apsaras
of Angkor, dance and music, sensual movement of
the universe itself subjected to a mathematical rhythm
by a miracle of the mind. They are probably the
same persons who are now seizing upon rehabilitated
intuition to enthrone it in a region outside of the
intelligence, and are thereby condemning it to death.
Man is unable to preserve his equilibrium. He has to
divide himself into halves and project himself now
toward one of the poles of his soul, now toward the
other. He who believes only in science is like an
orchestra musician who imagines that the whole symphony resides in the mechanism of his instrument.
He who believes only in intuition is like an orchestra
musician who imagines that the symphony continues
when all the players break their strings and their bows.
Man cannot admit to himself that intuition is only a
flame spurting forth at the point of contact of an
infinity of previous analyses and of accumulated
reasoning, and that it delivers him from criticism
through the faculty that it has, in action, in art, and
in science, for generalizing and for choosing.

For five centuries, the rôle of the European hero
has consisted precisely in maintaining within himself
the harmony between the intelligence and the heart,
a harmony which will assure to the reasoning individual
access to one of those moments of certitude seized
upon by the people in order to exhaust the climax of
love which, once every thousand years, perhaps, makes
it think and act like a single hero. This is true even
in the France of the eighteenth century, when Diderot
has his presentiment of the monotonous movement
which always goes beyond so-called moral progress,
and which is ceaselessly giving birth to new forces

against which this pretended moral progress is forever struggling, and when Lamarck gathers together in his rational differentiation of the organisms the elements of the biological symphony which he proposes to the future. All the conquests of reason, all its stored-up knowledge, contribute to the nourishing of an instinct. Plato the Sophist stood at the threshold of the innumerable avenues that lead to the new growth of popular genius which was named Christianity. And Plato's point of departure was the popular Hellenic genius arrived at its maturity. Feeling, the point of departure of reason, is also the point at which it arrives; and the gaining possession of consciousness brings us back to fruitful unconsciousness wherein the great peoples, like the great individuals, spontaneously create ideas and images in their mature years with as little effort as they created children in their youth. It is to obey the command of life that reason finally comes, not through cowardice, but through courage, to a new mysticism. It is in vain that pure science advances; it thrusts back the mystery, it does not destroy it. Once the threshold of mystery is crossed, art regains its whole dominion.

The modern world is so complex, so uncertain in its directions, so diverse in its elements, the field of society is so upset, the destinies of Europe have been rendered so precarious by the greatest war in history, such a whirlwind of conflicting interests and ideas sweep it along, that its morrow is obscure. And yet the needs of the European crowd remain what they were. When whole peoples take part in war, which but the day before yesterday was the game and means of the aristocracies, war has more influence upon their common evolution. Is not war itself a phenomenon outside of consciousness, a terrible biological crisis in which the individual disappears, in which there burst forth only those blind powers of collective life destined to destroy or to renew from top to bottom the faculties of energy and of love that take part in them? As the intelligence was outstripped by life, moral consciousness was overflowed by war. In the wind which shakes the vine branches, under the whirling rain of grapes and of flowers, Dionysiac intoxication bounds to the sound of cymbals, laughter, and gasps of love. But the claws of the panthers tear the naked limbs. Death and resurrection turn in the bacchanale. If the European soul is not annihilated, the men of Europe will build.

The nineteenth century, especially in France, is a cathedral dispersed. It must be erected. The non-existence of architecture in the last hundred years is very significant. The reign of the individual brings with it the downfall of the monument. We have seen that very often in history—after Egypt, after legendary Greece, when Japan had emancipated herself from China, and when the Renaissance caused the stained-glass windows to descend from the churches and ground them up on canvas, and when their statues descended to ornament its avenues and gardens. If the reign of the individual ends by his being given back to the multitude because he becomes too densely peopled himself to contain himself, architecture, the work of the anonymous crowds, will be reborn, and painting and sculpture will re-enter the monument. The whole art of to-day, even in its most transitory forms, is obeying an obscure need of subordination to some collective task still unknown; and this need suggests to our art—confused and diverse though it be in appearance—the direction of its lines and the quality of its tones. Whither do we go? Wherever the spirit of life wills it.

MODERN ART

The marvelous envelops us and we breathe it like the atmosphere; but we do not see it.

CHARLES BAUDELAIRE

RODIN

ANTWERP.

Chapter I. FLANDERS

I

HE day when, far from the Flanders
of his ancestors, Rubens was born,
Antwerp was still to be rebuilt. His
resigned and courageous mother had
shared the exile of his slightly mad
father, who had become the lover of the
wife of William of Orange after having been one of the
closest companions of that hero. When Rubens was
ten years of age and his mother, who had become a
widow, brought him to Antwerp, there was still the
threat of fire beneath the ruins of the great port. It had
not forgotten the stake and the gibbet, the statues
torn from the temples, the sea of blood that had been
shed and the livid face of the Duke of Alba in his iron
armor.

Only after two and a half centuries, when liberty was conquered, would Antwerp regain its position in Europe. For the artists, it was no longer the live city which had tried, with Quentin Matsys, to escape from the Gothic spell of Bruges and to enter the modern spirit through individual effort, and which, with Breughel, had succeeded in doing so. It was that very effort, however, which had brought forth the Beggars. Rubens had been conceived in the thick of the storm; within him he bore, together with the wild hope of the people and the energy of its most splendid moment of activity, all of its past conquests. The decadence of Flanders and of Antwerp could affect only those who were to come after him. He was to profit by the brief moment when Spain loosened her grip a little, and to send forth, like a flood, the mass of life that for two centuries had been accumulating in the granaries, the barns, and the ships of the country, and in the hearts and minds of men, through the labor of their fields, their cities, and their ports.

He did better than that. No country was placed more advantageously than Flanders for the gathering together of the currents which for two centuries had been crossing the Occident in all directions. For a hundred years Bruges had served as a bond of union between England, the Baltic, Venice, and the Orient. Antwerp was the first commercial port of the world under Charles V. It drained France by the Meuse and the Scheldt, Germany by the Rhine, and the Indies, Italy, and the lands of Spain by the sea. At the critical hour when the north and the south found themselves face to face in their age-old activities, when the problem of religion was opposing the social idealism of the Latin countries to the economic realism of the Germanic countries, Flanders, the heart of the universal empire of Charles V, was quivering from all the shocks

RUBENS. His wife and children (*Louvre*).

which the arteries of commerce brought upon it by merchandise, books, and soldiers. Struggling both for its independence and in support of the Reformation, it remained a country of the Empire and remained Catholic. It was natural that the man who expressed with an eternal force this unique moment of its life, should infuse southern intellectualism into the substantial, fat, and moving matter of the north.

The painters of Flanders had been trying to accomplish this for a hundred years. But Bruges was no longer sufficiently alive at the beginning of the sixteenth century for her Romanized masters, Jan van Mabuse and van Orley, to be able to assimilate the soul of Italy deeply, without danger. Antwerp, on the contrary, even at the end of that century, had not yet attained a degree of maturity sufficient for the Italian soul to penetrate the original nature of Flanders. The attempt of Quentin Matsys was premature; Martin de Vos, Coninxloo, Francken, and the good portraitist Pourbus were not, as men, big enough; the task of Breughel, a Hollander by birth, who released the spirit of the north from its primitive matrix, was too all-absorbing for him to attempt to find his agreement with the mind of the peninsula. Rubens had scarcely to listen to his two teachers, Otto Venius, with his Italian tendencies, and van Noort, with his Flemish tendencies, to discover in himself the destiny meted out to him by fate; the eight years he passed in Italy in the intimacy of the giant realizations of Tintoretto and of Michael Angelo, his repeated journeys to Spain, to France, and to England, the seven languages that he spoke, his superb manner of life and his two marriages for love permitted him to fulfill this destiny with unparalleled generosity and with royal abundance.

What a life! He was the only hero of humanity, doubtless, to unite the splendors of external life with the splendid images of it which he made. The period, in which the aristocracy had for two hundred years been receiving its education in art and had been charmed by his taste for the sumptuous, had conspired to have him maintain, until the end, his exceptional balance between moral health and sensualism. He was like a king of Flanders; he represented it to the kings.

RUBENS. The Landing of Marie de Medici, detail (*Louvre*).

His great dinners, his receptions, his fortune, his castles, his luxury, and his embassies, none of these could detract from him. Never even does he consent to admit to us that he suffered from his second marriage when, at the age of fifty-three, he married a girl of sixteen. From his very disquietude he drew forth a multiplied force and spread across the future the joy which he could not ask from her and which he could not give her. He ended his triumphal existence by triumphing over the anguish which he could not have failed to feel.

If in this exceptional man one desired to find only the highest expression of the Flemish nature which he unites with universal nature, one would perceive only one aspect of his work, the most accessible, in truth, but not the most essential. One would have to turn to Jordaens, who came fifteen years after him, a pupil of van Noort, as he was, but who, while turning toward him at every moment, was able to live and act with such confidence in his strength that, outside of Rubens, he remains the most robust interpreter of Flemish paganism.

Almost never did the feet of Jordaens leave the soil of Flanders. His eyes almost never pierced beyond the opal space of Antwerp. Almost never did they see anything beyond the going and coming of the ships through the luminous mist on the muddy river, and the products of the sea and of the countryside that were sold in the market place. His canvases heap up masses of living matter. His confusion is a force. A heavy rhythm gives to his blessed orgies an accent of ponderous joy which approaches the general idea, the unconscious symbol. Everything drinks and eats, all the mouths are open, all the nostrils and the eyes and the throats. Dogs, cats, and chickens wander among the gluttons and the gormandizers, snapping, picking, and licking the bones fallen under the table, the sauces that have been spilled, and the beer and wine that have overflowed. Flesh has the thickness of pumpkins that have opened, human fat is in layers like sausages, the skin of the women is as warm as the sides of soup pots, their hands lie on their breasts with the bunches of grapes from the baskets, faces and coppers glisten, and the smacking of lips and the slapping of hands on thighs are rhythmed by the gurgle of the bottles. Men

RUBENS.   BACCHANALE (*Hermitage*).

and women clink their glasses while they sing, and
bang the metal lids of the coffee-pots, and the rumbling
of the stomachs, brought about by the heaps of food,
is accompanied by the squalling of indecent babies, in
the obstinate chorus of the drunkards and the gossips.
Here is nothing but eating, feasting, gluttony, and
lechery, in which an innocent old faun, with a shining
face, a trembling hide, and a flapping belly, takes part.
He has just crossed the threshold of the Flemish
houses, for which he deserts the immense poem of the
fields and the broad nudities of a mythology less
heretical than one thinks: the backs, the bellies
shining in the light, and the robust limbs of the women
who milk the heavy udders of the goats amid the
foliage, the vine branches, and the plowed land.

II

And now, through the most far-reaching lyrical
movement that has ever flowed from a painter, through
a metaphysical feeling about the universe so evident
that it vibrates from one end of his work to the other
like the steady sound of a great river whose voice is the
same though it reflects a hundred skies, though it
bathes a hundred shores, and gives its water to a
hundred cities—Rubens rendered divine that mass of
animalism which Flemish art would have remained for
us if Jordaens alone had lived. He accepted the
domination of the elementary forces as if to get a better
understanding of them, and guided them from within
their very centers of action with the formidable ease of
a being who feels his life to be sustained by them and
who participates in their life. At the moment when the
reorganization of the Churches and the organization of
the great nations, contrasting with the anarchy and the
vitality of the sixteenth century, were demonstrating

the necessity of maintaining political unity in the social body, Rubens, who was very much of his time, who consented to place his genius at the service of monarchical centralization and of the religious Restoration —Rubens was affirming, as the century before had done, the eternal quality in the animal forces and the immortal presence of nature in the hearts of the heroes.

He is the central fire that will fuse, in a fruitful equilibrium, the Renaissance and the modern world. The plastic arabesque had been, with the Italians, the especial instrument for expressing the instinctive need to unite dispersed individual energies and for expressing the desire to establish a general meaning of the structure of the universe. With Rubens the

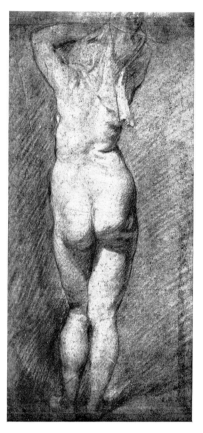

RUBENS. Study, drawing (*Louvre*).

arabesque will find in the roots of instinct itself the inner unity of the world, which the Church and the monarchy are trying to reconstitute from without. It transmits the soul of the philosophers and the artists of the

Renaissance to the eighteenth century, whose painters
will base their work precisely on that work of the
master of Antwerp, and press into the living wave
which the arabesque brings to that work, the naturalism
of Rousseau, the universalism of Diderot, and the
transformism of Buffon and of Lamarck, at the hour
when Harvey is describing the circulation of the blood
in the arteries and when Newton is born to describe
the circulation of the spheres in the heavens. The
arabesque is no longer a merely sensual expression as
with the Venetians; it is no longer satisfied to ask, as
the Greeks did, that the higher forms of a harmonious
imagination express in ideal fashion the passage of
the forces through balanced volumes, which continue one another and reply to one another. It accepts
all the aspects of the world without discussing their
nature. The formidable complexity of the sensations
accumulated by a thousand years of silence, the vast
treasury of forms heaped up by the Middle Ages, and
the enormous mass of matter of the north—all this
was to be given a sudden headlong movement—without discrimination by the arabesque, which turned it
in the direction indicated by the mind of the south.
With Rubens it enters the intimate substance of life
to stir it to its depths. Heavy with flesh, with earth
and air, having the decisiveness of lightning, the undulating line which runs through his pictures in every
direction sends back to the depths the movements
of their surfaces and determines the surfaces by the
movements of their depths: it is the mind itself, gov-
erning the sensual flood which nourishes it. Rubens
handles the forms of the world as though they were a
malleable paste, which one lengthens and shortens,
which one reduces or separates, which one drags and
distributes throughout the whole work, as a god,
recreating life, would impose a new order upon the

Rubens. Portrait of Helena Fourment (*Uffizi*).

tumult that life would have as it issues from him.
Everything in life is evolving. It is simply a force
in incessant transformation which germinates and
expands and dies in the infinite world of forms, allowing no chance for the mind, which is aware of all this,
to arrest its movement between the forms for a single
moment or to isolate it from the complex ensemble
which all, without an instant of repose, assist in forming and in destroying. Whether he paints myth, history, landscape, the market, sport, fighting, or portrait,
Rubens has no other subject than the indefatigable
pursuit, through a thousand symbols, of nature in
action, of the dynamism of life, whose immense river
sweeps through him without his ever being able to
exhaust its overflowing waters and without any de-
crease of his power through his attempts to exhaust
them.

Everything that came before his eyes during his
whole superb existence became an element, at once
fiery and docile, of his unified and dramatic conception
of nature. Never did he study anything for itself,
for the moral and material life which radiates from
any object when one studies its secret life. The human
face, for example, which he knew well, which he handled
as a sculptor kneads his clay, from which each day he
drew his unerring effects of sentiment—the human
face never interested him for the external or the profound character which it might have revealed to him.
It was of little importance to the constructor of worlds
what happened under foreheads other than his own
and what the eyes, fixed on his, revealed of an enigma
foreign to his own. Human eyes and human foreheads
entered the symphony like an instrument which he
knew how to make resound, at the place and at the
minute when he desired it to resound. When a gust of
feeling caused him to stop for a moment in the mirac-

ulous voyage which he was making among the forms,
surrounded as he was by matter and by mind, cleaving
his victorious passage amid flesh and amid trees,
dragging earth and heaven after him; when he looked
at a woman's face or a flower or a cloud with a concentration that stopped him in his course—he recovered
himself so quickly, he surrounded his distraction with

RUBENS. Philopoemen (*Louvre*).

such a display of orchestral sonorities, that it was no
more than a single voice in the chorus, mingling with
the others and lost in the furious tumult of oratorical
exaltation. His universal tenderness veiled his hours
of abandon. Like those who love everything that
lives, everything that dies, everything that is, he seemed
indifferent to the intimate dramas of the heart. He
had no time to stop to choose. He opened his breast
to all.

The mind which directs and maintains this whirlwind of life in a circle as sure as the gravitation of the heavenly bodies, rolls with it from form to form as if their very intoxication were producing the lucidity of that mind. Wine and the juice of meats and of fruits circulate through matter with lyric movement to give to the skin its red, to put saliva on the lips, to return into the soil with the stamping of feet, to evaporate into the air with the sweat that forms in drops, to pass into children with the milk from blue-veined breasts, to enter the animals through the grasses which they crop and the bones and debris which they devour, and to pass once more into man through meat and bread. And humanity, whether it loves or eats or drinks or breathes the air and the sunshine of heaven, whether it lies down or walks upon the earth, participates consciously in the universal exchange; and if earth ferments, if unhealthful vapors crawl, if the salubrious wind rises to twist the trees and make them creak, if the clouds carry through space the water that has been drunk up from the flanks of the soil, if the streams sink into subterranean caverns that they may cause a spring to murmur among the distant grasses, we know it when we observe a breast swelling above the curve of an arm, or a back mottling as the blood flushes its fat and muscle, or a mouth opening under a tuft of red beard, and the furious movement of a hand that takes, offers, or threatens is re-echoed to the very horizon.

This man had the right to love all the aspects of matter, putrefaction, and life, since he mingled the mind with putrefaction as well as with life, and since it is the mind that gives their movement to both. He had this right because he saw that life is born from putrefaction, that putrefaction germinates in life, and that life and putrefaction pass steadily from any point in space to all the others. Never did an artist have within

him to that degree the sensuality, always present,
and renewed and insatiable, which is to be ranked with
sacred things because it indicates to us—at every
step that we take, every time that we open our eyes
or our nostrils, or that we listen to the great murmur
about us—the constant solidarity which binds us with
everything that is and which causes us to assimilate

Rubens. Entry of Henri IV into Paris, detail (*Uffizi*).

ceaselessly everything that is, in order to carry it up
to our creative brain and give it back to men in co-
ordinated images. He could not conceive an object
separated from the others. His immobility turns to
movement and his coarseness becomes radiant because
he knows no bit of space but has its echo everywhere,
no fraction of time that does not continue within
himself, because he has never viewed anything in
nature without seeing higher forms germinating inces-

Rubens.   The hunt (*Antwerp*).

santly from common forms and without discerning in a bestial gesture a harmonious movement. He descends into the charnel house or lifts himself above it at will, at a single flight; and when he descends into the charnel house, he has, on the feathers of his wing, a reflection of the sun, and when he mounts he has flesh and blood in his talons. Without other transition than the play of values, the continuity of volumes, and the echo of tones, he passes from the profile of a bosom as full as a ripening fruit to a hanging breast, from a belly cut by folds to a luminous and hard belly, from the face of an old man with flabby skin to a woman's face whose pearly skin is flushed with blood, from flesh shot through with flame to dry bones, from a limpid brook to a muddy pool, from a sky all of silver to abysses of darkness. But the same wave circulates everywhere, swelling out the forms of youth when the withered forms are about to dissolve in it to make young forms again, absorbing the withered forms with the voluptuousness which it drew from the young forms. In the symphonic movement, the wail of the violincellos is never veiled by the stridence of the brasses, the sonorous wave joins despair and hope, and the weight that causes it to descend is balanced by the one that causes it to rise.

This man from whom, for two centuries, all the painters will come forth is yet the ruination of theories and schools. Life carries him along without his having the time to stop and give its final formula. With him it is a perpetual dawn; he is never without order and lucidity, but he is tireless in breaking every frame that he himself has made in order to overflow its borders, and with such abundance that as he advanced in age and rose into the light it seemed that the forms pressed themselves together ever more densely so that he might have the joy of triumphing over their

disorder with greater ease and ardor. There have
been loftier characters, subtler intelligences, more
passionate natures—there has never been such a
harmonious ensemble of all the essential faculties
which make up the superior man. In his magnificent
life of a king of art, he appears simple and good, steady
in his relationships, full of cordial nobility and of
affability, and quite without anything incomplete or
bitter. He had no need of heroic character, for he was
too well balanced to abandon his strength for the
charms of honors and of women. He had no need of
an exceptional profundity of mind, for the images of
life organized themselves in him naturally, according
to the rhythm they take as they pass through our
senses, and because he created with the ease of a rutting animal. He had no need of an uncompromising
passion because everything powerful or comprehensive
in the Europe of his time smoothed his path for him
without his having to demand it.

That fire, that inexpressible movement, that unbridled transport of passion which one sees in his slightest
sketches was no more than the passage through him
of universal life, forever whirling him forward without
his making any effort to summon it to him and without
his being able to restrain it. It was from him that
there poured forth those trees twisted by flame, those
torrents of light and shadow, that moving modeling
which sculptures and rolls the fat flesh, knots and
unties the muscular limbs whose embraces seem to
bring his mind into being, those full breasts of women,
those heavy udders of the cow from which he sucked
life, those overflowing still-life pieces, those fish, meats,
and pumpkins, those fruits of the earth and of the
trees which he brings streaming down or which he
crushes upon his canvas with sunlight and blood.
What did it matter if he addressed himself in the

language desired by this century to the most conventional century, the one most fascinated by fine speaking and oratorical emphasis, and if, in order to stir it, he employed the melodramatic means which it demanded of him, eyes reddened by weeping, prostrate bodies,

RUBENS. The Earl of Arundel and his wife (*Munich*).

supplicating hands, people kneeling theatrically, and athletic cadavers hung from crosses? The boiling torrent of life swept the theatrical attitudes along in its ascendant power, and they disappeared in it as the gestures of singers are effaced when five hundred musicians accompany their voices. The sonorous

JORDAENS. Fecundity (*Brussels*).

wind blowing caused the mantles and draperies to flap, tearing them from shoulders too broad and from settings too pompous, when they masked the blue perspective of the plains stretching away through vapors to the horizon with the curve of the earth, and set in movement by their wandering mists, by their volcanic undulations, and by the wind which blew across them. He had appeared between Rabelais and Bossuet and embodied them both to the tenth power. He drew after him in his train such masses of fat and grease, of ruddy flesh into which the hand could plunge, of unbound blond hair; such elastic surfaces of bare backs, of heavy hips spread out in the light; such heaps of fruits, of vegetables, and of pungent boughs of apple trees and bitter boughs of oak—that, in order to bring this ocean of matter into the modern world, he had to assume the solemn gestures and the bands of lace of the masters of the pulpit and of the confessors of kings. He served the banquet of the century in his own silver vessels, amid brocaded hangings and tall armchairs already occupied by lords in court dress, by women in décolleté, and by grandiloquent bishops. But he had seen the blood flowing through the bluish veins of the beautiful breasts that were offered to his eyes; he had seen the august jaws cracking bones, and the fruits, which he threw with both hands upon the table amid the meats, were moist with dew and swollen with sugar and with juice.

He maintained in his life and transmitted for our need of unity and of rhythm the substance amassed by the Middle Ages and the order introduced into the mind by the Italian masters. In surface and in depth, he mingled and interwove living nature with the continuous lines which for him represented its direction. His influence was enormous, it still endures, it has become a part of our activity for all time. But he had exhausted life for more than a century; the painters of Europe after him appear stricken by a sort of lethargic stupor from which neither Watteau nor Goya could tear them away, and which the France of the nineteenth century alone managed to shake off.

Flanders especially was crushed by it. Aside from Breughel, who is a complete realization and who moreover marked out his path, the whole sixteenth century of Flanders seems to have had no other function than that of announcing Rubens. The sons and the nephews of Breughel had gathered only a few brilliant flowers from the borders of the terrestrial Eden which Rubens entered alone, cutting the harvests, shaking the fruit trees, drawing after him the animals he dominated in order that he might feed upon their flesh or flatter them with his hand, and dazzling the women he loved without letting himself be conquered by them. When he had entered this garden, all the others picked up the grains and the leaves which he let fall unnoticed at each step, because his two arms were fully laden and because, although he was capable of absorbing all that he carried or of decorating his magnificent house with it, he knew too well that, so far as he was concerned, the branches, the ears of corn, and the flanks of the women would not be exhausted. When death laid him low amid the vines, his two feet upon the soil and his brow in the light which was ripening everything around him that his eyes had seen, the race of pupils that surrounded him, finishing his pictures, living upon his flaming sketches, and gathering up the notes in his albums to decorate a palace—the race of pupils could do no more than despoil him of his mantle and force open his fists, still filled to overflowing. Eden was dead with him.

III

Jordaens himself, so strong and so free, could not escape the overpowering memory of him. But at least he illumined his soul with the flame of Rubens instead of gathering up his bones. He brought even more sun into the flesh of his big women, he caused more

JORDAENS. Three Musicians (*Prado*).

blood to flow under their skin, they radiated a greater amorous power, and he discovered in himself, as he watched the passing of the god who opened upon life his two generous hands, rustic poems which he had barely suspected. He saw fauns, their hoofs clotted with mud, sitting in Flemish cottages into which cows and chickens came behind them; he saw the fauns partaking with the peasant of the juice of grapes, and bread rubbed with garlic. He saw more liquid light in the eyes of the girls and more furtive grace in the smile of their mouths. The spirit of the world passed through him in a broad flash.

The others divided up the universe of Rubens. Snyders gathered into biblical arks the beasts scattered through the three thousand canvases of the hero. Of the immense spectacle of the world into which Rubens had plunged, the skies, the seas, the nude women, the living woods, the springs and the meadows, the marble palaces and the cottages which he had dissolved in the blood of his veins to spread them forth upon the canvas to the beating of his heart, Snyders retained no more than messes of fish and the pork shops of the streets, the palpitation of the pearly bellies, the glistening tremor of the scales, the slimy motion of the great cylindrical bodies, the thickness of the meats, the warmth of fur and feathers heaped up pellmell, an odor of the sea and of clotted blood floating amid the russets of autumn game, and the blues and greens of seaweed and of ocean depths. Even so it was too much for him. Fyt helped him in his work. Crayer, who also delighted in fish, the sea, and the meat of the butcher shop, closed his eyes timidly so as to leave to them this domain, and thought it his duty to confine himself to equestrian portraits, monarchical triumphs and pompous theologies against a setting of twisted colonnades and brocaded hangings. The good painter Jacob van Oost left to him the athletic nudes and the muscular melodramas that he might shut himself up in his dying city of Bruges with the enriched middle class who draped themselves in the mantles and the doublets in which Rubens had dressed his princes as they appeared silhouetted against the grandeur of the skies. Van Dyck seized upon hands and faces, despoiled the soldiers of the harness of war in order to get a better view of their ankles and wrists, and dressed the divinities of pagan Flanders in robes of heavy stuff so as to have a more perverse pleasure in undressing them afterward. Where, before, there had been sureness of gesture, ease of power, superb elegance of force in action, there were now prepared gesture, mannered grace, and the faded elegance taught by the servitude and idleness of courts.

The noble had doffed his armor. He had permitted his stronghold to become a pleasure house; he had

VAN DYCK. Portrait of the artist (*Private collection*).

given over to the king his bridges and roads in exchange for finely embroidered garments. But deep within him there was still the vigor of a cavalier, even though a touch of corruption was visible at the tips of his fingers and in the pallor of his face. From the south to the north van Dyck's gaze roved with easy and careless penetration. In Italy he discovered, in great sad palaces, the grandsons of a violent aristocracy abandoning itself to its morbid decline. The grandsons of a brutal aristocracy, which was giving up its struggle for power against the merchants, brought him to England.

In the southern country—nervous faces, marked by the inner storm which can no longer vent itself; in the northern country—pale faces with blond hair, long pale hands resting on the hips as men stand in proud resignation when forced to shut up their idle strength in great parks full of leaves rotted by the mist that rises from the lawns drenched with moisture. On every hand, men standing apart from the torrent of the century, isolated in their pleasures, isolated in their boredom. The master had treated with the great; the pupil was treated by the great. His taste, his easy culture, his elegance as of a musketeer, and his dressmaker's talent rendered him indispensable to them. He employed the strength left him by the artificial life of an artist overpraised by idlers and too much loved by women, to become the painter of society and of fashion, the first in date and of importance. For a proud or delicate head outlined against a great living sky, for a fair hand holding a batiste handkerchief, for a flash of comprehension which one day turned a charming and silly face into the incarnate symbol of the old races devoured by their time (which they imagine themselves to have dominated while in fact they have not even tried to understand it)—he frittered away a talent already weary from playing with doublets, from trying on gloves and then tossing them carelessly aside, from turning lace into foam, from the madcap elegance that made him don his broad-brimmed hat with its waving plume, from pointing out the toes of feet shod in soft leather while his hand rested on a tall cane and he twirled his mustache.

Perhaps he did not understand that successes and pleasures sucked his pale blood little by little, and if he suffered, it was because he felt his decline without knowing its causes and without being able to win back his strength. Like all sensitive beings who have become

men of pleasure, he is sad. There are more blacks and grays in a single one of his canvases than in all those of Rubens. He never knew the sensual joy which that master lavished everywhere. He never had his broad pagan faith, nor any other to replace it. In his religious pictures, his insinuating and insipid sensualism is the mark of his full consent to be the painter of the Jesuits whom Rubens had served, indeed, when he filled the churches with enchanting virgins, which they ordered from him, but whom he had pro-
foundly combated when he upheld, con-
trary to their beliefs, the revolutionary force of life and carried it across his century. Van Dyck flattered the convenient devotion of those who no longer believe. Through his religious pictures he consented to play the rôle in Flanders—with more

Van Dyck. Portrait (*Lille*).

grace and more frequent evasions, it is true—which Bernini was to assume in Italy with noisy grandilo-
quence, Lesueur in France with insipid sweetness, and Murillo in Spain, with his dubious and unhealthy sensualism. Philippe de Champagne, who was about of his age, was forced, in order to maintain his position against the tendencies of the century, to make a severe and continued effort, and more so because he had received, as van Dyck himself had, the pagan education of the old Flemings and saw on the horizon of his

youth the tumultuous passing of Rubens. With one of those sudden breaks of equilibrium which only the great mystics can force upon themselves, he forgot even the joy of painting, which is the whole reason for existence of the masters of his country. He fixed his eyes upon the wooden crucifixes nailed to the bare walls of the Jansenist cloisters. He painted flesh

PHILIPPE DE CHAMPAGNE. Nuns of Port-Royal (*Louvre*).

clothed in gray fustian; he covered with cold ashes the kneeling portraits of the martyrs of Christian doubt. Rubens had conquered without a struggle, without even feeling their fetters, because his life swept everything along, the impedimenta of the allegories and the need for dogmatic demonstration which his time imposed upon him. After his death, we undoubtedly enter a century when art will no longer live—or rather, will no longer try to live—save through formulas, pedagogical preoccupations, theories, and moralizing intentions.

The century, besides, will take as its field of action another soil than that of Flanders, which scarcely sufficed, after the visit of Hercules, to nourish Jordaens. Van Dyck was unable to live there for more than six years of his maturity. Philippe de Champagne deserted Brussels for Paris. Victorious Holland sapped the life of the Low Countries. When she did not send her painters to Flanders—as, for instance, that strange Brouwer who died at the age of thirty-two after haunting the taverns of Antwerp in order to catch sight, among the shadows, of faces filled with joy, grimacing pain, or comical attention as they appeared suddenly, and who was perhaps brushed by the great invisible pinion which was to lift up Rembrandt—she imposed upon the last Flemish artists her most undeniable faults. David Teniers was seized by her love of anecdote and spread forth motionless dances, silent orgies, and dead kermesses in landscapes, gentle and gray. A tremor as of sorrow, pale and cold, passed over the Flemish soil. Its free spaces, where the mists of the Scheldt and of the North Sea had furnished amber and opal to its artists from van Eyck to Rubens, were to burn out completely. Their last flicker vibrates over the battles staged like quadrilles and the burlesque fortresses which van der Meulen humbly offered to the king of France, and over which a few blue and delicate vapors arise amid the slender trees. Flanders had given enough to the world. Her confused life, heavy and rich, her life swelling with blood and sap, drunk with strength and sweating with its odorous fecundity, had caused its spirit to pass, through Rubens, into the veins of the future.

BROUWER.   The Surgeon.

THE POLDER.

Chapter II. HOLLAND

I

OLLAND, which borders on Flanders, bears no resemblance to it. From the first, as soon as one approaches the mouths of the Germanic rivers, the aspect of the country changes, the plain descends below the sea-level. Holland devotes itself to stock-raising and agriculture; Flanders to manufacture. And then Flanders remains Catholic and, until the nineteenth century, is subject to foreign government. Holland, from the beginning of the seventeenth century, is Protestant and free. Where Antwerp is swept along amid the attraction of the civilizations of the south, Holland takes possession of herself in a sudden accession of strength which bursts her bonds.

From that moment is to be dated her escape from the despotism of the Renaissance men of the south. The Italians treat their country as a pretext, the artist makes abstractions, he invents, the world solicits him incessantly to find a direction for the appearances which it offers him and to find intellectual value which shall aggrandize the forms whose meaning he desires to generalize and whose sense he desires to follow in order to elevate the race and exalt all its desires. In the wake of the Italians Rubens drags the strength of the north. The Dutch, on the contrary, take their country as their subject. They "paint its portrait." It is the country that they love, because they have suffered in order to gain possession of it and hold it, because it feeds them well, because they have worked to improve it, to clear it up, and to protect it against man and the sea. For ten centuries they struggled to get possession of its mud, to build on it, to set up their towns which will sink into the bog or which an inroad of the sea drowns out in slime and quicksand. Life had been too hard for them, and is now too good for them to seek outside its every-day aspects the education of the mind which it can give to those who live in freedom, in idleness, and in the passionate stimulation of the southern countries—and who are tormented by the needs of an imagination left to itself or whose will power tortures them to restrain its own excesses.

As soon as she had seized her liberty, Holland emerged no more from herself. She does not seem even to have had to struggle to preserve the right to say that which she thought, or rather that which she saw, of herself. She watched herself live. The only thing she did not perceive was the war which she was obliged still to keep up against richer neighbors so that she might be allowed to dry up her polders and found her markets. She was not moved by the spectacle of her heroism; she was not conscious of it. She saw therein a means of winning her right to live as she saw fit, as a busy tradesman, as a careful and clean housewife, loving good food, comfort, domesticated love, fine clothes, and white linen, all of which bore witness to a healthy existence and a self-interested probity. If ever there was a people naturally sociable, of sentiment but slightly complicated, permanently balanced, and which readjusted itself without effort or shock, it is this one. Its greatest man, or rather its one really great man, here appeared like a monster. It certainly made him see that.

Holland carried on the practice of painting in the way that she fought, in the way that she carried on and still carries on the practice of trade. With her, that function did not correspond as in

FRANS HALS. Descartes (*Louvre*).

other places to a frenzy of conquest which announces itself from afar by feverish tremors and leaves behind it fatigue, sadness, and often death. She began suddenly, she stopped suddenly. It is like the joy of a young animal that snorts and skips, and after becoming aware of its health and its vigor, of the suppleness of its muscles and the depth of its lungs, no longer thinks of anything but grazing. When she no longer knew how to paint, she felt no remorse. Her art had manifested a moment of its power, broad, peaceful, positive, and

joyous—and that was all. When art no longer manifested it, this power continued; but instead of expressing itself through color and form, it expressed itself
through more ships on the sea, more merchandise in
the ports, through a greater number of canals, more
solid dikes, and more of well-being everywhere.

These forces, as has often been said, arose from the
magnificent effort which Holland had made to tear

FRANS HALS. The Lady Regents of the Hospital (*Haarlem*).

herself free from the foreigner. When men for forty
years have armed themselves every day to earn their
bread for the evening and the right to be alive at
dawn, when they have gotten up in the night to go
through fierce storms of wind and water in order to
slip a torch into the portholes of war-vessels, when
they have seen the stake set up for them on every
public square and a gibbet at every crossroad, they
may, if they have not weakened, regard with pride
those who will be born of their valor. All the painters

of Holland were sons or grandsons of the men who had made the Republic. Mierevelt, the first, is born in 1567 on the eve of the insurrection; the last, Hobbema, in 1638, when Spain is quite vanquished, when the Dutch East-India Company floods the ports with produce, when the Netherlands feel themselves sufficiently strong to control their sea whereby they block the Thames with de Ruyter's vessels and hurl that sea through the broken dikes in front of the soldiers of Louis XIV. Between Mierevelt and Hobbema come Frans Hals, van Goyen, Rembrandt, van Ostade, Albert Cuyp, Ruysdael, Terborg, Pieter de Hooch, Vermeer of Delft, and a hundred others. The Beggars of the sea have hurled the power of their fight into the wombs of the women.

To be sure, in this country where everyone may without effort be a painter if he opens his eyes, some men had done painting previously to the two generations which were born of the conquerors. But their voices were isolated and without echoes. In the Holland that was forming, the few little peasants who had been awakened by chance by the great diffused light which floats from the mouths of the Rhine to the dikes of the Zuider Zee, had gone on foot to Bruges, to Ghent, to Antwerp, or to Brussels where peddlers and traders from the coast had told them that those who made pictures for donors and brotherhoods gained a generous livelihood. In the fifteenth century, if van Ouwater, a pupil of van Eyck, did return to The Hague, Dirk Bouts lived at Louvain, Claus Sluter went as far as Dijon, and Malouel as far as Paris. In the sixteenth century, Cornelissen and Mostaert remained at home, but looked to Antwerp; Pieter Pourbus lived in Bruges. Anton Mor served Spain to the point of acquiring her arid strength, her dry ardor, and her somber and nude character. Lucas of Leyden, even if he did not leave his home, was solicited now by Antwerp, now by Germany, which triumphed completely when Dürer came to see him and when they had exchanged their ideas concerning the manner of cutting into copper and wood.

VAN GOYEN. The Skaters (*Orléans*).

And yet, if there was in Holland, before the war, a genuine Hollander, it certainly was this good engraver of blond landscapes and of the joys of the people in which, at times, the verve of van Ostade is forecast. Had he not died at the age of forty, had he been able to see Pieter Breughel, who had deserted for Antwerp the

landscape of Breda over which floats the golden mist
from the rivers, we should doubtless have known
sooner the face of the Netherlands. But he disappeared
at the moment when Italy was becoming the fashion in
Flanders, when Jan Scorel was trying to introduce
it at Utrecht, when Holland seemed to be accepting
Charles V and renouncing the pride of seizing liberty.

The insurrection which put the Netherlands into
possession of their independence was so thoroughly
significant of their maturity of mind that painting,
though scarcely born, made itself completely master of
its means. Between the sons of the insurgents and the
first Dutch painters who were looking toward Italy
and Flanders, there is a half century of silence. Holland
has no primitives, even less than Venice. The painters
of the brotherhoods are already modern men. Frans
Hals, from his first work, is a great painter; he knows
all the laws of plastic polyphony, he has freedom, ease,
a powerful and direct feeling for the permanent and
complex solidarity of form, color, consciousness, and
space; and, from his first moment, he is a Hollander.
And thenceforward, neither with him nor with any of
those who are to appear, will one find a trace of those
Italian rhythms with which Rubens and his successors
animate the matter of the north. Dutch art is of a
single block, remains until its last hour within the
material and moral limits of Holland, and, from the
beginning to the end, reveals the inner forces brought
violently to the light by the revolution. It is the most
strongly and uniquely national affirmation that history
has to show.

II

The artists who were born every day and everywhere
from the energy of the revolt, behind the shoulders of
the dikes whence one sees only the sky, and on the banks

of the canals where the sails pass against the hedges, had the desire to paint almost as soon as they opened their eyes. But only to paint. Not to imagine or to demonstrate, not to seek, beyond the life of the senses, for the world of ideas that it contains, but to paint—to fix the shadow of the sails on the water, the shafts of sunlight in the mist, the black and white spots of the

VAN DER MEER. The River in Winter (*Amsterdam*).

cattle in the polder, or the blue nets that dry in the forest of the masts. And when they were called to the large commercial cities, where the middle class, enriched by trade and consolidated by victory, was broadening its ranks, they brought with them, cool and fresh, the harmonies of their sky. Besides, the water-ways which ran through the country crossed and re-crossed in the cities, amid the houses of brick and glass;

the big full-bellied boats discharged upon the narrow
docks the flour, the milk, the butter, the fodder, and
the flowers which they brought from the fields. And
then the west wind, blowing over the lacy gabled
roofs, the canals, the short bridges, and the plane trees
of Amsterdam, Leyden, Delft, Dortrecht, and Haarlem,
carried with it the same great clouds which poured upon

PAUL POTTER. The Wood at the Hague (*Berlin*).

the low plains the water with which they are so gorged
that most of the mills turn to relieve them of it.

The peaceful pride of having won the right to live at
their ease urged the solid Dutch middle class to utilize
at once and for their profit, that desire for painting
which the rising generation was impatiently manifesting. They enjoyed their wealth, and in every way they
could. Already they were no longer the rising Holland

of the solid black effigies of old Mierevelt, nor even the severe assemblies which Ravesteyn, another painter of brotherhoods, was furnishing at the same period, and still less the attempts which Cornelis Tennissen made under the reign of Spain, a half century earlier. Now, when the civic guards, who were fortifying or reorganizing their companies everywhere, went forth to practice with the arquebuse, they hung their rapiers from silken scarfs, they put great waving plumes on their felt hats, and they unfurled embroidered standards. No mere boastful display was this, but the joy of fortune acquired by the calm strength which they retained amid the greatest perils. They were strong men. War, commerce, orgy—nothing disturbed their innocence. When returning from exercise they ate and drank as one eats and drinks when one is rich, when one leads a powerful life, when one breathes sea air and has walked in the mist that rises from the damp pasture land. A silent complicity was being brought about between them and those charged with painting them. Some, to tell the truth, did not understand them entirely; others too well. They did not pardon Rembrandt when he took it upon himself to take possession of them like a material that one works upon and bends at will to identify it with one's being, to knead it with light and gold and recast it into life as if it were another life that was to be mingled therewith, even though, in its passing, he caused the lightning of the mind to flash forth. When van der Helst dressed them in satin, placed them before him in their magnificence, all in front view, all of equal importance and quite proper despite their beer mugs and their weapons, they were so well satisfied with the painter who reproduced them so faithfully and so splendidly, that we cannot help considering him a little too much like themselves. Frans Hals, on the other hand, gives them just the value which we set upon them, or rather it is through him that we know their value. Never has

there been better painting than his, never has the sur-face of life been expressed with greater simplicity and power, nor has the order of importance of the elements which reveal life to our eyes been more accurately as-signed.

When he had passed the evening in exchanging blows and coarse words with his wife and the night in waiting for his wine to settle, one would have said that on the following day his mind was clearer, his hand firmer, his eye more fit to seize the moving harmonies that en-tered his studio with the spice-dealers, the money-changers, the brewers, and the drapers returning from their arquebuse shooting, and with the broad oppositions by which he introduced into painting a source of life so savory that he exhausted it to its depths. This drunkard flooded with fire everything he touched with his brush. Doubtless, between two sit-

QUELLIN THE ELDER. High Relief from the front of the Palace of Amsterdam.

tings, he sat down also to the banquet table, amid those red-faced strong fellows with their hair cut in a

brush, their short, pointed, blond beards and their upturned mustaches. And when the faces had reached a
point where they were round and full, when they reflected the joy of the well-filled stomachs and the easy
digestions, sword belts were strapped on again, felt
hats were donned, the big silk bows that crossed jacket
and doublet were puffed out. Then the blue, orange,
and red scarfs, the green plumes, the black cloth, the
fluted ruffles of collars and cuffs, the silky undulation of
the banners, hung in disorder over the tables or carelessly folded to mingle their colors, everything seemed
to receive—through the fists grasping the spear shafts,
through the temples swelling under the shadow of the
large hats, through the hands pouring red wine and
receiving it in crystal glasses—the wave of hot blood
which rolled in their arteries.

When he was seeking the colored surfaces of the
world, Frans Hals painted the ruff of a collarette or
the fringe of a scarf with as much delight as he would
the radiant smile of a servant girl, the burst of gayety
of a blond youth, or the full-blooded face of a civilian
officer. But this great virtuoso changed, which is
not frequent with virtuosi. It seems that after his
sixtieth year a kind of remorse seized him. Was it
perhaps that he had become intimate with Descartes
of whom, at about that time, he painted the portrait
which showed so clearly the restless and obstinate
spirit of the philosopher? Was it perhaps that the
poverty in which he died in the almshouse and his
intercourse with old men and sick men had constrained
him to look within himself and in consequence to turn
upon the outer world eyes that were more clear sighted?
Suddenly one sees his palette, not darkening—it retains
all its limpid splendor, its transparence, its frankness
—but suppressing all the intermediary notes of the
keyboard, bringing to black and white (both infinite

REMBRANDT. The Entombment (*Munich*).

in shades, pitch, and sonority) the whole expressive
repertory of the colors of nature. Is there more "soul"
elsewhere than in his "Regents," or especially in his
last picture, the "Lady Regents," which he paints at
the age of eighty-four, when he is no longer sure of his
hand? All painters know well that the word has no

REMBRANDT. The Lesson, drawing (*Private collection*).

meaning unless one employs it with reference to the
quality of painting. But sometimes, it is true, old
men learn; they humble themselves, they confess that
they have not understood or that they have understood imperfectly; they return to the school of nature,
through the door of the heart. Almost all the masters
have known that second innocence and have perceived

without apprehension that they have felt themselves becoming unskillful once more. Titian presented that great spectacle; we shall meet it again with Rembrandt and also with Velasquez. The surface of the world seems to efface itself from their eyes, and if the spirit of the forms appears to them more clearly, it is not that the spirit departs from the forms; it is that the master has discovered, on the contrary, the constant solidarity of the forms and of the spirit, because the inner logic of life imposes itself on him and because the accidental recedes in the measure that he understands the law. That is what impresses us when we see the last work of him who was, until nearly the end, the most exterior of painters. There is nothing attractive in what he views: an austere room in an almshouse, aged hands, aged faces, and the growing shadows of the days, the end of these lives and of his own; but matter and thought are now no more than a single thing all the more beautiful because when he knows where strength lies his hand weakens.

It was only natural that the painters of Holland, when sixty years old, should paint the portraits of these five or six grave personages, clad in black and white, and assembled around a table. They were aging at the same time as their sitters. Those who had seen war and made war, those who, in their maturity, had engaged freely and without disquietude in military exercises, commerce, and the pleasures of the table and of love, considered it proper, when their skin had lost its freshness and was hardening and becoming gray, to turn to philanthropy and administration. The old merchants and their wives busied themselves with good works. Each age has its pleasures. And Holland is a wise nation which, without difficulty, reconciles good living, the hierarchy of the bodily functions, and the social order that like the others is rooted in the economy and evolution of the country, with the Commandments of the Scriptures. And it is very fortunate that it is so, for this gives to art, which has recounted to us her life, that steadiness, that peace, that powerful tranquillity which presents a contrast, so perfect and so instructive to the mind, with the fever and pain concealed in Mediterranean art. All those who, before and after the "Syndics" of Rembrandt and the "Lady Regents" of Hals, painted those solid reunions of figures on which the materialism of commerce and the equanimity of soul, which comes from physical and moral health, had left their mark until the coming of wrinkles and white hair—Verspronck, Thomas de Keyser, Santvoort, Flinck, Elias, Jacob van Loo, and Jan de Bray especially—had so complete a vision of that society that one feels they approved of it, and one understands, when one sees them, that no external shock could have disturbed their harmony with it. Rembrandt apart, they are in no way different from those who posed before them. Social Holland is a magnificent work of art in itself, and one cannot object to her artists' accepting their place in the self-satisfied middle class.

III

The close resemblance of these painters to that which they represented enables one to understand why the eyes of those who see in the work of art the image of historical and geographical surroundings should have invoked their testimony. Van Ostade idled in all the villages, he entered all their houses. He is curious about everything. He goes to sit down at the inn, he enters the kitchen, he goes down to the cellar, he explores the barnyard. He peeps through a shutter to watch the children at school. When a fiddler sets the lads and

REMBRANDT. Portrait of Hendrickje, detail (*Louvre*).

lasses dancing under the plane trees of the square, he
hurries to the door and installs himself in the front row.
Every time that the dentist or the barber operates,
he is there. All inert things—an old vat, an old tub,
a broken earthenware pot, books on a shelf, plates,
bottles, the pellmell in a studio, a kitchen, a tavern,
a forge—are his friends, all of which a ray of the sun
from the window, the reflection of a hearth where
roast fowls are turning golden in their streaming juice,
the sheen from a copper saucepan or from a red-
hot iron on the anvil, animate so that they may take
part in the affairs, the noise, the silence, the life of
the moment. Everything lives, everything has the
same right to live and to live unconventionally. People
drink, eat, sing, laugh, love, and console themselves
in all candor. And if social discipline and the rapidity
of intercourse have introduced more restraint into the
villages, if their life is less innocent, there is still in
the Holland of to-day enough to explain all its artists
in the ensemble of their tendencies, and even to describe
them in the most minute detail of their realizations.
The joyous power of the Dutch temperament in effect-
ing its conquest has declined a little, to be sure, but if
the reading of the Bible by the old people is listened to
more decorously, it is not more fully obeyed the moment
that instinct pierces the crust of hypocritical conven-
tions and the apparent unity of morals. On the feast
days of the people and on feast days in the home the
same full-blooded health overflows at meals, in gestures,
and in speech. The old masters would recognize their
race here, and the setting within which its strength
expands; for the absolute plain crossed by white sails,
the four hundred mills with the red wings that turn
around Zaandam, and the space are still there. Van
Goyen, for example, is the Low Country itself—a strip
cut out from its earth, with a great stretch of sky.

That golden spray of water which bathes everything, those great lingering shafts of sunlight on a corner of a pasture outside of which everything plunges into luminous shadow, those skies filled with white clouds which at the same time allow the light to pass through, and, causing the ground to dazzle with liquid and powdery gold, make us wonder, when we have crossed

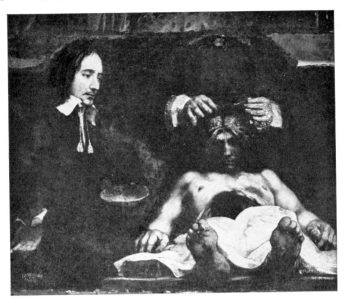

REMBRANDT.   The Autopsy (*Amsterdam*).

Holland, whether it was van Goyen who revealed them to us or whether it was the flat country which unrolls from the island of Walcheren to Groningen, and from Amsterdam to Breda.   In winter, when the canals and the ponds freeze over, if one goes to see the skaters fly and disappear among the bare trees and the houses capped with snow, one finds him there again, and van Ostade also, and van der Meer of Amsterdam, the

lover of immense horizons—who have all come, blowing on their fingers and stamping their feet, to try to
fix the crossing of the little black silhouettes against
the uniform whiteness and the pink and icy sky of
glittering afternoons. When one has seen the departure of the heavy vessels bending under their sails,
their pennants crackling, when one has seen the movements of the waves and the immensity of gray space
in which an uncertain golden glow is born, it is because
one has looked at the sea in company with the van der
Veldes, from the top of the Scheveningen dunes. One
knows Paul Potter without ever having met him if
one has strolled along some inclosure where the bulls
and the cows wander to nourish their blood and their
milk from the ever moist grass and the salty wind from
the sea. His painting is steeped in the breath of their
lungs, in their silvery slaver, in the sweat that evap-
orates from them, in the humidity from their nostrils;
and their hides take on the dull splendor which he gives
to the dust-enveloped plain whose transparence grows
dimmer little by little without ever vanishing in the
vapors that thicken with the distance. All, even the
most humble and the most unknown among these
artists, have carried into their painting something of
the vast opalescent mist in which the slightest spot of
color takes on an admirable value. Holland is drenched
with water, water rises from the soil and from the sea,
water unites the soil and the sea with the sky which
one never perceives save through its impalpable veil,
which the gold of the sun, the silver of the dew, and
the pale emerald of the waves tinge simultaneously or
by turns. Every little drop of vapor is an invisible
device for reflecting, breaking, and refracting the
light. A vast prism floats and transfigures everything
and sheds the glory of the daylight upon everything
which, away from here, is shadow and darkness—to

things which, everywhere else, one does not see or which one conceals.

Confined to his hut by the gloomy days and the long nights of the bad season, the Dutch peasant finds again, when the ice melts, when the earth moves, and when the first shoots pierce the frost, the ever-living enchantment of the rebirth of the world. In the distance melting into the vapor which rises from ditches and canals, the yellow and green pasture land stretches out and mingles with the cattle that graze in herds or lie down on the ground, with the colts that gallop and the sails of the boats and the wings of the mills, gilded or darkened by rays of light or passages of shadow. At times, when the earth is covered with steam, it remains invisible to the height of the grasses, and the animals and objects seem to float over it. Rain and sunlight merge; the nearness of the sea brings about unexpected slanting illuminations; the water, spread out everywhere, gives its liquid depth to the greens, to the blacks, to the reds, and to the blues which the meadows, the fields of flowers, the herds, and the houses scatter throughout the polder, without their ever ceasing to be at once brilliant and blurred in the shining fog. From afar everything appears like a brilliant spot which an uncertain fringe renders iridescent at its edges and then mingles with the air saturated with watery vapor. Form floats. And when the Hollander tries to fix it in sculpture, he seems still to paint rather than to carve. Quellin the Elder has not the sense of clear-cut profiles and well-defined masses. Space engulfs and melts his decorative sculptures. But seen near by, he is Rubens. The modeling moves within the contour, the softly filled planes flee and undulate under the tremble of the flesh. The blood beats in them, the milk rises in them, the light of Holland spreads over them its iridescent mist which is the milk and the blood of its fat pasture land.

REMBRANDT. Bathsheba, detail (*Louvre*).

It was but natural that the eyes of those who live amid this feast of moist shadow and sunlight create anew for the repose and continuity of their sight—in dress, ornament, habitation, and all their domestic objects—that concerning which the spontaneous harmonies of space never cease to teach them. They paint everything—the houses, the mills, the inclosures of the gardens and the fields, the pails, the milk boxes, the casks, and the full-bellied boats which go right into the cities to mingle in the black mirror of the canals their red or green reflections with the multicolored tremble of the clouds, the belfries, the brick façades, the window-panes, and the tiles of the roofs. Along the roads one sees green wagons with orange wheels; blue or green barrels with red hoops are piled up on the

REMBRANDT. Self portrait, detail
(*National Gallery, London*).

barges. The geraniums and begonias with which the windows flower are in earthen pots or painted wooden boxes. When one opens a window or a door painted a turquoise blue, in one of those clean villages where the wind strews the leaves of the plane trees on the flat brick pavement, one catches a glimpse of a room calcimined with yellow or with pure blue. In certain localities they paint even the trees. On their broadcloth suits, or on their velvet skirts, on their neckerchiefs, and on their bodices printed with bright colors, the peasants wear silver belts and the peasant women wear clasps and pins of gold. Around their necks all have coral necklaces in several bands, jet necklaces when they are in mourning. In Friesland their headdress is a silver helmet. The ports are full of brick-red sails and blue fishing nets. Until nightfall all Holland is a liquid painting, and evening itself gives to things a depth of color which one scarcely finds again save on the lagoons of Venice, on the dusty plateaus of Castille, or, in certain spring and autumn twilights, in the atmosphere of Paris. One needs to have seen at The Hague, toward the fall of evening, how the white swans absorb all the dying light under the deep trees which gather the silence around the broad sheets of water.

IV

In reality every Hollander is a born painter, and this could not be otherwise. In order that these original gifts may ripen in a few brains and be organized there, it suffices for a moment of enthusiasm or a brief need for effort to stir one or two generations. There is not a country in the world where history and the soil have more directly determined the plastic expression of life. And whatever may have been said of this,[1] Rembrandt did not escape the rule. Only, there must be no misunderstanding. What the thousand painters of Holland take as the subject for their canvases, Rembrandt takes as the element of his visions. Where the others see facts, he seizes secret relationships which identify his supernatural sensibility with the real, and transports to the plane of a new creation everything that he has

---

[1] Among others, Emile Verhaeren, who affirms, in his fine book on *Rembrandt,* that the mere fact of the appearance of a heroic genius suffices completely to demolish the theory of environment.

REMBRANDT. The Three Trees, etching (*Chantilly*).

religiously borrowed from the Creation we all know. And as those among whom he lives are indifferent to him, as his strange vision passes over the heads of the crowd, he seems to be outside it and even to stand facing it in a state of permanent antagonism. And yet he speaks its language, he tells us about it and thus about himself, who gets from it that which has made him suffer and that which has made him understand. He had to know both its love and its hate before dominating its sentimental passions, the better to accept it as an ever-living necessity and to merge it in himself with the other images of the world and so lift it up with them to the impartial power of his mind.

Whence, then, should Rembrandt have taken his gold and his reds, and that silvery or russet light in which the sun and the spray of water mingle, if he had not always lived in Amsterdam, in the most populous and most sordid spot in the city, near the boats pouring upon the docks red rags, rusty iron, pickled herrings, gingerbread, and the royal train of carmines and yellows on the day of the flower market? Through the fermentation of the slimy streets of the Jewish quarter, where colored garments hang from the windows, re-kindling with their burning gleams the reddish shadow, he went along the streets of water which lap and reflect the flowered façades and the dyed cloths, until he came to the edge of the Amstel, where, in the flaming evenings of the maritime cities, the big ships were discharging embroidered cloths, tropical fruits, and birds from the islands. Where else should he have gotten his desire for imaginary voyages, for glimpses of distant seas, for that magical Orient which he perceived as a spray, dancing in a shaft of sunlight, when he caused a ray of his light to descend to the deep cellars into which filters the dampness of the canals? And when he entered those dens where the usurers of the

REMBRANDT. The Beef (*Louvre*).

Ghetto weigh gold in the scales, where the poor heap up
by families, dressed in reddened tatters or in cast-off
Indian tinsel which they had picked up, where, in the
darkness, the second-hand dealers heap up iron
cuirasses, damascened arms, and wrought copper and
leather, how should he fail to surprise the gestures
which people make so unguardedly when settled in
their misery—the mothers with fully exposed breasts
suckling their little ones, the old people dying on straw
mattresses, the sores wrapped with dirty rags, and the
innocence recovered through hunger and love?

From the external and joyous vision of this picturesque universe revealed to him by his idling, by
his purchases in the shops, by the piling up in his
studio of heterogeneous collections—Venetian pictures,
weapons, furs, jewels, and stuffed animals—he goes
onward to his almost jealous contemplation of the
human face and gesture in the light which he composed
in order to illuminate them with all the harmonies of
the most distant suns and the most poignant darkness;
and he has not told us what roads he had to travel on
this journey. It is the secret of his suffering. It is for
us to accept and to understand when we look within
us, if we also have suffered. We know that he was
married, and happy to be so; that he loved his wife
Saskia with all his senses, perhaps with all his heart;
that he covered her with jewels and that he painted
her nude, dressed, and wearing a great hat. We know
that he was rich, or at least that he lived like a rich
man with her, and that, when he became a widower,
he was pursued by creditors and tracked from one
lodging to another; poor at last, abandoned by his
friends, given up to drinking, perhaps, he lived from
day to day with his son and a servant, his mistress.
And we know that the farther he plunged into his
solitude the more populous his solitude became. We

know that expression became more concentrated and more intense at the same time that the superficial harmonies, almost violent at first, wild with the joy of painting, with laughter, and the splendor of jewels and wine, grew reserved little by little, and finally sank their torrents of sparks, their reddish golds, their pale golds woven with blues, their green golds and their burnt-out greens shot through with gold, into the same dull and ruddy mass in which, since he no longer possessed jewel caskets, he had mixed the dust of his rubies, of his topazes, and his pearls, with the inexhaustible treasure of the sun and the shadow which he used royally and lavishly. We know that the imaginary architectures which Lastmann, his feeble master, was already trying to erect in fantastic lights,

REMBRANDT. Study, drawing (*Louvre*).

were being effaced from his dream at the same time that, to his startled soul, reality was revealing itself as more surprising and richer. We have seen the disappearance of his unreal mosques and synagogues, of which a few immense pillars and a few giant arches, covered with tracery and lacework, emerged from the shadow, thanks to a ray from above lighting up, on the pavement below, a group of Oriental kings; but

meanwhile the life around him was appearing little
by little, and the structure of the world was affirming
itself in more grandiose fashion when, in a dark attic,
he divined the presence, barely visible, of some spec-
tacle-maker in meditation. At its romantic beginnings,
this dizzy imagination sought to embrace everything
in the universe and in life and to transmit the whole
by forcing its effects through hallucinating contrasts of
light and darkness, of humanity, and of legend; and
each thing had its distinct rôle—darkness, light, humanity, legend. He played like a magician with these
scattered elements in order to astonish those about
him and to dazzle himself. At the end, the universe
and life had reconstituted themselves in a logical
order; the shadows and the light, legend and humanity,
were becoming part of himself, everything was coursing
to the center of his being, and, when he looked at
objects, he no longer invested them with his dreams
and his rays of light: he wrested them from the objects
themselves. At first, life was a marvelous tumult,
and it was his problem to cause everything ever seen
to enter into it, everything that ever was read, everything ever heard, everything guessed at. It became a
rapid vision between two confused eternities, something fugitive, forever impossible to seize, an illusion.
And it was in that phantom-like illusion that he suspected the truth. Young and rich, he made brilliant
portraits of himself, in which the aigrette of a turban,
the plume of a velvet cap, the gloves, the gold chains,
the spirituelle mouth, and the curled mustache showed
his satisfaction with himself. At that time he felt only
a few things and thought he knew everything. Old and
poor, he had a cloth wrapped round his head, his neck
and hands were bare, and a worn coat was on his
shoulders; but doubt, grief, awe before the mystery of
life, and the disenchanted certitude of the vanity of

VAN DE VELDE. The Sea Fight (*Amsterdam*).

action, all floated before the restless eyes, the sad mouth, and the furrowed brow. And now that he was feeling everything, he thought he knew nothing.

And yet, from insouciance to disquietude, from the impassioned and truculent painting of his first efforts to the hesitant but essential form of his last, it is the same central force which governs this mind. One follows it within him from form to form, with the shadow and the ray of light which circle around, illuminating one thing, hiding another, causing a shoulder to jut forth, or a face, or a raised finger, an open book, a forehead, or a little child in a manger. It is the same central force which tries to choose, to look upon the world as an inexhaustible repertory of moving symbols which the will seizes upon, but learns to utilize at its fancy only when it has penetrated the intimate powers manifested by space and by the volumes peopling it. In the silent man who wanders through the dirty streets and paints but few portraits other than those of his son, his servant, of some poor man he has met, or of himself, there lives always the imaginary voyager from the Orient and from Venice, who has followed, with the returning ships, the eternal movement proceeding from the heart of the cities to the uttermost parts of the sea; and in his mind the distant mirages of the infinity of the heavens still extend to the infinity of the waters. In the soberest portraits of his sixtieth year, where the gold and the red tremble in the limpid depths of the blacks and whites, the old alchemist finds himself once more, he who had caused fairies to appear in the mist of the west, who penetrated with flame the foggy winter of the cold countries, and mingled with the filth of misery the gems of mythical treasure, the purpled fruits which drop of themselves from the branches, the pollen of poisonous flowers, and the feathers dropped from the wings of birds of

fire. If he consents to live between a damp stairway
descending from the street and an air hole from which
the daylight falls, it is because the sounds of the pavement cause the hundred thousand sonorous orchestras
of enthusiasm and memory to leap within him, it is
because the light of day fills his inner sight with the
illuminations of setting suns and with fêtes which

VAN OSTADE. Gathering of peasants (*Munich*).

traverse and transfigure his desire. For him everything is now bathed in that radiance of which the
luminous mist, the quivering reflections on the canals
with their oily mottling, the glittering downpour,
the frost of the fields, the immense vibration of tropical
suns and the phosphorescent nights on the oceans of
the south have created the very atmosphere of his
thought and his sensation. Now all life starts from
this inner radiance whose splendor, in turn, is what

slowly reveals life, from the point of greatest brilliance to the regions of greatest darkness. That which plunges into the light is the reverberation of that which the night submerges. That which the night submerges prolongs into the visible that which plunges into the light. Thought, vision, words, and action unite this forehead, that eye, this mouth, that hand, with the volumes scarcely perceived in the shadow: heads and bodies bending over a birth, a death struggle or death itself. And this is so even, and perhaps above all, when the only instruments of his work are his steel point, his copper plate, and his acid—nothing but black and white; even then he handles the world like a continuing drama which light and darkness model, hollow out, convulse, calm, and bring to birth and death at the call of his passion, of his sadness, and the desperate desire for eternity and the absolute which overwhelms his heart. A lantern, a face lit up, darkness becoming animated, some beings leaning over a cradle on which all the light falls, a cross from which a corpse hangs, a miry road running alongside a pool, a cluster of trees, an obscure sky, a ray of light over some meadow land, the empire of the wind discovered in a flying cloud: here are nothing but black strokes crossing one another on a glowing page, and the tragedy of space and the tragedy of life make the sheet writhe in their fire.

When he was following the teaching of Rubens and of the Italians, as in that "Anatomy Lesson" at The Hague, which is only a good school picture—cold and of an even, waxy material—he arrived at laborious groupings from which almost everything that is his own disappeared, the anxious and direct sense of life, the atomic vibration which runs through his whole field of vision, the lightning illuminating that which he desires to be seen and the darkness veiling the things that he desires to keep silent. When he had followed out the moral bonds which unite the forms among themselves, when he had well observed how a woman holds a child to which she gives the breast, how she dresses it, how a little one takes its first steps, how two heads bend one toward the other for a confidence or a confession, and all the essential gestures which no one notices, he recreated from within out-

PIETER DE HOOCH (?). The reader (*Richmond*).

ward—and without seeming to notice it—the great harmonies of form. The real mystery of life is that a gesture is beautiful as soon as it is true, and that to a deep functional truth a deep continuity of movements and volumes always responds. One must follow Rembrandt from his humblest notes, made every day with a flying hand, to his most carefully thought-out works. A hundred times he had seen people bending over the same task, auditors around a teacher, spectators and assistants around a surgeon, women around a mother giving birth. He had seen that if each one is at his task, the masses organize by themselves, following an irreproachable equilibrium, that the light falls where it should and ignores that which it should, because it is advantageous that it illuminate one point in the scene and that shadow reign elsewhere. And, in the very intensity of application to works of humanity which group men and women around daily events, he found the power of his expressive volumes. If the man who thinks is not always united with the man who feels, the man who feels, if he will only plumb his own depths, invariably finds there the harmonies which attach the humblest sensations and sentiments to the loftiest thoughts. Giotto, when he grouped people around the death of heroes, had felt those secret harmonies which Michael Angelo hardly ever suspected. But his language is still meager, the masses are only indicated, they do not always respond fully and organically to the profound impulsion of the sentiments which animate them. With Rembrandt, on the contrary, the very substance of the souls with the gesture passes uninterruptedly into the material. Whatever his tool, whether he made use of etching or oil painting, whether he had at his command all the colors of the prism or only the shadow and the light which are at the disposal of the engraver, the luminous palpitation and the instinctive movements which are inappreciable for others reduced the universe, for him, to an uninterrupted circulation of animate molecules of which he himself forms part. To the limit of the invisible he pursues the living presence of all the points which his eye can reach. With his colors he incorporates not only the fat and the blood which he catches from the butcher's stall where the split beeves display their purplish muscles, but also a little of the fog, a little

PIETER DE HOOCH. In the House (*Amsterdam*).

of the night, a great deal of silver, a great deal of flame, and a great deal of gold and of the sun. There is something of all this in each one of the materials of his pictures, whether it is the flesh of men or their glance, the crushed stubble at the edge of a road or a few tufts of reeds in a plain, the shrouds wherein the dead are laid, or the silks and furs in which the living are dressed, or the space all trembling with eternal vibrations whose source and goal he finds in each fragment of things. It was in the same period, in the same city and the same quarter, in the heart of the same swarming and miserable life, surrounded by the same shadows and the same lights that Baruch Spinoza was meditating his book.

METSU. The Sick Child
(*Steengracht Museum, The Hague*).

Because Rembrandt is the only one who was always present in everything that he looked at, he is the only one who dared to mix mud with the light of the eyes, to introduce fire into ashes, to cause a pink or a pale blue, as fresh as a flower, to glow in a shroud. When he comes, all moral categories disappear, to let the triumphal torrent of life, ever reborn, pour through the night, spurt forth from sepulchers, and cover putrescence and death with phosphorescent shadows in which new germs unfold. He has no need to put a nimbus around the head of Christ seated at the table of a peasant or entering a cellar where the sick and infirm languish, for the most discouraged hearts to hear the lyric song of hope born again from themselves. He has no need of a thinker to cause thought to float over a face. An old pauper, with his furrowed visage, the tendons of his neck, and his rags suffices to evoke something poignant and gentle which he never defines; and his servant, baring herself in a miserable room, has enough sap under her skin to make the place flame as with a torch of voluptuousness. The force of life which dwells in him rolls into withered flesh and covers rags with purple. If Christ had not existed, Rembrandt would have found other legends through which to recount, from the cradle to the grave, the human drama that he was living, or else he would have done without legends and would not have placed under his pictures the titles which they do not need. In the birth of anybody, in the repast of anybody, in the death of anybody, he finds himself. His humanity is actually formidable; it has the inevitable accent of the plaint, the love, the continual, indifferent, and dramatic interchange between everything that is born and everything that dies. He follows our course toward death by the traces of blood which mark it. He does not weep over us, he does not comfort us because he is with us, because he is ourselves. He is there when the cradle is illumined. He is there when the young girl appears to us leaning on the window sill, with eyes that do not know and a pearl between her breasts. He is there when we have disrobed her, when her hard torso trembles to the throbbing of our fever. He is there when the woman opens her knees to us with the same maternal emotion with which she opens her arms to her child. He is there when the fruit drops from her ten or fifteen times in her life. He is there afterward, when she is mature, when her belly is deeply grooved, her bosom droops, and her legs grow heavy. He is there when she has aged, when her furrowed face is surrounded with a cap and when her bony hands cross at her waist to signify that she has no resentment against life for having dealt hard with her. He is there when we are old, when we look fixedly toward the approaching night; he is there when we are dead and our corpse offers its winding-sheet to the arms of our sons.

When, toward the evening of life, he painted the "Syndics of the Drapers' Guild," he had attained the

TERBORG.   Boy hunting Fleas
(*Munich*).

power to fix average humanity in the eternity of life. Such a force, mastering the soul of the world, giving to the every-day event the importance and the majesty of the mind, recreating the face of men in the simplicity of their habitual existence elevated to epic height by the invisible effort of the intelligence and of love, has in it something terrifying. With Rembrandt we no longer know the true value of words, doubtless because they have only that one value which we can place upon them. Is an art like his objective in which the inner drama so silently animates face and gesture, where the heart of an all-powerful man never ceases to beat within the forms that appear, where the night which he dissipates or thickens at will is always illuminated by his secret presence? And when that man reaches the power of manifesting his grief, his pity, or his pride without telling them, through his recital of the most ordinary and the most hidden acts of life, or in painting a mere portrait, can one discover in his language philosophic intentions which he would doubtless have been surprised to have attributed to him when he was caressing with tawny shadows the belly and the breasts of his servant? There is in this a terrible mystery of which Shakespeare, before Rembrandt, had caught a glimpse. Whereas every living spirit, worthy of domination and strength, struggles unceasingly to individualize himself, to separate himself from the world, the supreme individual no longer separates himself from the world; he accepts it wholly. The world merges with his being to such a degree, all external movements re-echo in his flesh so suddenly and so intoxicatingly that he no longer distinguishes that which is himself from that which is the world, nor realizes that all the things of the world are hymns which are within him. It is because there was, between the world and himself, a pitiless interchange, a kind of silent frenzy of desire, reborn immediately after the possession. When he had not succeeded in dragging to his room some outcast in order to lure to his mouth and his eyes all of his old tired soul, when he did not find his old brother there, battered and hollowed out by work, or his son Titus with his eyes of shadowy flame, or Hendrickje always ready to leave the stove and her dishcloth to put an amber necklace around her neck, undress, and give her flanks to the embrace of light and of the mind, he must needs, to appease his fever, stand before a mirror, grimace, laugh, look grave, feign fright,

TERBORG. Portrait (*Berlin*).

or give utterance to his suffering. Life for him was a continuous surprise and discovery. It did not allow him an hour of respite. All his misfortunes, his misery, and the oblivion into which he slipped were nothing as compared with the increasing torture of being unable to grasp the flight of things and to perceive the time which was left him to live and to learn, becoming briefer and slipping away more quickly, in the measure that the universe widened its limits and flowed back into him, ever more moving and more complex and more secret. The approach of death is not really dramatic save for him who feels that he will never possess life.

V

In an attempt to circumscribe this nature, so human, which is to say, so ready at all times to recognize itself in all men and to recognize all men in itself, people have gone to the point of trying to make it the expression of the Reformation. They have not realized how far its intoxication in welcoming all things, its sensual generosity, its powerful pity, and that superior unmorality in which Spinoza would have recognized his respect for the rôle which evil and corruption play in the universal organism, were separated from the spirit of the Protestant beliefs. In Holland, as elsewhere, the Reformation was, in its origin, the assertion of the national temperament and a political movement taking the pretext for outburst which the Reformers offered. The Dutch peasant demanded above all that he be allowed to dry up his polder, milk his cows, make his cheese, grind his wheat, and sell his cattle. And Dutch painting expressed, above all, the forces freed by the economic and national insurrection. Considered abstractly and separated from the vital movement of which it is only one aspect, a religion has never created

TERBORG.   Woman combing her child (*Steengracht Museum,*
The Hague).

artists and its power of fecundation, precisely, dies when it triumphs. Dutch painting disappeared with the energy of the emancipation, while Protestantism remained alive. If it had a rôle in the genesis of painting in Holland, it was to demonstrate that the religious spirit, of which art is the supreme expression, is everywhere superior to its sectarian forms. In its iconoclasm, Protestantism prevented Dutch art from illustrating the Scriptures for the ornamentation of the temples and the edification of the believers. Dutch art had its revenge in turning toward space and life and in edifying the artists, who are the eternal believers.

If there is, in Dutch painting, a man impregnated with Protestantism, it is Ruysdael. It is also Albert Cuyp, no doubt. But Albert Cuyp, after all, is perhaps just a good Hollander who tried to say about Holland everything that could be said, and thereby forced his language a little. In his work he gathered together the diffused blondness of the landscapes of van Goyen, the sumptuous materiality of the early Rembrandt, and the fineness of color of Terborg; he accompanied Paul Potter to the paddocks, he followed van Ostade and Hondecoeter into the barnyards and the stables, and he went with van der Velde to look at the sea, without gaining from them their mysterious power, or their simplicity, or their intimacy, or their familiar good-nature, or their cordial optimism. A shade of solemnity hovers about when the lords go hunting or supervise their fisheries, when the herds climb a hill crowned with walls in ruin, or when evening falls slowly over his imposing landscapes where animals are lying down. One would say that he prepares for Louis XIV a Holland made aristocratic and ready to turn that king out politely. He is the painter of the rich, and he knows how to act his part. He is even proud of it. Which is what the Reformation leads to when one accepts without regret its social consequences of economic individualism and family egoism, as it leads to Ruysdael when one studies the question of his principles and closely observes the workings of his inner being in order to judge his acts with severity.

For Ruysdael, the man, flees the rich, and fine materials, and the whirl of life, and luxurious repasts. He is always grave, he is often sad, he is sometimes tiresome, and he is the only one who tries to convince, to abstract, and to demonstrate. And what is more, he has character. But one must not forget that he appears at the moment when Holland begins to feel the fatigue of painting. His artist's sensibility warns him that there is a certain diminution, or at all events, disunion, in the energy of the nation. Where did he get those tortured rocks, those furious cascades, and that harsh, lusterless color which one might say was dried by the wind? When he approaches the sea, it is only to look upon the tempest, the waves assaulting the piers, and the sky and water mingling in the spray of the downpour and the breakers. When he crosses the polder, the daylight is livid among the stripped branches and the trunks twisting above their roots halfway out of the soil. He quivers with the earth when a black cloud passes over the sun. Trees uprooted and shattered by the torrents, herds returning with the storm over trembling wooden bridges, and poor huddled houses; he sees in nature only that which responds to the dramas of consciousness which must have shaken him. The vast world is gray, there are flights of black birds against the big clouds which fill the whole sky. His universe, given over to the tragic elements and wherein man and life are only poor ephemeral things drenched by the rain and beaten by the winds, permits us to divine the secret illness which he does not confess, and beside it the romantic battle pictures of Wouwerman,

Vermeer of Delft. Young woman putting on a necklace (*Berlin*).

bathed in clouds of smoke and showing men hanged and
walls in ruin, disguise, for the joy of those who delight
in fine military painting, the real physiognomy which
is being assumed, in the eyes of a powerful man, by the
sinister aspects of the road.

As the joy of painting seems to grow with the contemporaries of Ruysdael the nearer they approach the
hour when painting is suddenly arrested, the work of
this great poet of space forces us, each time that it
presents itself, to inquire into his life. And of that we
know nothing save that he had but little success and
died in the poorhouse. To be sure, he saw the dikes
cut, the polder inundated, and the new generation
obliged to regain everything from the foreigner and the
sea during the prime of his life. But the old springs
still have their temper, the peasant and the fisherman
have kept their weapons furbished, and among those
painters of his time who stay indoors to seize there
the harmonies of home life or who fix the image of water
and clouds on a square of canvas the size of their two
hands, not one experiences that sentiment of melancholy impotence which makes an intellectual drama of
each one of his pictures. If Terborg is a little older than
Ruysdael, he dies in the same year and, like him, is
present at the drama of the great wars. Brekelenkam,
Jan Steen, Metsu, Pieter de Hooch, and Vermeer of
Delft are about of his age. But Jan Steen, the carefree
spirit, never ceases his laughter, and, say what you will,
it is without bitterness. The others do not leave their
households, which the well-varnished furniture fills
with blond light, save to go to look at the round arms
of the servant girl who is washing the doorstep from a
full pail, or else at the neighbor opposite who is making
lace behind the painted inclosure and the little window-
panes set in blue frames. The people have become rich,
and well-being has come to the clean little houses

where the luxuries of the home are being developed in egoistic fashion. Jan Steen is the only one who has discovered that he has had enough of housekeeping, of letters of love or of business, of living in the intimacy of the family, and of smoking a lonely pipe; he has seen all he wants of plying the distaff at the fireside and rocking the crying baby. He brings home people who drink, sing, break the dishes, and relieve themselves in the corners of the room. And that is not enough, if we are to believe the legend. He turns innkeeper. He helps his strong lads whom the drunkards follow to the cellar staircase, and the young fellows who are in a hurry to get upstairs to the floor above, in setting up the rickety tables where artless gluttony will soon put his customers at their

VERMEER OF DELFT. The Alley
(*Six Collection, Amsterdam*).

ease. He roars and gets drunk with them, he plays dice and cards with them, he is their friend; before his door he sets up stands for the minstrels who play their bagpipes, beat their drums, and scrape on their fiddles. He does not fail to come in haste when the tooth puller with drawn face and enormous pincers searches the mouth of a poor devil who howls and stamps his feet, to the great delight of the gossips and the children.

This moralist is probably a man of the most vicious
life. But he never loses his head, and he sees what the
others do not. He is present, as if by chance, at the

VERMEER OF DELFT. The drinkers, detail (*Dresden*).

comedies of married life, and he knows far better than
the constable how to pounce on a couple of wenches
who are picking the pockets of their customer when he
is dead drunk. And the cut-purse and the thimble-

rigger interest him infinitely. Never does he become angry, never does he preach; his indulgence is illimitable. It is because he needs it himself, as he weil knows. He is their accomplice. His clearness of eye, which delights him, shows his frankness. If he had not lived their life, if he had observed their innocent sports from the outside only, he would note with greater attention and more discreet pleasure the rare play of the tones under the caress of atmosphere; he would be more of a painter than he is, but doubtless less living, as well. All classes and all environments have their own painters in this period, or rather, in all classes, in all types of environment painters are born who never cease to belong thereto, who have no wish to escape from them, and who die after performing their function, like the banker at his counter, the shoemaker in his shop, the butcher in his stall, the miller in his mill, and the fisherman in his boat. And so Holland herself, her villages, and the people of her fairs, the pavements of her cities, their hovels, their shops, their almshouses, the homes of their citizens, their storehouses, the traffic of the canals and the roadsteads, the doubtful resorts of her harbor towns, her solid virtues, her gross vices, and her violent and heavy life of joyous effort in commerce and war, the whole country comes down to us, overflowing with action and enjoyment, economical and prodigal, without a single one of its gestures or one of its minutes being forgotten, dissimulated, or misunderstood. Were it not for Ruysdael, and above all Rembrandt, this would be the least mysterious mirror, but also the most faithful, which man has ever held up before the face of his days.

VI

Only, after Rembrandt, and even with Ruysdael, the painting of Holland lost the conquering force of the generation which issued from the founders. Jan Steen has no longer the truculence of Frans Hals and his pupils, Brouwer, van Ostade, and the first vagabond painters who rolled their candid life through the evil places and the inns where they paid their shot by painting a sign or the portrait of some bully. The painting of Holland knows now that van Tromp and de Ruyter command the winds and the wave; it is happy, it isolates itself, and perhaps it is just that absolute and passive beatitude which tortures Ruysdael. One can foresee that the coldness and the petty, anecdotal spirit of Metsu and the glassy dryness of van Mieris will succeed, all too quickly, the absence of disquietude and the splendid materialism of Vermeer and of Pieter de Hooch.

When these bourgeois painters had discovered silvery grays, and blacks upon dull reds emerging from the penumbra, when they had surprised, in a room filled with blond ash color, the acts of the family seated around a beautiful tablecover, with an inkwell or an open book on the table, or with a workbox or a musical instrument, they could do no more than sit down before silver compote dishes, decorated plates, and crystal glasses. The gold of a lemon, the skin of a roast fowl, the topaz or the ruby of a wine maintained there under their eyes the familiar harmonies which the waxed floors, the satin dresses, the velvet curtains, the earthenware pots, and the copper vases realized in the house. Terborg lent to the bourgeois families, who live in these interiors so charged with their artless egoism, such rare and sober elegance that it seems to emanate from his almost muted symphonies.

One cannot conceive portraits more aristocratic than those signed by this painter of the most materialistic and positive among the peoples of the earth. He is a Titian of the north, less decorative, certainly, and less

broad, and less lyric, but on the other hand carrying
the contrary virtues to the highest point of distinction.
A small personage is alone, standing in the center of a
little picture.   Dressed in black, almost always, with
rare grays insinuating themselves throughout the
whole, living like flesh and blood, precious as a fine
pearl, it seems that through the taut structure and the

JAN STEEN. Epiphany (*Brussels*).

density of the harmonies which he concentrates in that
tiny space, he summarizes in his discretion the unexpected image of intellectual Holland. By himself alone
he represents the silent and proud reserve of the spirit
in exile amid the surrounding coarseness. All Terborg's
models, his cavalrymen, and even his prostitutes bear
that imprint. And yet, by a singular paradox, all of
them, even the lowest and most vulgar, are themselves

and at home.   The expression is concentrated and fills the forms to their depths; it is distributed with equal attention over busy hands, foreheads bent under shaggy mops of hair, the happy and peaceful faces of the mothers, and the astonished or mischievous faces of the children. The light does not obtrude itself, it is never indiscreet; but it follows lovingly the line of the comb in the red hair, it touches the amused grimace, it shines in the eye of the dog who is being relieved of fleas, it lights up a jewel against a moist skin, and it carries on the mood of gentle excitement which envelops everything and is awakened and maintained by every incident of the homely and continuous drama of the inhabited room, the window which lights it and the commonplace actions which take place there each day. A transparent atmosphere caresses the gilded napes of necks bending under the carefully arranged hair.   In the air dazzled with pale gold, the discreet glow of a silvery skirt, of a cherry-colored bodice, of steel-gray breeches, of a boot of tawny leather, or a pearl hung from a blue ribbon and glistening on a blond cheek mingles with the sonority of the harpsichord itself to surround and penetrate with their soft tones the velvety peacefulness of lives unrolling in security and comfort.

Pieter de Hooch prefers to look out through the window whence one perceives the canal, and on the other side of it, the little triangular houses of red brick with their painted shutters.   But into the street he carries on the intimacy of the dwellings where buxom young mothers with bare arms wash and comb little girls with long dresses and round pink faces and bushy red hair. He carefully follows the soapy water which streams from the pavement of the dining room, to filter in between the stones of the quay.   When he is seated before his door and chats with his neighbors, he has to give a glance through to the back of the open rooms and look on at the household work. At home, he cannot bear to have a single door closed; he watches the laundry and the shining kitchen. Not satisfied with being present at the doctor's visit or watching the child being dressed or listening to the thin song of the spinet, he must follow the light as it roams through

RUYSDAEL. Haarlem Lake (*Brussels*).

the corridors, following from room to room the black and white tiles of the floor, lighting up the coppers, and awakening—with the carpets, the upholstery of the furniture, the half-drawn curtains of the alcove, skirts and doublets—the discreet life of the reds, the grays, the oranges, and the blacks, which it bathes and turns blond, gently and evenly. With him, with Terborg, and with Vermeer, everything lives and speaks; we see that the teapot is warm, that the chair has just been used and the tapestry work has just been left, that the andirons are awaiting the feet which will rest upon them, and that all these things which are kept so clean are yet a little bit worn, and that the wandering shadow takes on the warmth of the hand.

Vermeer reaches the point of painting the radiant silence which emanates from these friendly things, and the very welcome which they extend to you. That woman and that mirror are used to each other; it was also that woman who moved that ball of thread; and if that curtain retains that fold, it is because each time she raises it she touches it in the same place. Those rare pictures hanging on the wall have, with their muffled harmonies, awakened in the pearly amber of the room a few almost imperceptible echoes of the world of misty gold which begins across the threshold; slowly and peacefully they have formed her vision. Everything is heavy with memories of her, of her perfume, of her warmth, of her habits, of her breath. If anyone but she were there, the light entering by that window near which she places herself to read or work would not soften as it passes through the glass, it would not caress so lovingly the hand and the inclining forehead, it would not mingle with the golden strands of the hair. The light itself is a friend of the household. In the glass or the case of a clavichord it sketches the shadow of a familiar profile, it tints the bare wall as it would tint a pure water, and across objects which emerge or grow dim, it carries the mystery of the growth or decline of day.

No one has penetrated farther into the intimacy of matter. As he crystallizes it in his painting, as he permits it to retain its grain, its thickness, its dull inner life, Vermeer has multiplied its qualities through all the limpid brilliance and the warm transparence which it takes on through the sight of the painter whose eyes were probably the clearest that ever have been. There is so deep an agreement between the material and the harmonies which accompany it that they seem to come from within, to be born spontaneously from the mass of objects, like a fruit coloring in proportion as

RUYSDAEL. View of Haarlem (*The Hague*).

its juice mellows. The color is kneaded into the tissue of things, into that rounded face flushed with its young blood, into that hand resting on that golden bodice; those reds and those blacks are as unfathomable as translucent stones. He did not paint a silk dress, lace, eyes, lips, cheeks, the velvet of a mantle, or the plume of a felt hat without his bearing in mind the cattle in the fields against whose emerald they look like black diamonds. After the rain, everything opaque in the atmosphere of Holland assumes a liquid and luminous depth which Vermeer incorporated with his color as if it were powdered pearls and turquoises, vibrating like the molecules of living organisms. He mingles the turquoise and the pearl with everything, with the soil, with dirty waters, and with old

ALBERT CUYP. Starting for the ride (*Louvre*).

walls. The blues and reds of roofs and shutters, their disturbed reflections in the blue water, and the trees whose dark foliage is blue, form, in the only landscape which we have from him, a miraculous harmony. The milky blue of Delft ware, with which the very paving stones of the city seem to be colored, floats through the picture and is barely affected by the pearly grays and pinks which the light and the clouds temper in a vibration of silver.

Vermeer of Delft summarizes Holland. He has the qualities common to the Dutch, and in him they are gathered into a single sheaf and at a single stroke raised to the highest power. This man, who is the greatest master of the beauty of pigment, is without the least imagination. His desires never go beyond that which his hand can touch. He has accepted life in its totality. He gives it out again. He has interposed nothing between himself and it, he limits himself to restoring to it the maximum of splendor, of intensity, and of concentration, which an ardent and attentive study discovers in it. He and Rembrandt are the opposite poles; for Rembrandt is the only one in his epoch to go against the stream of splendid middle-class materialism which surrounds him, in order to attain, through it and all bathed in its strength, the infinite lands of contemplation.

And yet the painter of Delft, like Terborg, like Pieter de Hooch, like Brekelenkam at times, like that Karel Fabritius so mysterious and so powerful, and who died too young to gain possession of his own nature, felt the genius of the master. Almost all the painters born in Holland contemporary with Rembrandt and after him recognized him as being the only one whose indifference to the approbations and the hatreds of the crowd rendered him capable of understanding it and worthy of dominating it. Only, carried along by his strength, and strong in his very strength, these men fought in their own station and during their own time, sure of acting in accordance with his dictates when they were no longer observing him. They had confidence in themselves. . . . The weak men, on the contrary, those who never took their eyes off him—Gerard Dou, Ferdinand Bol, Salomon de Koninck, Flinck, and Maes—were devoured by him. Ferdinand Bol carried his golden atmosphere, like an intruder, in among the abundant forms which Rubens, the other king of the north, imposed upon his weakness. Gerard Dou thought that in order to make a home scene, a hand, a shoulder, or a face stand out more strongly from the darkness, he had to wait for night, light a candle or a lamp, and reduce to an amusing or sentimental little story the human and dramatic enchant-

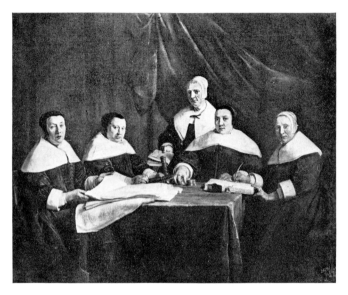

JAN DE BRAY. The lady regents of the Hospital (*Haarlem*).

ment to which life, in revealing itself, always transported the old man with the oil-stained handkerchief bound around his forehead as he drew from some dark hovel the splendor and the heat and the fecundity of the sun. The flame of that sun showed Nicolas Maes no more than the anecdote, enveloped in the silent intimacy of Terborg or of Vermeer. The "chiaroscuro" which the old masters of the Netherlands, especially

Honthorst, were already trying to borrow from Caravaggio, and in which Rembrandt had seized the law of
nature itself—chiaroscuro was emerging once more,
with the last artists of Holland, from the actual inter-
changes of mind, matter, and space, to sink to the
level of a school process, to immobilize the world and
dissociate its elements. In this period of the death

HOBBEMA. The Avenue of Middelharnis (*National Gallery*).

struggle of Dutch painting, following immediately
upon the last two defensive wars, the men who abandon their studio and go forth from their houses are the
only ones still to express something of their country.
They will look again upon the sea from the dike which
is being repaired, upon the grassy fields which are being
dried up again, and the cities and towns which are
building up their brick walls again and restoring their
canals. Such are van der Heyden and Gerrit Berck-

Heyde, who paint the street, the market, the public square, and the intimacy of the narrow façades behind a curtain of trees. Such are the last painters of the van de Velde dynasty who, after having boarded the warships, after having breathed the smoke of powder and conflagration amid the thunder of the cannon, have seen the big ships of commerce taking the sea again with their pennants flying, and have seen the long waves and the banking of clouds in the breeze that plays through the great spaces of the heavens. Such is Hobbema, who passes his life in the polder, still drowned in places by swamps and encumbered with rotted trunks; he goes forth among the slender trees and along the broken roads, stopping each time that a clearing opens amid a little wood or that a farm sheltered from the west wind by a few thin elms appears beside a pond. He finds again the eternal and monotonous landscape, the muddy and grassy soil, the lightness of the blond mist. Holland consents to abandon painting, but upon condition that the last of her painters record that she has not changed, that she is pursuing her task, that her cattle are increasing, that her mills are still turning.

TOLEDO

Chapter III. SPAIN

I

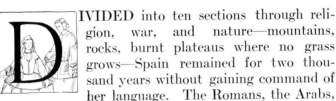IVIDED into ten sections through reli-
gion, war, and nature—mountains,
rocks, burnt plateaus where no grass
grows—Spain remained for two thousand years without gaining command of
her language. The Romans, the Arabs,
and the French had, by turns, affirmed their domination through their imposing architectures, upon which
the Spanish soul, still obscure and fragmentary, im-
printed only furtive traces, until the hour when Catholic, political, and military unity interpreted its need
for action. Then there was something like a tragic
conflagration. The flames spurted forth from the
shadow and pierced the walls in order to gain the
summit of the towers; a frenzy of cruelty and melancholy passion appeared everywhere; the naves and

choirs were encumbered with tortured altar-pieces
and with stalls hollowed out with carvings; the alcazars
and the mosques were seized and Christs of wood and
altars of gold were set up in them. Everything pointed
to a somber aspiration toward suffering, through which
the voluptuous desire to enter upon life sought to
punish itself even before life was mastered. But the
painted idols which the artisans of the people had
been carving to place at the crossroads ever since the
first centuries of Christianity, the Calvaries, the niches,
and the thin, bleeding gods hung by the nails in their
hands, sinking on their spreading knees, could neither
inspire in a people unused to great abstract constructions the power to build a fitting sanctuary, nor check
the invasion of the less terrible images which the
enriched cities and the triumphant monarchy summoned from abroad. The union of Castile and Aragon
and the conquest of Granada did not bear fruit until
later, and then only in a few solitary minds which
wrested the soul of Spain from the foreigner only to
render it a secret cult in their proud meditation. Spain
has no collective expression defining for the future that
jealous unity which it affirmed, sword in hand, upon
the routes of the world.

Its sudden expansion through war subjected it for a
hundred years to the peoples it had vanquished. The
annexation of Flanders, the war with France, and the
conquest of Italy deliver Castile to the Flemings and
the French, and the eastern sea-coast to the Italians.
The infiltration did not, moreover, wait political events
before coming about. Jan van Eyck came to Castile
soon after finishing the painting of the "Mystic Lamb"
at Ghent, and, through Luiz Dalmau, the painter,
conquered Catalónia. Later, the French sculptor
Philippe Vigarni brings to Toledo and to Granada the
knowledge of the men of the north, which his brother,

SANCHEZ COELLO. The Infanta Caterina Micaela (*Prado*).

the painter Juan de Borgona, a hard, tense draftsman, tries to place at the service of Italian idealism. Bartolomeo Ordonez, a sculptor of Barcelona, goes to Carrara in search of marble from which to carve his overloaded tombs, hollowed out like a piece of goldsmith's work, and Gil de Siloe peoples the chapels of Burgos with them. Ordonez also brings back the theatrical redundance and the grandiloquent mannerisms which are beginning to decompose Italy. Damian Forment, confronted by her, restrains the rude strength of his native Aragon. The power necessary to isolate themselves belongs only to the free spirits of culminating epochs made aware, by invulnerable pride, of the dangers of these contacts. But when a race is developing, all its energies are concentrated upon conquest and expansion. The Primitives, suddenly transported to a world which is descending the other side of the slope, allowed themselves to be dazzled by the skill and the audacity of the decadent artists. They think that they can learn. They abandon what they know. They give over to the men of civilization the control of their senses.

For a people without character the defeat is a decisive one. A people bent on defining itself, on the contrary, suddenly perceives that it has as yet said nothing about itself and employs the instrument which it did not forge to explore its depths. When Alonso Berruguete, the son of a good painter-workman who had helped with his ingenuous collaboration in the works of Juan de Borgona, had learned in Italy the speech of Michael Angelo, the Renaissance could penetrate no farther into Spain. The ease of Berruguete in making a torso twist from the hips, in sending a face back into the shadow of a shoulder, in furrowing a muscular belly with darks and lights, and in pursuing the most terrible and most grave reality in a cadaver

stretched upon the ground, bears witness to the fact
that Spain is reacting at the very moment when she
seems to be surrendering herself. She utilizes a style
which she has learned, and which she will try to forget,
only to deepen her faith in an ever-increasing cruelty.
Berruguete had just died when Juan de Herrera constructed the Escorial. Spain has no architecture.
But if there is a monument which interprets the efforts
she had to make in order to resist the invasion of the
complicated and declamatory styles born of the meeting of the Gothic men, the Arabs, and the Renaissance
men, it is that monument. It is arid. Its long walls,
bare and gray, are of a frightful sadness. It arises from
a desert of stone, alone with the somber sun. Philip II
died there in a cell without an opening to the sky.

Toward the end of the violent century which had
seen Spain seizing Portugal and the two Sicilies, dominating Germany, vanquishing France, thrusting back
Islam, conquering America, and launching the Armada
against England, Philip II summoned, for the purpose
of ornamenting his tomb, certain bad painters who at
Genoa were prolonging the death struggle of Rome and
of Venice. He was following the example of his father
who had secured the service of Titian. But Titian
had just died a centenarian, and Philip II, accustomed,
since his childhood, to the magnificent forms which
Italian art at the moment of its full bloom had been
unfolding before his eyes, preferred, as always, the
reflection and the husk to the somber spirit whose
outline was being traced in the wake of the armies,
the missions, and the ships starting forth at his command upon every path of apostleship and conquest.
It is possible that Anton Mor, the Hollander turned
Spaniard, who was so profoundly impressed with the
pale faces and the feverish glances seen at his court,
and that the Castilians, Sanchez Coello and Pantoja de

la Cruz, whose sad and haughty spirit had bowed so spontaneously before the harsh etiquette which held the bored infantas upright in their stiff dresses, had declared themselves unable to decorate the walls. Morales, the mystic and barbarous painter of Estre-

MORALES. Pietà
(*Academy of St. Fernando, Madrid*).

madura, was not made for this task, either, and, besides, he was about to die. But it was already known that there were good painters at Valencia. At Cordova there existed a flourishing school. And above all, there was, at Toledo, an artist, who had himself been formed by the Italians, and who was painting, at the moment when the Escorial[1] was being finished, one of the greatest works of painting,[2] revealing, at a single stroke, the soul of Spain to itself—he, a Greek reared in Venice, at the very time that the Spanish hesitated to affirm it.

II

Philip II was certainly not capable of raising his funereal piety to the level of the passion which filled

[1] Built from 1563 to 1584.
[2] "The Burial of the Count of Orgaz" dates from 1584.

the little church in Toledo with faces made livid by
the rush of blood to the heart, and with eyes of fever
and of wild adoration, and with bony hands all lifted
toward heaven. Otherwise, something great could
have resulted from his meeting with Greco. When
Theotocopuli arrived in Toledo, hardly twenty years
had elapsed from the time that Ignatius of Loyola,
his thigh broken and rebroken, had dragged himself to
the altar of the Virgin to lay his sword upon it. Don
John of Austria was nailing the banner of Christ to
the topmast of the vessels which he was to lead to
Lepanto. Teresa of Avila had just finished burning
the last ashes of her flesh. For forty years she had
welcomed the flame of the south, the scorching of the
rocks, the odor of the orange trees, the cruelty of the
soldiers, the sadism of the executioners, and the taste
of the Host and of wine in order to torture and purify,
in the fire of all her senses turned back toward her
inner life, the heart she offered to her divine lover.
Within the country, the Holy Office never allowed the
fire to die out around any stake. Abroad, the captains,
dressed in black, led their lean men, fed on gunpow-
der, to fight, rosary in hand, against the Reformation. The Duke of Alba deluged Flanders with fire
and blood. The flames of torture and of battles at-
tested, over all the earth, the fidelity of Spain to her
vow.

The Cretan, who still saw in the depths of his memory
the red and narrow gleam lighting up the icons in the
orthodox chapels and whom Titian and Tintoretto
had initiated into painting in their Venice, where the
bed of purple and of flowers was already prepared for
royal deaths, brought into this tragic world the fervor
of ardent natures in which all the new forms of sensuality and of violence enter in tongues of fire. In reality,
this young man of twenty-five years was old in his

EL GRECO. View of Toledo (*Private collection*).

civilization, a thing full of neuroses centuries old, and
subjugated by the first shock of the savage aspect of
the country in which he was arriving and by the
accentuated character of the people amid whom he
was going to live. Toledo is made of granite. The
landscape round about is terrible, of a deadly aridity,
with its low bare hills filled with shadow in their hollows, with the rumble of its caged torrent, and with

EL GRECO. The burial of the Count of Orgaz, detail (*Toledo*).

its huge trailing clouds. On sunny days it shines with
flame, it is as livid as a cadaver in winter. Only occasionally and slightly is the greenish uniformity of the
stone touched by the pale silver of the olive trees, by
the light note of pink or blue from a painted wall.
But there is no rich land, no leafy foliage: it is a fleshless skeleton in which nothing living moves, a sinister
absolute where the soul has no other refuge than
the wild solitude or cruelty and misery as it awaits
death.

With this pile of granite, this horror, and this somber flame, Greco painted his pictures. It is a terrifying and splendid painting, gray and black, lit with green reflections. In the black clothing there are only two gray notes, the ruffs and the cuffs from which bony heads and pale hands come forth. Soldiers or priests —it is the last effort of the Catholic tragedy. Already they wear mourning. They are burying a warrior in his steel, and now look only to heaven. Their gray faces have the aridity of the stone. Their protruding bones, their dried skin, and their eyes, deeply sunken in their hollow orbits, look as if they were seized and shaped by metal pincers. Everything which defines the skull and the face is pursued over the hard surfaces, as if the blood no longer coursed through the already withered skin. One would say that a cord of nerves went forth from the vital center and was drawing the skin toward it. Only the eye is burning and fixed, expressing the will to reach the fire of death by dint of rendering life sterile. One follows the glance inward, it leads to the implacable heart. The mouths are like slits. The hair is thin through fasting, asceticism, and the slow asphyxiation rising from braziers burning in closed rooms. The wind of the desert seems to have passed over the scene.

When the red robe flooded with gold and the golden miter of a bishop spread forth, on backgrounds uniformly gray and black, the sumptuous memories brought back from Venice and the Orient, one would say that the painter was playing with his power of controlling the voices of the world in order to give more accent to the dull splendor of the gray faces, and to the harmonies of death and dust which mount like a hymn to the silent joy of offering in sacrifice to the divine spirit of life all the joys which it spreads before us. Remorse at having been born pursues the painter until the end, but when he expresses it in his art, the magnificence which it takes on avenges him for his terrors. Whatever the elements of the higher equilibrium which a great artist pursues—almost always

EL GRECO. Portrait of an unknown man (*Prado*).

unknown to himself—whether the most completely purified mysticism or the most violent sensualism guides him, he is not a great artist unless he realizes through them those mysterious symphonies in which both the

matter and the soul of life seem present and mingled
forever with all eternity. It is not necessary that
above Greco's groups, spectral angels of superhuman
size should arise, or that, behind his drooping Christ
there should be enormous grayish clouds which isolate
Him from the universe; the somber glow is everywhere,
in the raised foreheads, the hollow orbits, the arid
earth, and the habits of black velvet. It is in him, the
ardent center of all these things, a profound and living
poem fashioned by the encounter of obedience and
liberty, of the broad and voluptuous world whence he
comes with the harshest soil and the most tragic people of Europe, of the severest spirit of western Catholicism with completely disordered memories of Eastern
orthodoxy.

Never did the Christian ideal express, with greater
anxiety, its impotence to divide life into two sections.
The spirit tries to tear itself away, but in vain. What
is beautiful in the divine forms is always borrowed from
the science he possessed of terrestrial form, and it
always returns to them. At the end of his life he painted
like one in a hallucination, in a kind of ecstatic nightmare, where the preoccupation with expressing the
spirit alone pursued him. Deformation appears in
his pictures more and more, lengthening the bodies,
attenuating the fingers, and hollowing the masks. His
blues, his winelike reds, and his greens seem lit by
some livid reflection sent to him from the near-by tomb
and the hell caught sight of from eternal bliss. He
died before realizing the form of the dream which
haunted him, perhaps because he himself was too old,
and no longer found in his hardened bones and in his
irritated and weak nerves the power he had possessed
for seeking, in love of the world's appearances, the
means of comparing and supporting his vision. And
yet, what an effort! When we enter one of those

EL GRECO. The Nativity (*Metropolitan Museum, New York*).

Spanish churches where, on days of service, the gleam of the tapers and the vapor of the incense make us forget for a moment the horror or vulgarity of the images of which we catch a glimpse, we must also carry on with ourselves one of those combats which leave us enervated and somewhat shaken with that intoxication in which the ecstasy of the paradise desired effaces the soul and the body of those who try to forget. He alone could see arms lifted as if to raise the weight of the heavens and to draw aside its veils. Standing at the foot of the Cross, he alone was able to pierce the shadow which rises from all sides like an accomplice to hide the murder; and it is with a terrible glance that he follows the phantom horsemen who enter a hollow road. He alone has seen among those who will to know no more of the earth, forms drawn out as if in prayer, aspiring wholly toward something higher, hands which seem prolonged into supernatural lights, drooping and emaciated trunks, and also young nude bodies which he cannot tear from the innocence of life, but around which circles a phosphorescent glow which comes no one knows whence.

At the remote origin of that invincible elegance which never left him, however much he was gripped by the need to express more than he could, one found the Greek, the Greek of the forgotten ages, the Hellene. The wraith of the gods which still wandered on the shores of the southern sea had drunk a strong wine from the golden cup of Venice and had permitted itself to be carried along, still not entirely consumed even by Greco, to the burning deserts of stone where the aridity of things offers the mind no other avenue than that of death. It was that wraith—it could not die, it had survived the twelve centuries of constraint imposed by the degenerating Orient upon the Byzantine images—over which one would say that there mounts a

long pale flame, like those wandering fires which dance
upon the marshes. It is the witness of the impotence
of genius to detach itself from its roots, and of the
majesty which it assumes when it consents to nourish
itself from them. Greco must have fasted and worn
sackcloth. He must have followed, with bare feet,
the processions across the powdered granite with his

El Greco. Christ driving the money changers from the temple
(*Private collection*).

ankles cut by shackles, bearing a heavy metal cross, and
masked with a monk's hood in order not to have the
pride of his humiliation. He must have passed the
burning nights, when passion is compelled to roll in the
torture of voluntary chastity, so that in the morning
he might carry his exasperated strength into the ever-
livid faces intent on heaven and into the garments,
always black, which bear witness to our grief at having

lived. No matter. He had a daughter. He loved
children and women, and ever the burning shadow and
the bare landscape. His whole will to be superior to
life crossed and recrossed the powerful center of the
life which, when one has felt its burning, sends its lava
into death itself and the eternal shadows and the dust
of bones.

Beyond existence, when our memory is burnt out,
there is, to be sure, nothing of us that remains. However, if somewhere there is a place where shadows
wander, if in some sinister valley there are cadavers
which stand upright and living specters which have
not yet lost their form, Domenico Theotocopuli alone,
after Dante, has entered there. One would say that
he is exploring a dead planet, that he is descending into
extinct volcanoes where ashes accumulate and a pale
half-veiled moon sheds its light. But all of that has
been seen by him. Spain presents such aspects under
the snow, in winter, or in the torrid days when the sun
has calcined the grass, when there is nothing more in
space than the vibration of silence coming from nowhere, to lay its deathlike weight upon the heart, and
when livid mirages and gloomy metallic lakes are formed
and effaced upon the seared horizon.

III

Greco delivered the Spanish soul. After him the
flame mounts, straight and high, to die almost suddenly. Nowhere else was there ever an evolution so
rapid and so brief, were there rarer and prouder spirits,
or was there a darkness more profound before the
sudden outburst and after the unexpected fall. Spain
is an apparition—emerging from the shadow and re-
entering it after having, with terrible violence and in
the light of gold and of swords, traversed history and

passion. Two or three men express this soul in less
than a century, and they rise to such a height that they
are among the few men whom man can no longer do
without. The constraint was so great that few souls
burst forth, but when they did there were such forces
within them that they shattered all the bonds of the
intelligence and the heart. Don Quixote was starting
forth on all the dusty roads, alone and free to act out
his dream, and master of the conquest of Illusion.

When Velasquez came to Madrid, he must have
passed through Toledo. He therefore brought to
Castile, which, little by little, was to exert so strong an
influence upon him, the profound teaching of Italy interpreted by a Byzantine who had grasped Spain, and
the spirit of Andalusia, where he learned his trade.
It was not from Pacheco, who scarcely knew the trade,
nor from Herrera, with whom he spent scarcely enough
time to learn the grinding of colors. But Pacheco had
fine pictures and received many artists. His studio
was considered the center of Seville, queen of Spain and
of America, the city of gold and of fire. Góngora
reigned there, Cervantes had come there. Pablo de
Céspedes, the good painter of Cordova, brought there
the ideas of the Roman masters. Flemish pictures
were shown there. There was a thorough acquaintance
there with the pictures of Ribalta, an old painter of
Valencia, greatly influenced by Correggio and the
Bolognese, but a robust and strong nature whom
Zurbarán consulted. Some works by Ribera, his best
pupil, must have penetrated there.

In any case, the first pictures of Velasquez and
almost all those of Zurbarán bear the imprint of the
science which defines Ribera and of which Martinez
Montañés, at the period when they were studying in
Seville, was also giving examples so severely honest—
the statues of painted wood in which he renewed the

EL GRECO. The temptation of Saint Anthony (?), detail
(*Private collection*).

old art of the Spanish sculptors, by borrowing from the Christian drama the elements of tragic naturalism the need for which they express. The pitiless realism of Spain went through and through the Catholic fiction in order to seek behind it that which is bitterest and barest in life.
In Spain, Catholicism is not, as in Italy, a political system, or, as in France, an æsthetic and moral discipline; it is a narrow reality which daily existence exhibits afresh. The sacred legend is history, living history. The Virgin is a woman of the people with a dirty child in her arms; the Magdalen a filthy girl, worn by debauchery and misfortune. They have all seen the heretic crucified or burned, they have smelled the blood of beasts which the burning sand soaks

RIBERA. The clubfoot (*Louvre*).

up. They have followed the red tracks of the nauseous carts which carry the dead horses out of the arena. The saint manifests himself to the Spaniard under the appearance of a beggar, of a cripple, of a blind man with his eyes covered with flies. The sores of the sick, the carrion drying or rotting in the sun, the dead mule skinned by a clubfooted man, the dwarf, the idiot, and the infirm—whatever is ugliest and most terrible on the earth—is the spectacle which feeds the soul, thirsting for obedience to a sinister destiny. Even to-day, in certain villages, the peasants take down from the Cross the wooden Christ of their Calvary and flagellants pray and bawl and fall on their knees around it. Cadavers of wax lying in open coffins are carried through the streets. Crucified figures covered with human hair and skin are hung up in the chapels. Valdés Leal, the painter of Cordova, painted biers torn open, dead bishops eaten by worms and fermenting in their purple —shining harmonies in the fetid night of a cavern.

It was in order to have the somber strength necessary to say all this that José Ribera departed in his youth for Italy, led a miserable life there, committed murder, perhaps, triumphed, and learned to follow obstinately the play of the muscular fibers, the tension of ligaments, of tendons ready to crack, and of the bony structure clearly seen under dead or dried skin. It was in order to give greater relief in the dramatic light to the projections and contractions stamped by suffering on limbs grown thin, on hollow torsos, on wasted chins, that he asked of Caravaggio how he sent back into the opaque shadow everything that did not express ecstasy or despair. His ascetics are covered with mud and dust. In the carrying out of his work he adopts the cruelty of his executioners and the obstinacy of his martyrs—that thirst for reality which makes brothers of the two types. One cannot reproach him for his too faultless muscles, because they will be broken on the wheel or hang listlessly away after having been broken. One pardons him for his bituminous and black backgrounds because sometimes he rends them in order to show there the vivid skies in which solidly modeled clouds trail.

One need but see those rough-skinned fingers and those knotty joints, those stained beards, those dirty faces, those wrinkles, those bared teeth, and those reddened and watering eyes to recognize how the pitiless will which they express gives to tragic life and

ZURBARÁN. Saint Bonaventure and Saint Thomas Aquinas (*Berlin*).

to death their nakedest aspect. When one looks for a long time, one sees, arising out of the depth of the reddish shadow like ripening fruits, tender faces of women already caressed by that condensation of amber, of silver, and of pearl which penetrates the flesh with Velasquez and Goya, and for which Murillo substitutes powder, rouge, and the smoke of incense.

Perhaps he should have lived far away from the School in his Valencian Spain where the palm trees and the orange bushes cast a shadow, warmer, heavier, and more odorous than in other places. But then he would doubtless not have afforded to the masters of Andalusia and of Castile the hard, firm structure which offers itself, from time to time, to support their miraculous and hesitating edifices.

It was in this sense that he was to influence the young artists of Seville, and with added vigor because almost all of them had received the counsel of Francisco Herrera, who was as much dominated by the masters of Venice as Ribera was by Correggio and the Neapolitan painters. Las Roelas, a priest of Seville who was considered by the Andalusian school until the time of Murillo, had transmitted to him its external formulas. Herrera opened men's eyes. Backgrounds came into existence in the depths of his canvases, and with them that trembling and delicate space which characterizes both the Venetian and the Spanish painters of the mature period, that space of silvery rose against which he could henceforward spread out, without fear of contrasts too violent and of oppositions too sharply defined, the brilliant colors imposed upon his taste by the savagery and the fire of his nature. After him the road is free; Velasquez and, later on, Goya, can come. That which is properly Spanish, not in the character of the forms of the country and the faces of the men which Greco had seized immediately, but in the very matter of the atmosphere and the mysterious, veiled bond between the surroundings and the spots which tell of objects, is outlined with Herrera. Besides this, a quickness of decision hurries him along. Of school composition he has assimilated everything that was needful to the Spaniards, who are profound impressionists, but inapt in giving a logical distribution to the masses and

ZURBARÁN. Saint Bruno and the Pope (*Seville*).

in imposing upon the forms the intellectual hierarchy which gives so dangerous a strength to Greco-Latin art. He has learned from the Italians the superficial arrangement of groups and the approximate ordering of the phrasing. Furious improvisation may play over these dead themes and, in an equilibrium swiftly attained, will raise Spanish passion until it staggers to its full height, like a wounded man drunk with pride who insists on conquering before he dies.

Zurbarán and Velasquez, who come from the same sources, are of the same age, and express that passion when it is free, even if it is not the most intense and uncompromising; both will abandon allegorical pretexts and conventional idealism. Both will agree to forget that which they have learned in order to attain directly that desire for reality imposed on all by their passion—from the executioner who prays and from the priest who kills to the king who lives as a prisoner and who is buried in fustian. Inasmuch as Roelas, Ribalta, Ribera, Montañés, and Herrera transposed the history or the legend which they relate into the scenes of daily life appearing to them in the crudest aspects, they will seek, in these very scenes, the motive for the poems in paint which will gain in veiled emotion, in intimate profundity, or in naked majesty that which they will lose in anecdotal interest or in picturesqueness. They will renounce the pursuit of the life of the imagination for which they are not fitted.

One cannot say that the people which conquered the ocean and America, which dreamed Don Quixote, a thousand novels and ten thousand plays, and wrested from its nightmare the etchings of Goya, was lacking in imagination. But its inventive faculty develops only in the direction of the life before it, which it searches or forces or disfigures without ever seeking in it the symbols of a form to be organized. It does not combine, it does not generalize; it creates its illusion from that which exists. The adoration of Goya for woman appears in the manner in which he speaks of her, not in the aspect which she has and which he leaves to her, an aspect frequently common and sometimes repellent. Don Quixote sees a queen in a tavern girl, a helmet in a barber's bowl, an army in a herd. To express his ideal, Cervantes can do no more than make of it the caricature of reality.

VELASQUEZ. The Virgin and Child (*Prado*).

The more the culture of Zurbarán and Velasquez develops, the farther they will penetrate into this pitiless probity. At the base of it, the one will find the bareness of rock and the virile coldness required to despoil their mystic envelope of the practices of annihilation into which Spain plunges after her expansion; the other will find the harmonies revealed by space when one understands how to contemplate it with that passion for isolating oneself in their echoes with which a musician listens to the sounds of the world. Education, race, and the period make fraternal spirits of the two painters. He who goes to live in the savage monasteries of the deserts of Estremadura sometimes opens a window in order to perceive in the distance that aërial palpitation which Velasquez causes to circulate around

VELASQUEZ. Portrait of Mariana of Austria, detail (*Prado*).

the forms themselves like a murmur of color. He who
is at the court, fettered by the ennui of its etiquette,
sees in princes the austerity which Zurbarán lends to
churchmen. But Velasquez flees from Spain at times;
he returns to it with horizons more vast, around him
space widens out to immensity, his soul seems to have
wings as he approaches his end, and, passing over
periods and peoples, his mind carries on its dialogue
with certain superior minds which all peoples understand and which no periods can exhaust. Zurbarán did
not cross the moral frontiers which Spain imposed
upon him.

He seems to obey monastic rule. The walls of the
cells, their tables, their wooden benches, and the fustian
of the cowls are not more bare than his strength. The
sterility of Spain is in his sepulchral cloisters where
meditation revolves around death-heads and books
bound in skin. The white or gray robes fall as straight
as shrouds. Round about, the vaults are thick, the
pavement is cold, the light is dead. Only at rare intervals does a red carpet or a blue ribbon animate this
aridity. The voluptuousness of painting reveals itself
in the hard bread and the raw roots of the meal eaten in
silence, or in a hand or the earthy face of a cadaver, or
in the mortuary cloth of silver-gray. But those
spectral visages, those lusterless garments, that bare
wood, those protruding bones, those ebony crosses on
which not a reflection trembles, those yellow books with
their red edges ranged in clear-cut order like the hours
which divide up life until the end into periods of dismal
observances, all unite in assuming the aspect of an implacable architecture which faith itself imposes upon
plastics, forbidding it everything which is not a rigid
line, a bare surface, an opaque tone, a straight shadow,
or a precise and hard volume. A monk in prayer
weighs so heavily upon his knees that his head, when

he lifts it, seems to raise the stone of a sepulcher. Those distributing or taking food invest the need to live with a solemnity which carries over into the table-cloth, the glasses, the knives, and the victuals. Those lying on their deathbed imprint upon the life surrounding them the ridigity of death.

In this severe painting, everything seems gray. One would call it the color of ashes. If the granite grays which form the very substance of Greco's painting, if the silver grays of Velasquez and Herrera and the pearl grays of Goya, did not leave in our vision their rare reflection, one would think that Zurbarán meant to give to the men withdrawn from

VELASQUEZ. Portrait of Philip III, detail (*Prado*).

the world, whom he has painted, the appearance of abandoned hearths and of braziers grown cold. But all Spain is gray. Its denuded plateaus have the aspect of a dead star covered with ashes by its volcanoes. Spain is a monotonous, deserted expanse rolling unevenly, in which, here and there, one imagines a herd by the dust that it raises. It is not only the flight of the clouds or the trails of snow on the mountains which

VELASQUEZ. The Villa Medici (*Prado*).

pour down upon the country that which resembles leaden dust heaped up in places. Toward evening, before they are colored with pink, pale and almost burned out, the hills at the horizon seem touched with silver. When one stands on a height overlooking the cities, one sees the gray expanse round about. The white houses painted with green gold, sometimes covered with granite, and touched with blue and pink, take on a surface like dull tin, occasionally darkened by the accent of a black cypress. An unhappy soil, horrible near by when it shows only its fleshless bones, mysterious from afar, delicate, and veiled with impalpable harmonies born of the varying shades of color in the cultivated land combining with the shadows of the clouds to bring their gentle vibration into the gray uniformity.

IV

This savagery and this subtlety are found in the painters. The work in itself is sinister, never masked; the deformity of face, of body, and of soul is paraded without shame. They do not discriminate. Death, horror, everything is good in their eyes, and everything collaborates willingly in their task. But as soon as one looks between the forms, the nightmare vanishes, something unexpected and unknown is unveiled—a circulation of aërial atoms, a discreet envelopment, a transparent and faintly tinted shade which floats around them and transfigures them. Velasquez, after the age of fifty, never again painted sharply defined things, he wandered around the objects with the air and the twilight; in the shadow and transparence of the backgrounds he surprised the colored palpitations which he used as the invisible center of his silent symphony. He was no longer taking from the world anything more than the mysterious exchanges which cause forms and tones to interpenetrate one another in a secret and continuous progression, whose course is not manifested or interrupted by any clash or any shock. Space reigns. An aërial wave seems to glide over the surfaces, impregnating itself with their visible emanations in order to define and model them, and to carry away everywhere else a kind of perfume, a kind of echo of them which it disperses over all surrounding space as an imponderable dust.

The world where he lived was sad. A decadent king, sickly princes, idiots, dwarfs, invalids, certain monstrous jesters dressed like lords whose function it was to laugh at themselves and make others outside the law of life laugh at them—all bound up in etiquette, plots, and lies, and united by the confessional and by remorse. At the gates the *auto-da-fé*, the silence, the rapid crumbling of a still terrible power, and a land where no soul had the right to grow. No matter. In a country, in a court where no one, the king least of all, could free himself or desired to free himself from any of the servitudes imposed by the strength of the soil and of the faith, the painter alone knew how to dominate the fatal character of the surroundings. For his needs he had mastered the grandiose and lugubrious landscape which undulates at the feet of the Guadarramas. Condemned never to paint anything but kings, buffoons, and beasts, he had seized upon the silvery matter which invades the azure of the plateaus of Castile, that he might mingle it with the pallid faces and the dark costumes of the princes, weave it with the air and the steam into flying names, and associate earth and sky with the light harmonies which a horseman, galloping through space, revealed to him alone, in the floating scarfs which traverse the armor, or in the waving plumes of his hat. He possessed everything that trails and quivers in a plain which the mists of the morning or the dust of the evening covers with translucent veils. It is because there is a rift of blue among the storm clouds that a pink ribbon flecks the cuirass of black steel with its unexpected note. In the drops of silver which spatter that cuirass there trembles the diffused splendor of the air. In the whole of a gray picture, with a gray horse—its tail and mane flying in the wind, with gray fringe floating, with a gray sky, a sea stormy and gray, there is just one pink knot between the ears of the animal who bears a proud rider dressed in red and black. The mountains, the blue plains, the distant streaks of snow, the grayish or somber undulation of the ground sown with cork trees and olive trees, are found again in all the grays, in all the blacks shot through with dim blues and with pinks, which the man and the rearing animal impose upon the landscape or receive from it. When there are flames and smoke in the plain, they barely veil the silvery tremble of the clouds, and their reflection does not darken the harmonies of the foreground. His sickly little princes are surrounded by a lyricism of color, contained, veiled, and secret as a great soul, by a diffused light, and by tremors which, running through it, surround their ennui with a retinue so charming that they seem to bear only the shadow of the pitiless crown.

A spirit of nostalgia floats in the air, one sees neither the ugliness nor the sadness nor the funereal and cruel direction given to that crushed childhood. Whether Velasquez followed his masters to the hunt or returned with them to the dark alcazar, he remained the silent friend of the dying race which only an intelligence of sovereign freedom could deliver for us from indifference and death. He alone knew, when he went through the livid corridors, how to preserve in his memory the image of a melancholy and subtle apparition, of a wandering harmony lending to the light the fugitive sheen which it turns on the things that present themselves to its

Velasquez. Antonio el Inglés (*Prado*).

kiss. For him alone the little infantas were not burned-out beings with greenish, sullen faces, martyrs swaddled in the robes of state which weighed heavily on their breasts and prevented them from playing, leaping, running, and enjoying the birdlike life of little girls. He loved them. He himself had had two daughters, one of whom had died as a child. On their wan faces he followed all the reflections of the pitying world which mingled with the pallid blood, with the moist lips, and with the astonished eyes, the silvery daylight shining from red curtains, from gray and pink bodices where at times a red or black ribbon alone gave a darker accent, like a corolla bursting forth in a field of young wheat. The blond hair and the pinks of the costume encircled the frail heads with a vague aureole which gave back to the amber air a little of the torpid and charming life stifling behind their foreheads. A transparent handkerchief, spread out like a butterfly's wing, gave glimpses of paler blacks under it, and more attenuated pinks and distant blues. Upon a dress of rose crossed by stripes of thin silver plates and enlivened by spots of mauve, he surprised, with a quickening pulse, a red rose in the childish fingers. The lassitude of those hands resting on the backs of chairs, or the hoops of skirts, filled him with an ardor so tender that, without ever confessing it, he lavished upon them all the deep caresses which the world of the air reserves for that which bathes in it. Under all that trembling silver, his hesitating red and pink appear like a bed of flowers covered with dew at the hour when the light of dawn shines on the hoarfrost of summer.

Velasquez is the painter of evenings, of space, and of silence, even when he paints in broad daylight, even when he paints in a closed room, even when war or the hunt rages around him. As they went out but little in the hours of the day when the air is scorching, when the sun dulls everything, the Spanish painters communed with the evenings. The education of their eye went on in the twilight, and it is then that the

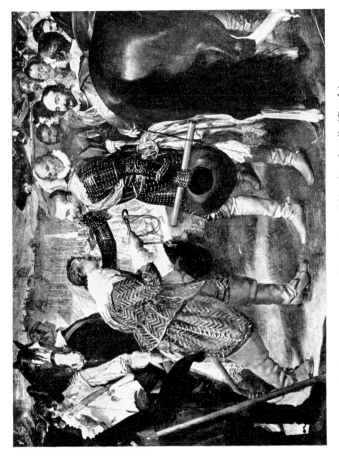

VELASQUEZ.   The Surrender of Breda, detail (*Prado*).

signification of Spain in color attains its value. When one has not seen how the night falls over the graded plateaus of Castile or of Estremadura, or over the red and gray plain of la Mancha, one does not know the dull accent, veiled and affecting, which the black capes and hats assume as they silhouette against white walls whose brilliance seems at that moment to be dimmed by a pearly silver. The air takes on an orange tint which reveals a profound intensity in the colors. The rising dust, bathed in the horizontal rays of the setting sun, envelops figures in a blur of amber which half effaces them and paints them against space in somber and trembling spots. Especially when garbed in black, they look like phantoms.

The nearer Velasquez approached his end, the more he sought those harmonies of the twilight in order to transport them into the secretive painting which expressed the pride and discretion of his heart. He abandoned broad daylight, he tended to seize upon the semi-obscurity of rooms where the passages of the planes are more subtle and intimate, where the mystery is increased by a reflection in a glass, by a ray of light coming from without, or by a girl's face covered with a bloom like that of a pale fruit which seems to absorb into its vague and lusterless light the whole of the diffused penumbra. The silvery shadow is rendered animate by the red in the blond hair, by the silver in the black hair, by the greens, the blacks, the pinks, and the infinite grays dispersed like a rain of petals falling where the harmony bids them fall: one would say that all was an apparition at the depth of a great invisible mirror, into which a serene evening enters very slowly. Visions seem to glide; an imperceptible balancing and swaying make one think of music, and when the apparition has disappeared, we do not cease to search our hearts for those beautiful fugitive shadows. They are vanished sisters whom we caught sight of before seeing them, and whom we shall see again without trying.

In fact, we are in the same space as they. These

VELASQUEZ. The Maids of Honor (*Prado*).

forms are the reflection which nature assumes in an obedient mind which accepts it in its every appearance, never modifying it to heighten its effect, but purifying it imperceptibly in each of the details which manifest it; and when it has been rendered for us in its ensemble, it has been made into something of slightly finer shades, something more aërial, more discreet and more rare, which is what gives it that exact and supernatural aspect. The mystery is almost terrifying. None of us can watch in the world the progressive spreading forth of the shadow and the light, the secret passage which causes one form to prolong another, without his eyes becoming wearied by the continuous circulation of an atmosphere whose density is all that gives gradation to objects and makes them turn and keep their place. But Velasquez sees these insensible things, and expresses them, without deigning to say toward which direction he is guiding us. He travels amid the fluid forces —inappreciable to another—which define the universe. That which we term line—a symbol permitting us to arrest in space the volumes which are never arrested at any precise point in space—that which we term a spot—the superficial illusion of an eye unable to grasp the flight of contours—that which we term form —an abstraction which does not take into account either the air or the light or the living spirit with which matter is animated—these are conceptions which Velasquez can dispense with. He arranges the elements of color in space following the order of surface and of depth dictated to him by these elements when he has assimilated them with his tranquil power of balancing sensation by taste and measure; and when he has finished his task, there has been performed the miracle of an admirable work wherein the artist does not seem to have intervened.

This feeling for *value*, this constant and apparently facile power of exactly proportioning the image to an objective judgment, is perhaps the mark of the freest intelligence, the one most serene and master of itself

VELASQUEZ. Portrait (*Louvre*).

that ever existed in painting. Raised to this height, virtuosity is a heroic sacrifice. One cannot say that Velasquez never reveals himself. Castilian pride, Andalusian temperament, Oriental fatalism, and Arab nonchalance are all affirmed or divined in those lofty and severe effigies which were painted between the death of Cervantes and the death of Calderón. But the psychological value never trespasses on the plastic value. It stands almost exactly even with it. It envelops itself and remains almost hidden under a precise play of shades and incomparable harmonies. He does not oblige us to see, in "The Lances," the cordial courtesy of the victor, the noble humility of the vanquished, and the spirit which transforms war and, despite the burned plain, the erect weapons, and the cuirasses, raises it above murder and hatred by the simple fact that, momentarily, it passes through a lofty and proud vision. Without saying so, he confides to the trembling water of a mirror the images of modesty or of power in its ennui. He does not compel us to notice the melancholy contrast between feeble princes or colorless queens and the animal that carries them, whose blood beats under the skin of its nostrils, its hocks and its rump, and whose mane flies in the heat of the race and in the steam of its sweat. He does not insist on the irony of the spectacle when he sees approaching an abject dwarf dressed like a prince and leading a formidable dog as tall as himself and threatening to growl, its feet firm, black, as strong as life when it yields to its strength. He scarcely smiles when he writes the name of Don John of Austria under the portrait of a weak-bodied, sneering buffoon, or the name of Menippus or Æsop under that of a beggar. When he paints an idiot, he does not say whether it causes him suffering; he makes the idiot's head and shoulders sway with the stammering of his songs.

When the king, with his long, sad face, is before him, dressed in black, he does not confess that it is his own majesty with which the king is invested. A distinction so royal that it never takes the trouble to try to impose itself, a grandeur detached from itself and conscious of being alone in knowing itself, raises to the level of his heart this world, which is dying little by little. This reserved nobleness is the last of his victories; and his supreme affirmation is the least openly avowed of all, and the most difficult to penetrate. Only a few bright spots vary the prison-like existence. First the sojourn in Madrid of Rubens, at the height of his powers, with whom Velasquez, who was then not yet

CARREÑO. Monstrous Girl (*Prado*).

thirty years old, established a friendship, and by whom he was counseled to go to consult the masters of Rome and Venice on how to discipline a natural generosity. Then the two journeys in Italy which he extended as long as possible and from which he brought back, with the friendship of Ribera and of Poussin, that which only a superior mind can discover there, the instrument with which to free himself. The remainder of the time he lived like a servitor, oppressed with idiotic duties, badly paid, dressed in clothing cast off by his superiors, and painting by accident, when he was charged with a portrait, a decorative subject, or one from religion or history. Each progression was for him not only a victory over himself, but also over the indifferent inertia or the hostile forces which surrounded him. He wrested each one of his works from a solitary and almost forced meditation, thrown back upon himself by the impossibility of finding a kindred mind and of confessing his real soul in any other way than through the works with which he was commissioned, into which he infused his longing and his silence, as if behind a veil almost impenetrable. He did not suspect until quite late, at the hour when the shadow of his days was lengthening along his path, the extent of his secret power to bring from the depth of his passion to the surface of life the image of his unknown illusions. And as his isolation and constraint increased with the years, his proud understanding grew apace, as if he had felt that he would not have the time, before death, to collect his forces completely.

V

Yet it is in this supreme gathering together of forces that Spain, before its sleep and in a last proud effort, lifted up its great isolated figure. "The Lances" and the portraits of the king and queen are the adieu to her age of strength. Now that Spain is vanquished everywhere, the grandiloquent "historical painters" and the manufacturers of heroic portraits are to multiply. Before Velasquez, only one man, because that man was a painter, de Mayno, had known how to subordinate the anecdote represented to the plastic poem which the contemplation of the forms and the sense of the fleeting harmonies of the space of Spain impose on those who neither affirm nor demonstrate before they have used

GOYA. The Majas on the Balcony (*Private collection*)

their eyes. After Velasquez, only one man, because
that man was a painter, Carreño de Miranda, still had
the power to arrest the fall of the spoiled princes, the
morose infantas, and the monsters of luxury, in order to
continue that history which is made only by those who
see and those who create. He shows us protruding
jaws, lifeless eyes, hanging lips, monastic robes—
the refuge of men of broken will, and of the shadows of
grandeur; malicious dwarfed women stifled in fat, mis-
shapen heads, and faces of crime and of horrible simplicity; after that there was nothing. Goya will not
come until a century has passed, and then as a kind of
miracle. The other followers of Velasquez, his son-in-
law del Mazo, the brothers Rizi, and Claudio Coello
are good, honest practitioners, of vulgar nature, and
heavy, coarse, or too clever in workmanship. Murillo
is not a great painter, because he is of a low mind.

He justifies the decision taken by Velasquez in his
leaving Seville and by Zurbarán in his returning to his
Estremadura. The bigoted and soft atmosphere of the
enriched city of Andalusia wore upon the nerves and
transformed the most virile beings into sensual women.
Herrera is still too savage to allow himself to be impressed, but Montañés possesses no more than a hollow
energy. Alonso Cano, his pupil and the studio companion of Velasquez and Zurbarán, is a bombastic
painter, and a soft and enervated sculptor, warped by
his morbid desire to erect effigies of ascetics with whom
he associates pale flames and tender colors, in order to
emphasize his effects. The streets smell of incense and
rice powder, of lemon flowers and sensuality. The
Jesuit is at his ease there; he controls the heart through
all the senses. Murillo, through his desolating painting,
overwhelms Ribera. His sick and his virgins are pro-
fessionals. The beggar is always picking his fleas, and
the Mother of God always has her eyes raised to heaven

and her hands crossed on her heart.   He prostitutes his
gifts as a painter.   Certainly, he expresses the ques-
tionable devotion of the city where, on saints' days,
idols are carried about, dressed up, and covered with
false jewels.   But he submits in a cowardly way.   His
sensuality is awakened only amid too-heavy perfumes
and in semidarkness.   He spoils everything around
him.   Valdés Leal, full of his Cordova, a burning city

Goya.   The Skaters, etching (*Private collection*).

where the Guadalquivir trails, over sand and rock, a
few narrow streams of stagnant water, forgets the
somber splendor of his visions in order to listen to him.
For he is insinuating, sanctimonious, and sugary.
His pictures are full of ambiguous shadows and of
spurious light.   He has certainly wandered around the
city on the evenings of feast days at the hour most
favorable for a glimpse, through the haze of the tapers
and the censers, of the pink and yellow façades.   He has
often seen, in the nave of the cathedral all ruddy with

lights, couples kissing on the lips, in the shadow of the pillars, at the moment when the Host is raised. The blood of the bulls has sent its smoke toward his nostrils, mingled with the odor of pepper and oil on black hair in which pinks have been entwined. But he has not felt the tragic joy and the distress of the monotonous rhythms of the dance of voluptuousness whose beat is followed interminably by the guitar and the clapping of hands. When a Christ on the Cross all smeared with blood is carried by, he has not heard, in the depth of his soul, how the song of a girl rises up, the sobbing, nasal plaint, infinite, arid, ardent, and sad as the desert.

He did not understand secret Spain. And when one knows the misery of Spain after his time, one cannot explain to oneself how the man who, in a half century of frenzied improvisations, sketched the most living physiognomy of that strange land, could come more than a hundred years afterward. Goya was from Aragon, to be sure, a province off the great routes and less exhausted, the place where the sculpture of the people had endured longest. But there was no crucible into which he could pour his lava. The house of Austria was dead from exhaustion; the Bourbons, emasculated and crushed by unhealthful devoutness, cloistered their secret vices in the alcove and the confessional. A bad German painter, Raphael Mengs, was their nearest representative for Velasquez. Spain was a lean beggar, draped from feet to chin in a patched old garment, worn and rusty. Why this sudden flame under the mask of carnival, this spark on the cold hearth? We always deceive ourselves about Spain. With a contemptuous decree, Napoleon annexes the sleepy thing. It sticks to him like a vampire, saws his tendons, drinks from his veins, and casts him off, drained of his blood, in a few months. That thing was not dead; it does not die. It has spasmodic crises which raise it up at a single

bound, impose it upon the world, and send it back to
sleep. It is like the Arab conquest. If the Inquisition
and the gold of America explained the ruin of everything and the apparent death, they ought also to
enable us to explain that savage vitality concealed by
the indifference, the immobility, and the exterior
fatalism. The Spaniards did not go to create gold in
the Antilles or the Indies, to be sure, but to gather it up.
Upon their return home they allowed tools to rust, undoubtedly, and the rock to take back to itself the earth
which had been stripped of trees, and the mind to
harden. And after that they stayed in their lair, cut
off from Europe. They no longer saw the sea, the
great civilizer; they no longer watched the departure
and the arrival of the ships. But then, why this awakening? And why this sudden energy, why the terrible
insurrection, Saragossa, and the sinister burst of
laughter, and Goya's torrent of pearls and of flowers,
if the Inquisition has broken down the entire strength
here? When the desire to expand and to conquer commanded the heart of Spain, the Inquisition was an instrument of discipline and of combat. It is a corset of
torture when this desire has disappeared; it grinds that
contracted heart. It is in vain that Spain goes beyond
her borders, she lives and goes to sleep at home; her
military and lyric expansion is not an organism that can
be controlled, but a spring which, after one release
always comes back into place for another. If some
external thing occurs to irritate her pride, she comes into
possession of her power and of her soul for a century or
for a day.

VI

With Goya, it was for a day, which is why he moves
so quickly. One would say that the old Spain, that

of the Holy Office, that of Don Quixote and the enchanted castles, that of Sancho and the unbounded earthy materiality, that of Arab magic, of the raucous and sad music, of the ingenuous cruelty, of the laughter at the gallows, and of the ardor for death, everywhere exhibiting itself or hiding itself, demanded that this man tell its story in haste, before the modern world should enter with the French. He gives us terrible approximations, horses and men ill formed, a species of tragic mannikins who live with a violent life, but which he has never time to refine and to set on a firm base. He interprets his rapid visions with whatever means come to him. His drawing staggers and stutters, but he never hesitates; with a single uncouth line he goes straight to his goal. It is a hasty edifice that he builds, with empty forms and with cloth puppets which he fills with his flame and his unbridled passion, as one stuffs a doll with bran. And yet the thing balances, an architecture is sketched, and also groups abruptly placed which a brief instinct for harmony distributes into blocks of shadow, brilliant lights, and subtle passages which leave in the memory no defined forms, but a persistent hallucination, a fluid whose lightning flashes everywhere and reveals life from within through the black hole of an eye, through a shoulder and an arm as they take aim, a stocking stretched upon the calf of a leg, a rumbling among the shadows, or a lake of silver whose gleam comes to the surface of the picture. Everything is approximate—the landscape, the gesture, the face, the costume. The intensity of the drama is increased thereby. For everything is drama, even a portrait. Now shadows appear, a nightmare coming from the depth of a people, its blood, its pride, its anger, its laughter, its vices, its voluptuousness, and its fervor, evoked in a mad whirl and hurled into the plane of life. Goya is a sorcerer who

GOYA. Queen Maria Luisa (*Private collection*).

boils herbs and who surprises in the burning vapor the dark spirit of the soil where they grew.

His most finished canvases resemble sketches snatched from space itself, like a great water color still drenched with water. The tremble of the muted harmonies which Velasquez had revealed to Spain becomes slighter and more uncertain. Everything trembles and glitters. The pink or gray silks, the blue or purple velvets, no longer merely suggest flowers hidden under the silver dew of orders, brooches, ribbons, and jewels scattered over the breasts and the hair, or around wrists or fingers. One would say that the inner skin of the oranges, the reflection of the flowers in pure water, and the very shadow cast by the rose of the infantas on crystal fountains were traversing the transparent and dancing air of torrid Spain, and quivering in the diamonds, and germinating as drops of fire in the rubies and the opals. The cloudiness of the pearl invades everything, penetrating the air and the

GOYA. SATURN (*Prado*).

GOYA. Portrait of an Infanta (*Private collection*).

bare skin, whose lusts are surrounded by it. The cloudiness of the pearl touches the beautiful arms of the women, the flowing arms, full as a living column, and swelling with sap and with blood. He finds the pearl once more in their gloves which reach above their shoulders, in their little satin shoes, their hair framing their powdered faces with a light nimbus, in the bodices pressed around their warm breasts, in skirts that draw around their bellies in an amorous caress, and in their laps bathed in shadow. He is the most intoxicating painter of carnal voluptuousness. He surrounds women with a kind of flaming aureole. They are all beautiful, even the ugly ones. The pearly glow on a shoulder, a moist mouth, gleaming teeth, or a downy and heavy arm suffices to fill him with fever. Their odor which he breathes, their breath which he drinks, wander in his very harmonies. He takes feverish possession of all the secrets of their flesh. The idea of violation haunts him, but he is held by their grace. He is bestial. But a kind of savage lyricism ennobles his bestiality.

And beside, he knows the danger. He has seen them tossing a disjointed puppet in a blanket. He must have escaped from them after furious debauches, and cast them all on fire upon his canvas, injecting his fury into their eyes which are like dark, hot coals, and their mouths, in which the blood beats. When they are old, he has his revenge; he deepens the hollow behind their collar bones, scrapes their bones, dislocates their jaws, pulls out their hair and all their teeth, reddens their eyelids, and wrinkles and tarnishes their skin. He shows skeletons in décolleté, in a fluffy cloud of silks, with flowers, muslin, and jewels scattered in profusion. Their rank does not frighten him. Infantas or queens, they are hideous and sinister if he sees them so; and if he desires them, he tells it. Moreover, they consent. Everything consents in Spain, upon condition that the

fire from within consume life to the end. Princes
adopt as their painter the man who knows them best;
they allow Titian, Velasquez, or Carreño to exhibit
them to the public. It is pride which sets them apart,
and then they abandon themselves, like other men, to
the frightful realism which permits Spaniards to manufacture invalids, to torture and be tortured with an
insouciance which is
called cruelty by
those who do not
understand, to stuff
back into the bellies
of horses the entrails
that were hanging
out. Goya is the
most implacable.
The royal family of
his country is a col-
lection of monsters
stupefied by the ac-
cumulation of phys-
ical defects, by the
practices of bigotry,
by furtive orgies, and
by fear. His generals
have faces like butch-
ers. The model gives
himself to the painter;

Goya. The Man with the Lizard
(*Private collection*).

a savage indifference to everything that is not brute
passion and instinctive life provokes sudden encounters
from which lightning flashes. When he has not a
woman, or when she does not show her arms, her breasts,
and her hips, everything is concentrated in the face,
which seems a condensation of space seized in flight.
The air quivers in all the flesh; the flesh quivers in the
air through its inner radiance. It is as if he had sur-

prised life itself. The eyes—the eyes of children especially—are dark holes opening upon thought undefined. Velasquez had seen that. With Goya, the mystery heightens—the form being that of an instant, a lightning impression, a rapid and profound moment, arrested in the flash of an eyelid, a burning shadow accumulating in the passing moment all there is of secret and spontaneous forces in a creative mind.

In Italy, where he passed several years of his youth, he had done hardly any copying, and indeed had rarely touched his brushes. He meditated much before the work of the initiators of painting, and enjoyed himself the remainder of the time. Save for Velasquez, who makes clear to him the true plastic sense of Spain, he knows no bonds of tradition, nothing but a frenzied thought at the heart of a world profoundly agitated by a passion so wild that it succeeds in fixing that world in its most clear-cut and most characteristic aspects. Before his fortieth year he will scarcely do more than begin to interpret the visions which since childhood he has been allowing to ripen through their burning contact with his vices, his anger, his hatred, his bravado, and his wild impulse toward love and toward liberty. And if echoes from afar run through him, as if veiled by the vibrant air and the dust—the melancholy and musical spirit of Watteau, the licentious grace of Greuze and of Fragonard, the sensual warmth of Prud'hon, something of Reynolds, something of Tiepolo— it is that, with a force the more tragic that he is so completely alone in the most compressed country in Europe, he represents a century everywhere determined to free life from the dogmas which stifle it, and from the aristocracies which are no longer worthy of directing it. He fights incessantly, against the monarchy that harbors him; against the Inquisition which does not understand him or does not dare to break his

GOYA. The Young (*Lille*).

brush; against religion, which was too deeply sunk in
the narrowness of the letter to grasp the heretical
symbols flashing through it; against the French when
they come to stave in with cannon shot that which he
loves and that which he hates. Everything serves
him as a pretext; his laughter and his fury pass into
his state portraits as freely as into his terrible etchings
where, at the depth of the blacks, one perceives the
movement of vampires, sinister apparitions, gnomes,
winged fœtuses, and undefined monsters, and where
the whites bring forth gleams of a powerful grace—a
breast, a woman's leg, or a pure arm gloved with gray.
He bounds from one idea to another, striking here,
caressing there; he loves, he violates, he crushes with
masked irony when men think him submissive; he is
filled with tenderness while he revolts; he does not
always know what he means to do or to say and, in
order not to falsify about that which he feels, he expresses it brusquely in jets of acid, no matter how, but
with the spasmodic strength that comes of nerves laid
bare and of passion that is stronger than fear. His
brush, his pencil, and his etching point race to follow
his thought. One thinks to follow it, and it escapes.
Is he Watteau when he mingles with the merry-making
of the people and surprises, under trees like those of a
theater, muffled figures and spangled dresses, when he
organizes games and round dances over which passes
the sinister breath of something that will never be
again? Is he Shakespeare when he follows witches to
their nightly revels or sees crossing the depth of nocturnal skies membranous wings and bloody phantoms?
Is he Rembrandt when, with a ray of light falling from
no one knows where, he illuminates a hunted and furious monster with a human pack behind it? Is he
Voltaire when he prostrates his crowds before a preach-
ing parrot, or shows women kneeling at the feet of an

GOYA. The Massacre (*Private collection*).

ass or before a scarecrow covered with a monk's robe? Is he Hokusai when he sees, appearing in the enervated night, a face or a form in which the most discordant aspects of the beast combine with those of death? Is he Dante when the war comes, when there are piled up in carts the cadavers of the massacred, which the soldiers violate and impale, when one sees emerging from a frame the muzzle of the guns turned on a heap of screaming flesh, when ropes or hands strangle, when a lantern standing on the ground lights up executioners as they bend over, faces torn with bullets, black mouths, lifted arms, and blood and brains spattered about everywhere? He is Goya, a peasant of Spain, jester and sentencer, a ferocious street-boy, an irate philosopher, a visionary impossible to arrest in one form, something gay, evil, lecherous, and noble, at the same time or by turns. He goes through the carnival, amuses himself with hot-blooded women and boneless puppets. His cheeks are red, but his gayety is funereal. One does not know whether he laughs with the others or whether he laughs at them, or if, under their laughter, he catches a glimpse of the teeth of a fleshless skull. He goes to see the killing of the bulls, the garroting of the bandits, and the bleeding of the flagellants; he mounts on the barricades, lashes the prince, and is hail fellow with the blackguard. He decorates his house with frightful figures, people buried alive and fighting one another, cannibals gorged with human meat and waving bloody pieces of it. He goes into a rage against his epoch and partakes with passion of its cruelty, its gallantry, and its tainted romanticism. He is a free spirit, and he is a rustic. He is, of all the great Spaniards who were subtle and savage, the most savage, the most subtle. He is full of darkness, but the flame illuminates him. His indignation kindles like that of a saint, but he has the sadism of torture, and when he says, "I saw that," in describing limbs torn from bodies, decapitated trunks, and heads hanging from branches, he exhibits the soul of an executioner. It was with fury that he lived the life of his sinister and charming land, and of his century, carrying on together its conscious debauch and its instinctive heroism. Driven from Spain by the priests, he died in exile, amid the Frenchmen whom he loved for their spirit of revolution, and whose bloodiest enemy he had been. When his coffin was opened, two skeletons were found in it. . . .

VERSAILLES

Chapter IV. THE FRENCH MONARCHY AND THE AESTHETIC DOGMA

I

HE cavalier king, the favorite of prelates who capture strongholds and command squadrons, had no painter of his own. Van Dyck, a Fleming, by the way, and, at bottom, light and servile, dwelt in England, where he had united his fortunes with those of that other gentleman-king who lived ill and died well. On the other hand, Marie de' Medici appealed to Rubens to decorate the Italian palace which she had just built in Paris. Italian plastics and Spanish literature were entering everywhere; the French mind was undergoing one of those crises, so brief and so frequent in its history, when it asks the surrounding peoples for weapons, which it will sharpen, polish, shape, and adapt to its hand. It was taking its repose through war, wherein its artistic faculties were developing through action, the joy of wild fighting, soldierly elegance, battles as courteous as tournaments, trenches opened to the sound of violins, and duels to the death which were considered a game.

The only man of that epoch to understand its ardent force and its dry grace kept away from the scene and detested the performance which religion and politics imposed upon his actors. Jacques Callot, who sees the poor world pillaged, broken on the wheel, burned, and hanged, weeps over it, is indignant, and rages against the unhappiness of the time. Jacques Callot curses war, but he loves the soldier. With his lean veterans in threadbare cloaks, his pikemen in their top-boots, their rakish felt hats and battered plumes, one would say that it is with a point of a rapier that he engraves his copper. The trooper, the trooper before the days of the uniform, who belts in his empty belly with a golden baldric, and the muddy swaggerer of whom one sees no more, when he advances, than the cock spurs and the eagle face, are brothers to the cripple and the beggar with whom he has tramped the roads, and to the wandering comedians whom he has heard rehearsing, in barns, the rôles of Scaramouche, Fracasse, and Arlequin. In their company he has eaten his soup from the top of an old drum. He has boiled herbs in the kettle of fifteenth-century witches, and the story-tellers of the sixteenth have regaled him with their half-spoiled wine. He has accompanied Jerome Bosch and Breughel amid grinning skeletons, the monsters, and the bloated personages of the side-shows. He has discovered Rosinante, of the knight Don Quixote, harnessed to the cart of poor Romanies. He has followed the musketeers from the Hôtel de Troisville to the Hôtel de Rambouillet. This lean wolf is a proud man. Had he not lived, there would have been a gap in this century, despite Cyrano, despite Théophile and Scarron. We should hardly know its setting. We should not comprehend the fever of living that there was between the ferrule of Malherbe and the ax of Richelieu. The official painters knew nothing of their age. Simon Vouet is a phrasemaker. The good engraver Abraham Bosse is a Boileau who would attempt to correct Molière and to tame Tabarin. Jean Boullongne, whose taste for the dregs of life might have brought him close to the crowd, thinks himself obliged to reside in Rome, and to employ his verve in aping Caravaggio. Italy will return our artists to us only after having misled them.

CALLOT. Drawing (*Uffizi*).

Indeed, they all go there, and any way they can go, on foot with bands of men picked up by chance, if there is no other way. Callot himself, when a mere child, goes there with some gypsies and stays there for twelve years. The other man of Lorraine, Claude Gelée, engages himself with a company of cooks in order to make the trip, and, having reached his goal, hires out as a domestic. Parrocel gets there only after having been a prisoner of the corsairs. Courtois leaves his native Burgundy at the age of fifteen to go off to Rome, live there, paint his romantic battles, and die there. The two brothers Mignard sojourn there for a long time, Nicolas for a third of his mature life. Sébastien Bourdon incurs the hostility of Claude by imitating his pictures there. Noël Coypel, who goes to direct the Academy there, brings with him his son Antoine, at the age of eleven. Duquesnoy of Brussels, Pierre Puget of Marseilles, Girardon, and the Coustous—all the sculptors of the century—go to take counsel from the shade of Michael Angelo, and lessons from the chevalier Bernini. Le Brun returns only after having for several years solicited the generous domination of Poussin, who will live there all his life in a little house on the Pincio, where, with Claude, he will represent the profound soul of France in exile under its own sky—René Descartes living in Holland or in Sweden, and Corneille being obliged to wrap himself in a Spanish cape in order that his passion might exert an influence there.

As the centralization of the monarchy had driven forth this soul from the woods and the river banks, as, with the disintegration of the art of stained glass, it had forgotten the profound fineness and the diffused illumination of its sky, and, with the progressive decline of its corporations of artists, the mysterious correspondence which unites the sculptured image with the inner fire of living, it seemed to be sending its two best painters upon the mission of once more learning from Italy the sense of light and of volume through which space and the form of the world shape our will. They had not, visibly, a great deal in common, neither in origin, nor in character, nor in culture. Poussin is a Norman, Claude is a Lorrain. The one is a great reader, the other hardly knows how to read, and writes his very name badly. The one is of a firmly ordered mind, meditative, a bit doctrinaire, tending to intellectual generalizations and plastic abstractions, pursuing in the universe the invisible plane which unrolled in his brain, always master of his vision, regular of face, that grave and strong face that is modeled like a monument. The other has ill-set features and a hunched figure, clumsy and heavy; he goes on from dawn to dusk as a beast goes to the drinking ford, and is kept above the level of labored work and of confused conception by a continuous lyric exaltation capable of carrying him, without apparent effort, across the threshold of the superior harmonies wherein intuition and intelligence are in close communion. But both were in love with rhythm and measure, at a period when the need for method and for style was everywhere reacting against the political and intellectual fermentation which had torn the sixteenth century from the organism of the Middle Ages; and both were determined to ask from Italy the discipline to which her masters, the first to free themselves from ancient servitudes, were tending irresistibly, amid the confusion of isolated researches and the antagonisms of passion.

It was they who were to gather together the secret teaching of Rome, so dangerous for those who are weak of will or of mind. Italy, debilitated by her effort, divided into twenty hostile camps, now sought in this teaching no more than a willing, hollow slavery, without hope of a compensating intimacy. Spain, exhausted by pride, refused to move. England was organizing her merchant class and the practical religion destined to enrich her. Germany, devastated, chopped to pieces, and emptied by a horrible war, no longer felt anything, no longer understood anything. France, who was rapidly mounting toward political unity through

POUSSIN. Echo and Narcissus (*Louvre*).

which she would try to gain a substitute for her lost
unity of soul, was the only one in Europe who could
profit by the intellectualism offered by the Italians,
and arrest the world, on its road to renewal, in the
illusion of an hour.   When, in the long-sustained
studies of Claude and Poussin, one has followed their

POUSSIN.   The tall trees, drawing
              (*Louvre*).

will to subject the tree
and the water and the
body and architecture to
the same profound law
of structural likeness,
which the one divines
and the other discovers
in a universe patiently
interrogated at all hours
of the day, we hear aris-
ing by itself the regular
and powerful echo of
the alexandrine of Cor-
neille, and the presenti-
ment of the geometrical
system which Descartes
will formulate, and we
catch a glimpse of the
overwhelming shadow
of the æsthetic and ad-
ministrative edifice which Colbert and Louis XIV will
build from top to bottom.

Only, the edifice is in process of building; it does not
yet inclose them.   Better even than in Poussin's
drawings—among the finest in the world, but where
the spontaneous force of emotion, of verve, and of
life never dissimulate his sculptural research—one sees
the character of the moment in Claude's drawings—
lines of fire, burning spots, strangely shaped and
powerful visions of the landscape before him, an intoxi-

cating apparition, moist in its coolness, bursting with
sap, bathed in air, in shadows, and in light, which he
hurls on his sheet of white paper with his black ink.
Their roots plunge to the richest and best-nourished
loam of their soil. They form part of a strength that
is growing, and not of a strength that is dying because
of its desire to become fixed. The passionate search
for a new equilibrium gives them nobility, and a flame
which holds the work upright and causes it to pass
beyond its frame, exalting the will and illuminating
the heart. Amid the rotting virtuosity of the Italians,
they preserve their calm, remounting to the great
works and remaining faithful to the mission which
France has intrusted to them. The problem is that of
establishing the structure of the world wherein the
French mind, which persists, will, with admirable ease,
introduce into its retarded evolution the old southern
rhythms renewed by Italy, and will play the rôle of
conciliator and arbiter between the men of the north
and the men of the south. It is necessary to give to
the whole of Europe something which shall replace, in
the body of the *élite*, the broken backbone of the dead
Middle Ages. It is necessary to impose upon humanity,
whose adventure has carried it out of its earlier paths,
the harmonious order which shall permit it, for a
century, to believe that it has found new paths, and,
in any case, to prepare for their discovery. The dawn
and the end of day, all that which gives to the
universe its intensity of sentiment, illuminate, in the
heart of a landscape redolent of the ancient world, a
humanity determined upon seizing, amid the gleam of
things, the magnificent appearances which sustain
its hope.

Oh, lyricism of Claude Lorrain, you did not know
what your rôle would be! You did not know what
your bristling masts, your pennants, and your sails

in the flaming sky would represent to us.   You did not
suspect the meaning assumed, in the minds of men who
had reached the extreme limit of intellectual anarchy,
by your straight-lined ray, sweeping along the scene to
the foreground, lighting a brief flame on the crest of
the hastening waves bringing to men the immense
weight of the water, the salt wind, and the horizon of
purple and of mist where the other face of the globe is
gradually sinking.   You knew nothing of that, you
only felt; when your eye, ever raised toward the circular line of the Roman desert, fixed a central point of
red and gold in the haze, whence luminous dust spread
out in every direction, and into an ever more tenuous
rain, you felt that banks of stone and a double row of
palaces, churches, and ruins, were giving to the flight
of your dream a regular form wherein it was perhaps
acquiring more of persuasive power and of the strength
that sweeps us with it.   It is always the same — that
dream; its power to stir us grows and swells from work
to work as we observe so much innocence and so much
incessant aspiration toward the glory of the daylight,
and note its determination never to abandon those
irreproachable avenues which lead to harmony, and
which betray nothing of the evil life, the doubt, the
struggle, and the suffering which they must, however,
traverse.   The standards are always flying from the
peak of the towers, there is always the forest of the
rigging, the oriflammes, and the foam caught by the
light, the rippling expanse that flees in the reek of
purple gold, and the molten sun which governs the
swelling or dying symphony according to whether it
rises or sets.   Claude permits Filippo Lauri to people
this world of glory, to garnish the peristyles and the
staircases of his temples with crowds, not even perceiving them in the radiance of the sunlight which bathes
everything in a translucent aërial mist whose fiery

POUSSIN. Mars and Venus, drawing (*Chantilly*).

center is merged with the center of his being. Claude dwells in the sun, he darts forth with its rays, and from the moment when it begins to set he never takes his eyes from the hills, the motionless tops of the trees, and the uncrowned capitals which it floods with somber gold, at the moment when it is about to die. This poor peasant lives in the heart of an impressive hour,

POUSSIN. Study of Evergreen Oaks (*Chantilly*).

which he does not hear sounding. The orb declines, the shadow, still flaming, extends over the ebullient youth of Occidental society, but it gilds a proud and regular fairyland of edifices and colonnades, a world of stone and of marble arising from the paved shores, toward which the ship of the spirit, believing itself at last and forever master of itself, approaches with majesty—black against the redness of the sky.

II

With Nicolas Poussin, the writing is of far greater
power. Here is a man who knows where he is going,
sometimes too well; he expounds and demonstrates with
an eloquence in which his compatriot Corneille could
have recognized his power of coining maxims, and of
inclosing, in a uniform and vigorous rhythm, everything which, in life, is unprecise and fugitive, in order
that he may impose upon it the form of his will. Heroic
and lyric unity is the sole point of departure; everything groups and orders itself around that. The
plastic unity is simply the result of an intellectual labor
of conscious elimination, and of construction through
the idea, wherein form and gesture, local tone, the
general tonality, and the distribution of the volume and
the arabesque respond to the central appeal of reason.
And, when one has looked for a long time at his direct
studies, their forms sculpturing the void like bas-reliefs
wrought by light and shadow, when one knows that
upon his return from excursions to the Campagna
where the wrecked aqueducts, the circular edifices, the
flat-topped pines, and the line of the pure hills impose
clear-cut contours and decisive formulas upon the intelligence, "he brought back, in his handkerchief, pebbles,
moss, flowers, and other things of the kind which he
desired to paint exactly, from nature," one cannot do
less than obey, as he did, that all-powerful appeal.
"I have neglected nothing," he said to his friends.
His character is as lofty as his faculty for comprehending, a faculty whose progression is the result of a desire
to comprehend the universe, and which is ever ready to
spiritualize its gains. Grapes, ripe fruits, bread, wheat,
the golden russet of autumn, or the pure water of summer, or the springtime foliage which the wind silvers
and sets trembling, are the sensuous center of his

abstract symphony, whose grave coloration responds to a preoccupation with voluntary unity; and this gives but additional splendor to that recumbent body of a woman, to that lyre of gold shining upon a dark bosom, to that copper, fired by the fall of day, or to that laurel leaf, gleaming like a green bronze. As Homer compared the waist of a girl to the stem of a tree, he rediscovered the form of columns in the feminine torso. His constant and faithful penetration of the world filled him with moral harmonies as well ordered as a temple, and the tree and the round breasts and the arris of a monument or of a rock against the sky, entered the rhythm of the dancers to unite their curve with the resonance of music, and to purify them as a whole by their passage through the mind.

Whether he carries his lucid revery over the stormy landscape of the bacchanals, under the gray and black clouds and the deep azure and the thick foliage, or whether he leaned over the waters in order to surprise, in their motionless darkness, the silvered silhouette of the gods, never did antique myth and Italian ardor fail to appeal to French measure and definiteness, in order to express the nobility of his calm sentiment. The regular tiers made by the houses on the hills, the straight front of the colonnades, and the enormous round towers crowning the heights, all lead him to rediscover in the disposition of the trees, the mass of the earth's undulations, and even in the form of the sky laden with powerful clouds, that architectural sense of the world which is peculiar to the artists of his race and which they translate with the same sustained lyricism and the same firm intellect, from the Romanesque church and from the Gothic nave to the gardens of Le Nôtre, to the château of Mansard, to the music of Rameau, to the palaces of Gabriel, and to the poems of de Vigny. Everything contributes thereto and sub-

POUSSIN.   The Massacre of the Innocents (*Chantilly*).

mits itself thereto. Human attitude and form are an
admission that there is, in the elements of nature, a
rigorous subordination which unites the movement of
the heavenly bodies with the succession of the seasons
and the beating of hearts. One finds this in the gesture
of an arm plucking fruit from the branches, pouring
wine into a cup, supporting a burden on an erect head,
reaping wheat, leading a horse to the plowing, casting

CLAUDE LORRAIN.   Landscape, drawing (*Louvre*).

a line into the water (while turning halfway around to
listen to a singer), bending a bow, shaking the thyrsus,
or placing upon a brow a crown of oak. From that
superb submission to the higher will which establishes
the hierarchy of Nature in order to bring forth intelligence as her highest function, every function borrows
an affecting purity. A yoke of galloping horses, an
ox raising its head, a mute herd under the moon, the
swelling udder of a goat to which a child is clinging, or
the muzzle of a horse raised above the water are

CLAUDE LORRAIN. Landscape, drawing (*Louvre*).

events that echo to the extreme limits of the waves of
secret harmony which the contemplation of the universe
causes to arise within us. The tree with the black
trunk, which mounts as pure as the column of the
temple, is a hymn of gratitude to the prodigious order
of the world. The giant voice of the gods murmurs in
it with the wind, and with the wings of the bees; and
the gleam of the daylight on the silvered bark and on
the edge of the trembling leaves is a glance of pride
from the royal orb. The earth, space, love, the games
of man and woman, the sacred submission of the
beasts, all is sublime and all is innocent. Everything
purifies itself and grows greater when one acquiesces in
everything, thereby bringing it into contact with that
which is highest and noblest within oneself, that which
has the greatest faculty for giving admiration.

This great man, like all the great men of his century,
is to be understood only upon close acquaintance. He
frowns on one's approach, his tone is severe. The
deep soul appears suddenly when one is almost ready
to give up trying to seize it, the idyllic, amorous, and
sensual soul of a being resolved to accept the poetry
and the immorality of the world upon condition that he
remain the master in tracing its sure courses and its
accessible summits. In order not to love him when one
has understood him, one must have failed to feel that in
his purified heart is reborn the illusion of the singers of
our distant dawn, whose desire perceived nude women
passing under the branches, and mirages trembling in
the water, when the labors and the games rhythmed by
the course of the heavenly bodies gave to life the appearance of a sacred poem which everything on earth
participated in ennobling. Pure arms open in space to
invoke voluptuousness or to cradle sleep; round heads
of children lie on the naked belly or on the warm
shoulder of the mothers; heads crowned with flowers

arise to look straight before them or to sink again on
swelling breasts; walking, and kneeling, and the suppli-
cation of hands, the whole of the drama and of the
eclogue, are inscribed on a superb scroll which passes
across life like an indefatigable affirmation of gratitude
and faith. Massacre as well as love is a pretext for
glorifying form, whose calm splendor appears only to
those who have penetrated the indifference of nature

CLAUDE LORRAIN. Drawing (*Private collection*).

before massacre and love. Two profound memories
haunt Poussin. He has seen performed, in the woods,
where the shadow is burning, the orgiastic wedding of
Titian and the universe. "The Fire in the Borgo" has
revealed to him how sculptural limbs, spread wide by
terror or made tense by prayer, can introduce among
men a harmony superior to pity, because it creates hope.
That was his starting point for the establishing of
French tragedy and for joining the wild soul, the musi-

cal and trembling soul of Racine, by way of the order created by Corneille.

And that is not all. His track is deep. All Frenchmen, down through the strongest and most radiant century of their painting, will follow it passionately. Here is the rosy child, the Dionysiac child of Boucher and of Bouchardon. Here is the religious sentiment of woods and meadows, the nude forms and the branches reflected in sleeping waters, the harmony of the bacchanal and the eclogue with the architecture of the clouds and of the thickets, the heroic tree with outspread leaves, Watteau, Vernet, Ingres, Corot, Puvis de Chavannes, Cézanne. Here are the downy colors of the ripening fruits of France to which Watteau, Chardin, Corot, and sometimes Ingres, will come to get the temper of their harmonies. Here are the raised arms, the convulsed masks, the tragic cadavers, and the sensual and funereal drama which thunders around Delacroix.

III

The dead masters apart, and the honest Domenichino, whose heavy labor he respected, Nicolas Poussin, who felt nothing but disdain for the honors with which people sought to embarrass him and who remained only two years in Paris, although he was lodged in the Louvre as first painter to the king—Nicolas Poussin despised the various manufacturers of sculpture and painting who surrounded him. When he had arrived in Rome, at the approach of his thirtieth year, they had elected with enthusiasm, as prince of the Academy of St. Luke, that Simon Vouet who later was to scheme to force Poussin to flee the court and thus reserve the pickings for himself. Which indicates the state in which he found painting there. The School was triumphing there in its narrowest and emptiest form. The French

painter knew hardly anything about the School.   But
the spoils of the heroes are the habitual food of the
parasites of the mind.   Le Brun had received in Rome
the counsels of the master whose example was later to
be monopolized by the Academy in Paris, to the point
of still calling him, after his death, "M. le Poussin."
The religion of the School was being established.   Its
dogma was passing from Italy into France, after having

been filtered and de-
canted by the bigoted
missionaries sent by
Colbert to Rome.
Nothing remained but
to adapt it to the im-
perious needs of the
French monarchy
which, for half a cen-
tury, would attempt to
impose upon France a
unity of action and
thought which was per-
haps necessary, but
from which she nearly
died.

To establish itself in
France, to organize it-
self, and to conquer

S. BOURDON.   Portrait of the Artist
(*Ecole des Beaux-Arts*)

there, the dogma found, indeed, an intellectual atmosphere which was particularly propitious.   The Cartesian method impregnated all minds.   What, then,
after all, was all this return to nature through generalizations which were considered to have produced
ancient art, if not the "reduction to the universal" to
which the whole system of Descartes was tending?
Did not Malebranche see in the irregularities of nature
the punishment of sinners?   And did not Jansenist

rigors represent an attempt to conduct the moral law toward the same absolute ends? The writers, and the best ones, precisely, affirm the superiority of the "ancients" over the "moderns." Tragedy subjects the exposition of psychological conflicts and even their unrolling, to inflexible rules. Mathematics—whose edifice will be crowned by Newton's law, regulating the order of the heavens—penetrates literature to the point of bringing Fontenelle, toward the end of the century, to set up "the geometrical spirit" as the basis of all action. Bossuet, hauled about in every direction by his need for controversy, always saves himself by invoking the necessity of keeping the Church immutable, and by placing dogma outside of all discussion. The true, the beautiful, and the good begin to be confused one with another. In short, in the freest natures, Molière, La Bruyère, La Fontaine even, something is appearing of the Cartesian rigor, in the architecture of speech, the precision of contours, and the clearness of avenues. And when the state, in the name of unity, tracks down Protestantism and Jansenism, it is itself penetrated by their logical thought and their thirst for demonstrating. The king is in no wise different from the men of his period. They recognize the period and they recognize themselves in him, which is what gives him such ascendency over the others and over himself. The irreducible alexandrine of Molière, of Racine, and Despréaux, the symmetrical battles of van der Meulen, the ritualized etiquette of his court, and the inflexible administrative organism on which his power rests, establish around his mind a network of precise images and of forms rendered hierarchical. The only profound drama of the century, the anguish of Pascal, is nothing else than a perpetual struggle between an immense aspiration toward love and the limits wherein it is inclosed by the rationalist

Hotel Sully, Paris, Windows and Dormer Windows.

method which his geometer's mind was forced to adopt.

A man astoundingly organized for the task holds all the threads of the system, which he renders more complete and more rigid each day, and more logically deduced from the premises which command it. Everything holds together in it; a broken thread may, and

The Basin of Apollo at Versailles.

should, compromise the whole. Colbert institutes powerful bodies which will be able, by themselves, to build bridges and cut roads on an invariable model, in order to regularize the diffused life of the country. He sees nothing but the straight line. River is joined to river or helped out in its unequal and sinuous course by paved canals which cross the hills, going by the shortest route. He protects the forests, in order to

LE BRUN. Group of Women (*Louvre*).

direct the regular cuttings of the timber there, which
shall go off to the maritime arsenals, and so furnish the
wood necessary for the construction of ships, whose
tonnage and form he determines, and which he launches
on an exact date, inscribing in lists, pitiless in their
exactitude, the men who will man them. For he must
force the springs, so that nothing shall be in excess; he
must make use of the public treasury, and the chain
and the whip to compel life to fit into such precise
frames. He gives to soldiers their uniforms. He rigorously organizes the protection of industries. He opens
manufactories in order to incorporate with the state
all the trades that he can seize upon. He subjects to
his control those whom he cannot deliver to the king.
He struggles against everything which combats or
balances the autocracy: the parliaments, the governments of the provinces, municipal rights, the synods,
and soon religion, which refuses to return to universal
and national Catholicism. He hates the press, he hates
the book—all that which can introduce a rift into his
system—or a wheel which he has not carefully tested.
He concentrates, in Paris, collections and casts, volumes,
manuscripts, medals, vases, statues, and pictures. He
administers the Fine Arts with as much method as the
Department of Roads and Bridges, or that of Finance,
or of the Navy. He extends his protectorate to literature and plastics, institutes pensions for the artists
who consent to obey, organizes and centralizes the
Academies, and creates other ones for the bodies that
as yet had none—the archæologists, the musicians, and
the architects. He makes a state institution of the
journey to Rome by founding a School there, admission
to which will be determined every year by a formal
examination, and which shall be an æsthetic convent,
with obligatory mass, fixed hours for rising and retiring, and inflexible surveillance over the elected in-

mates. That is not enough; we must go back to Byzantium to find a precedent. It is prohibited to open free studios in France; he reserves to the Academy of painting and sculpture a monopoly in teaching. . . . One day, he will have a member of that academy banished for five years for a pamphlet which the artist was suspected of having written against Le Brun.

Art, which Colbert wished to protect, is thus menaced, and tracked to its living sources. It does not as a whole, however, die of this; something of its profound disquietude survives, a general idea which all the adherents of the system are engaged in propping up everywhere for fifty years. It was the invincible need of the century itself which placed above the Italian School, evolving according to hollow formulas in decadent surroundings, the French æsthetic dogma, an outgrowth of the concrete and living foundation of the race, and pursuing the systematization of art to the point of travesty, at the same time that science, philosophy, theology, and society as a whole, under the shadow of the centralizing monarchy, pursue the moral and material unity of the nation. The irreducible Gallicanism of the king and of the clergy of France is a manifestation of that same desire, assuring to the French soul, after all, the right to express itself. Italian doctrine is only a frame into which it is necessary to fit in the whole mass of the great general effort, willingly or by force. The prejudice of the noble subject, the subordination of the accidentals of color to motionless form, the hierarchy of the styles, and the strict obedience to the proportions of the antique, all must, however, pass through the clarity of French reason in order that it may adapt to its needs abstractions too distant and absolutes too isolated. The education of the will, slowly given by Descartes and Corneille to minds full of knowledge, and to energies

well ordered, imposes, even so, upon the ensemble of
the edifice, an imposing character. The economics of
Colbert, the art of Le Brun and Le Nôtre, the military
science of Turenne, the exegesis of Bossuet, the architecture of Hardouin-Mansard, the criticism of Boileau,
the comedy, the tragedy, the verse, and the prose are
all laid like an homage at the feet of a king made for

The Pont-Royal, Paris (1685).

his time, modeled by it, and convinced that he directs
it. And when all this results, despite numberless insufficiencies of detail, in setting on foot a system which
holds everywhere, the system borrows from its unity a
strong intellectual life. Unity, after all, is one of life's
essential characteristics. In this case, to be sure, it is
from without that it is gained, from a theoretical point
of departure and by means of artificial processes. . . .
It manages, however, to raise an edifice which all minds,

momentarily uniform, have labored to build. Catholicism employs its habitual method. It monopolized the
spirit of the commune, and the Renaissance bears its
stamp. It will rationalize itself to combat the tendencies of that period by making itself master of the
weapons forged by the Renaissance in its fever and its
torment. All will crumble; but what a work! The

HARDOUIN-MANSARD. The Place Vendôme.

artist, the poet, the soldier, the writer, the priest, the
artisan, the clerk, and the noble — each one traces his
straight course to the same central point where all
meet and where the king unites all the reconciled
dogmas in his solitary majesty.

IV

He is surrounded in it by hierarchic gardens graded,
from terrace to terrace, as they rise around circular or

rectangular basins and lines of decorative baskets, marked by rows of trees cut by straight avenues, and forming an architecture of forests and of fountains wherein the thickets and the spouting water take on regular forms to oblige the world to recognize the order at the summit of which he stands. Everything mounts toward the king, the monumental staircases, the statues of bronze and of marble, themselves occupying, in the distribution of the jets of water and of the cascades, a rigorous hierarchy, and offering their docile material to commands from above. The liquid masses and the trimmed walls of the foliage make vaults, cradles, crowns, and avenues; their solemn hymn lifts up and hovers with a great cold murmur, from the well-raked gravel and from the close-cut grass, to the long, austere façades which align the superimposed windows in three rows. The copper and pewter figures in the sheets of water send the faintest of dull reflections to the clear-cut curtains of boxwood and yew which, with black strokes, unite the russet masses of autumn vegetation with the dark branches of the summer. It is a fragment of the universe stylized like a temple. Garlands of metal and garlands of leaves stretch from tree to tree and from column to column, forming, among the pierced walls of marble and of verdure, theaters where the violins mingle their plaint with the sound of the water. The ballet, ordered like a rite, unrolls its figures of animated geometry to the sounds of a music whose symmetrical grace has the nudity, frail and firm, of the circular colonnades from which the paths radiate. In the evening, fireworks prolong into the darkness the play of the straight lines and of the perfect curves, in order to demonstrate to the mind that the order of life has not changed its direction.

All around Paris, in a radiating crown whose elements are connected by imposing avenues and, here

PIERRE PUGET. Maternity, terra-cotta (*Aix*).

and there, at a greater distance, scattered in the
environs of the large cities, the art of the gardens makes
of France also, in the general misery of a soil that is
scarcely cultivated, a vast system of aristocratic oases
wherein the Cartesian order, the Catholic order, the
monarchical order, and the æsthetic order express
themselves in solidarity and with a rigor well relieved
by space, by shining waters, and by verdure, in which
appear the luminous notes of statues, railings, and
staircases. After all, with the open spaces, regular,
square, or polygonal, of Hardouin-Mansard, surrounded
by mansions of moderate height, which are related by
their bodies, their two wings, their pediments, and their
great windows, with the straight street and the road,
it is the representative art of this century of will and
reason. Everything in it is geometrical, the abstract
line, the vast ordered space leading to another space
by a corridor bordered by the colonnade of the trees,
and the broad roads and clearings, all permitting us to
maintain order in the confusion offered by the senses
to the brain. The square, the garden, the street, the
bridge, and the road are lines drawn by the intelligence
between the accidents of terrestrial nature and the
mystery of habitations and of forests. The road
especially, whose two sections are joined by the bridge
—the august bridge, in which the two finest elements
of building, the vault and the wall, are fused—the
road bordered by the strength, the coolness, the silence,
and the regular majesty of the trees, the road covering
the earth with its network, and espousing its curves
the better to dominate it, the road, a horizontal architecture, is one of the noblest forms of the peoples'
faith in themselves. It is a challenge to death, for it is
to survive those who trace it and who harden it with
stone. It confronts man with man in the marches of
war and in the exchanges of peace. It embraces, like

arms, the cities which it cradles and presses upon the
bosom of the soil. Like arms, it is laden with branches,
with sheaves, and with vines. It offers bouquets of
parks, of villas, and of gardens. It has the candor
of obedience, the firmness of logic, the rectitude of
mathematics.

And yet, if the mind desires resolutely to place
itself face to face with all this order, which was already
being sketched under
Henri IV and Riche-
lieu, and which goes
on like a straight-lined
boulevard, cutting
through the confusion
of wars, popular re-
volts, and political dis-
orders, from the Place
Royale to the Place
Vendôme, something
embarrasses it in its
admiration and re-
strains it from loving.
It cannot really aban-
don itself to the ab-
stract intoxication of
comprehending, except
before the military
walls, set up with

COUSTOU.   Nicolas Coustou
(*Versailles*).

mathematical rigor by Vauban, to withstand cannonades
and assaults. Here, at last, adaptation gains its
majesty. The star of stone, of earth, and of water
girdles the outer city, crowns the island of granite,
and terminates the acropolis, like a thought issuing
from them in order to justify them. Reason protects
life; there is no question, as in other places, of life
being barred in by reason. Form does not consent to

subordinate its functions to pure intelligence save when they together express some profound organism growing within the crowds like a bud on a branch. In the French cathedral, the statue, the stained-glass window, and the carved foliage caused the mass to blossom; the spirit came from the depth. Here the spirit comes from without; it is no longer more than a parasite. The extreme abundance of allegory is the first thing to proclaim the propensity toward general ideas of an epoch incapable of discovering them in the forms and of completely expressing them through the means offered by the forms. At Versailles, everything is built abstractly; not a detail issues from a spontaneous volition or from the needs of sensibility. The decorator is not free to play his rôle as he understands it, within the limits set by the direction of the work and by the genius of his chief. The chief, who himself obeys dogmatic and political considerations foreign to the purpose of art, intervenes in every detail to obtain the submission of the artist in everything. And if the ensemble preserves the order of a theorem, it cannot pretend to the abstract limpidity of the theorem, since it works on the plane of life, and therefore breathes a dull sadness. It is a manuscript written in a fair handwriting into which no one has emptied his heart.

v

The bas-relief of Girardon, into which passes something of the sensual and melodious passion which conceived "Andromaque" and "Phèdre," is in exile in the gardens of the king. As it is of the robust lineage of Jean Goujon and of Ronsard, it would be at home under the branches, if its beautiful nude women disporting among the reeds did not have the effect of a free irruption of life in the too perfectly clipped alleys

GIRARDON. The Bath of the Nymphs (*Versailles*).

which mount toward the too-severe façades and the cold vestibules. Trembling water, undulating grace. . . . It is, perhaps, in the twilight of Versailles where the harmonies of autumn were calling, each year, for the coming of Watteau, the first great divine breath. But it stands alone. With Poussin dead—who, moreover, had lived but little in France—the plastics of the century will have neither its Molière, nor its La Fontaine, nor its Pascal above all, nor even its Bossuet. On the other hand, it will have its Boileau. We need not be astonished at this. The strongest power has only an uncertain influence upon the dawning and the progression of the great personalities of literature, whose work bears within itself its origin and its goal. If it can, in hours of political anarchy and of intellectual disorder, allow the great personalities of plastics to grow like the others, in hours of exaggerated centralization and unification it drives into canals and hems in the development of the arts whose fundamental function is to build and to decorate. The system of the century, which already very strongly reacted upon the writers and the poets, had to bring the painters and the sculptors into almost complete subjection to its law. The great men did not find their place in it. The mediocre men gained through it.

We see Pierre Puget wandering, like one accursed, from Toulon to Genoa, from Genoa to Marseilles, from Marseilles to Paris, where he is condemned to repress his soul and abase himself constantly, in order, despite his revolts, to obey the common rule; and despite his disgust, he must submit to the school formulas which his visible anguish tortures and falsifies everywhere. He is not even at his ease amid convicts; he stifles. He begins things, and abandons them. He tries to model the whole of Marseilles like an object. His desire is to draw vessels, build them, and decorate

LE SUEUR. The Death of Saint Bruno (*Louvre*).

them. He conceives galleys and three-decked ships where the cannons coming from the portholes act, as do the masts and the sails and the oriflammes and the grandiloquent sculptures at the stern, as decorative elements. With his tridents, his sirens, his Amphitrites, and his Neptunes, he struggles on in the seaports, among the clerks and the engineers. He fails in all his projects. "The marble trembles before him, . . ." but he is determined not to take account of this trembling of the marble in order to impose upon it, in spite of itself, the swollen rhetoric of the century, to waste his time, and to scatter his pride in every trade. As a civil and naval architect, a painter, a sculptor in stone and in wood, he works himself out of breath to gain a spiritual domain which he could have assured to himself by a patient and passionate penetration to the depth of a single one of these forms of thought. A few powerfully sketched works are all that give up the secret of the greatness he felt in himself, but upon which he imposes a frame which stifles it and convulses it at every point. The spirit of Michael Angelo wears itself out by trying to lock up its flame in the grimaces of Bernini.

In this he is the opposite of Le Brun, who is devoid of passion, and works without disquietude and at his ease, and who governs the whole of art. He has no other reason for existence. Fed on Descartes, an æsthetician, an historian, an archæologist, and, into the bargain, a well-taught painter, he exercises, in the name of Colbert, a kind of viceroyalty over what is called from that moment on the "Beaux-Arts," and represents, in France, the Doctrine which he knows how to adapt in its entirety to the functions demanded of it by the deified monarchy, in order to attain the material and philosophic conquest desired by the French mind. Not more than a few isolated men resist: Mignard

THE BROTHERS LE NAIN. The Forge (*Louvre*).

follows only half-heartedly; Philippe de Champagne, a Fleming, moreover, and but little attracted by the School, cuts himself off in his jealous Jansenism. Le Sueur lives apart, knows almost nothing of Rome, never having made the journey, and, in this century, communes with the spirit of Fénelon through his mellifluous grace, the measured, decorous, and discreet appearance which he gives to French mysticism, and through his sweetish suavity, which falls like a rain of fine ashes on his pale blues and his grays. All the others obey: Mansard, the Coustous, Coyzevox, Girardon himself, and Louis XIV first of all, who thinks that he is commanding. The royal manufactories and the academies are under the orders of the first painter of the king. Le Nôtre furnishes him with the frame that he needs. When he takes part in the work, he can certainly do portraits as robust as those of Sébastien Bourdon and Claude Lefebvre—good painters—or of Coyzevox and the Coustous, good statue makers, and of all those solid workmen who painted well and sculptured well, as men wrote well, and built well, as men spoke and conversed well, as they preached well, as they commanded the armies and the squadrons well, and fought well in their century. But that is too slight a task. He needs immense surfaces in order to spread out his learned and flat painting; he seeks in the battles and the history of Alexander a necessary frame for the bombastic odes which his position and his faith command him to address to Louis XIV. And if his plan includes some room to be decorated, he rises to an effort as superb and as empty as the pompous eloquence to be expected of the artist who solves everything and directs everything. . . . Here are long vaulted halls of gold where ornaments in relief make a rich frame for red and somber paintings, cut-glass chandeliers, waxed floors, and tapestries: the reliquary is ready for the

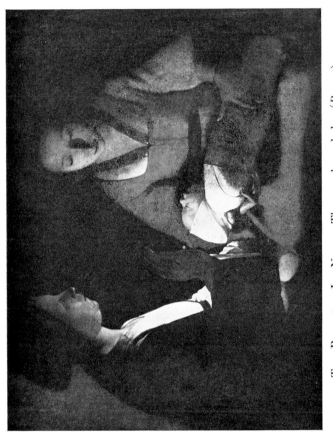

THE BROTHERS LE NAIN.   The new-born baby (*Rennes*).

god. . . . Hyacinthe Rigaud, an acute psychologist, certainly, will be able to embalm him alive in his glory, not a hieratic glory, to be sure, for he has never stepped outside of his century and his society, and he justifies them and summarizes them in their solemn unity; Hyacinthe Rigaud will find all the elements in readiness for his dithyramb. The face, the hand, and the foot will be given a purely monarchical significance. His whole science is employed in painting outspread brocades, mantles of velvet and ermine, and the insignia of nobility. Fingers are never posed on anything but scepters, globes, and crowns; high heels point the tips of the toes at an angle, and flowing wigs deploy the whole of this magnificent stateliness around foreheads, eyes, and lips. Life has fled the depth of souls, and silence reigns in France, as if the aristocratic sentiments of its *élite* were scandalized by the surrounding tumult, which the death of Rubens, of Velasquez, and of Rembrandt has not yet quieted, and which German music will soon animate once more.

In reality, the period here expresses, with Poussin himself, and with Jean Goujon before Poussin, the fatigue of an extremely intelligent people which is trying by all possible means to conceal its fatigue, and which gives to the forms which it uses for that purpose a majestic exterior and a systematic development which create the illusion sought. It attempts to arrest individual research, which the following century and the Revolution will unchain anew. Instead of seeking a new organism through the individual, it imposes upon the individual a unity issuing from above. France pays—royally—for the glory of having been the first, after the Crusades, to set in motion the movement of the Occident. The stylization of the mind, which she had been seeking since the introduction in her land of Italian idealism, was only an attempt to arrest life in formulas, an attempt destined to be very rapidly checked, but participating, even so, in the qualities of harmony, of clarity, and of measure which remained, despite all, the privilege of the soil.

And so we have before us merely a façade, like those great colonnaded walls which mask uncomfortable apartments, like those imposing manners which ill conceal coarse and dirty habits, like that splendid display of wealth and force which did not prevent La Bruyère from evoking in terrible terms the misery of the peasants, nor the brothers Le Nain, above all, from recounting, in their little pictures which were not shown at Versailles, the story of the black bread earned by ragged men, with broken hands and bare feet, pictures which told how much majesty is given by exhausting and joyless work to weary attitudes, to clasped knees, to arms dropped in abandon, to eyes staring into emptiness, and to the profound play of light in poor dwellings. A great work, three-fourths of which is lost, a work of primitive power despite its learned structure, it sometimes makes us think of the grave statues of Egypt by its grand humility; an isolated work, and yet classic and of its century, through its form, but isolated in sentiment. When

H. RIGAUD.   Portrait (Louvre).

Louis XIV grows old, when his family crumbles, when everyone can see that he is mortal like the others, and that, after all, it is very fatiguing to keep a mask on for a lifetime, the lizards are allowed to run in the monument, the gilding and the stucco are allowed to peel off, and the wind, sweeping the dead leaves and the dust of flowers, is allowed to whirl in the cold rooms.

COYZEVOX.   Nymph with a shell (*Versailles*).

If he still stands erect, it is because the Jesuits have been summoned to prop him up.   But everything is cracking—ecclesiastical discipline, industrial power, the navy, the army, pride—and respect.   Ruin is everywhere, and persecution, and want.   Colbert's system, carried to the bureaucratism which causes the greatest sterility, brings on a tariff war, the paralysis of commerce, and the most extreme anæmia of the arts.   The king has no more money.   Let a fissure occur in an ensemble

so superb, and everything slips through it. . . . Louis
XIV, his great style, and the dogma, one and multiform,
which he represents, will spread, for a century, over
Europe, over poor Germany, respectful of so much
splendor, over wild Russia, decadent Italy, and drows-
ing Spain, while France, through one of those sudden
recoveries, one of those changes of front with which
she starts up again at the moment when she is sliding
to the abyss, goes off in another direction with a careless gesture and irony on her lips and in her eyes. The
disintegration which, from the beginning of the powerful masquerade, had been announcing itself tragically,
with Pascal, affirms itself ferociously with Bayle, who
no longer believes in anything whatsoever. Saint-
Simon scrapes the oozing bones, and pours vitriol and
vinegar on the wounds that will not close. . . . Mignard, though very old, reacts against Le Brun as soon
as he becomes his successor. Rome is now without
attraction; Rigaud dispenses with her, Jouvenet does
not go there, nor does Largillière. Coyzevox has
already something of the free and nervous look of
Houdon. The painters of the north return to fashion.
Largillière, who has studied Rubens at Antwerp and
several times made the journey to London to gather
up the trace of Van Dyck there, seeks to emancipate
himself, to loosen his hand, to bring air into his harmonies. A breath of romance and of the pastoral
lifts the curls of the wigs, and carries the eyes toward
the heavens. . . . The soul of Watteau sometimes
circles through the alleys at evening, mingling with
the laughter that is returning, with the tears that are
released, and with a sad and tender something which
makes the hearts tremble. . . .

THE PETIT TRIANON

Chapter V. THE RATIONALIST PASSION

I

HE sun which rose from the depth of Lorrain's canvases, amid their severe architecture, was Watteau. An autumn sun, lighting up russet foliage. A profound sigh of nature, delivered from a corset of iron, and at the same time dying from having been so long compressed, and giving herself up to the desires of the poet with the concentrated and fiery heat of a flame which is burning out. In reality, they are still there, the severe architectures; the fête of the Regency installs itself in the great palaces; Saint-Simon and Montesquieu, iconoclasts, both belong, by birth and by activity, to the castes which guarded and cared for the icons; and the teaching of the school, until the end of the century and

A Panel, style of Louis XVI.

beyond it, will reign officially. Its aspects are controlled by the mind. When Poussin gave order to his ideas and his images, he could not purge his flesh of the memory of the forms and the nymphs whom Jean Goujon and Ronsard encountered in the woods. When Watteau came forth from the alleys to explore these woods, full of forms and of shadow, the will of Poussin and the harmony of Racine penetrated there with him.

He arrived, with the freedom of the senses and with a thirst for mystery, in a world which had swept mystery from all its avenues and had forbidden the senses to go beyond the limits of reason. He accepted the exterior of this world, so as to keep intact his whole strength and his melancholy, and overturn their spiritual intimacy in order to send blood coursing through the marble of the statues, bathe the trees of the gardens with mist and light, and wring ardor and tears from the costumed personages who, for fifty years, had been crossing the stage, refusing to lend to it their dissimulated passion, and to borrow its well-schooled tremors. He still wears the wig, but he will have no more to do with pensions and offices. Instead, his lot is wretched poverty, a life of wandering, consumption, and the tenacious presentiment of death. That was enough to make him seek the shelter of the leaves, listen to music as it circled round, and surprise, in words overheard by chance and fleeting forms, the illusion of love and the flight of the hours.

What a mystery is a great artist! Whether Watteau wished it or not, his sentimental comedy in the eternity of nature is the image of existence of us all, seen by an ardent nature across his bitter destiny. Here is the confronting, without respite and with admirable love, of life, too short, and of the infinite desired. Trembling soul, adoring soul—the burned-out pinks and the pale blues quiver like his poor soul. He feels that he is

going to die. Between two flutters of an eyelid which
mark the awakening of consciousness and the repose
which comes too soon, he expresses the happy appearances and the poignant realities of the adventure to
which he is condemned.

The resigned pessimism of the Italian farce, the
cruel reality which prowls through the masquerade and

WATTEAU. The Italian Comedy (*Private collection*).

masks itself with black velvet, came at their destined
hour to afford distraction to a dying aristocracy and to
the profound man who hides this death struggle under
flowers. The whole century will feel it, Tiepolo,
Cimarosa, Guardi, and Longhi will reply, later on, to
Watteau, from the center of the fête; and from Spain
herself, somber, ruined, and seeming almost dead, comes

the bantering laugh of Goya. But with Watteau, it is
the prelude, intimate, delicate, drunk with tenderness,
wildly desirous of making the illusion endure. He listens
to the wind. He wanders and chats with the comedians.
Like them he embroiders upon any canvas. Never did
subject have less importance in itself. It is always the
same, like the relationship of man and woman with love
and with death. Since that is so, how monotonous!
The groups posed on the moss, like leaves torn dying
from the trees, or like ephemeral butterflies, will be
carried away by the breeze which hurries them on to
the abyss, with the forgetfulness and the phantoms, the
plaint of the violoncellos, the sigh of the flutes, the perfumes, and the sound from the jets of water. When one
isolates from its frame the talk of all these charming
creatures, dressed in satin, powdered, rouged, having
nothing in life to do but make love and music, everything expresses the joy of the instant seized on the
wing. Here is nothing but prattle, rockets, and cascades of laughter, and an intricate cross-fire of gallan-
tries and confessions. The round dance turns, the innocent games are organized and, when the concert begins,
the flute and the mandolin scarcely cause voices to be
lowered. Why does the ensemble give that sensation so
near to sadness? The spirit of the poet is present.
Slow steps and swayings, scattered words, necks that
turn aside to seize a phrase of gallantry, throats bending to escape or to offer themselves, inclined and
laughing faces resembling flowers only half open, all
will pass, all will pass! How quickly a society appears
and disappears under the trees a hundred years old,
which, themselves, will die one day! Nothing is eternal
but the sky, from which the clouds will disappear. The
costumed comedy reveals a terrible ennui with life; it is
only the song of the sonorous instruments which can
cradle the despair of those who have nothing to do but

WATTEAU. Fête Champêtre (*Dresden*).

amuse themselves. Not one of us will arrest the impalpable instant when love transfixed him, and he who
comes to tell of it with tones which penetrate one
another and lines which continue one another, still
burns with a desire that he will never satisfy.

To tell all this, he had therefore placed that which is
most fugitive amid that which is most durable among
the things seen by our eyes—space and the great woods.
He died at Nogent, under the fog and the trees, quite
near the water. He had brought back from his Flemish
country, and from a visit he had made to England, the
love of moist landscapes where the colors, in the multiplied prism of the tiny suspended drops, take on their
real depth and their splendor. Music and trees, the
whole of him is in them. The sonorous wave, rising
from tense strings, itself belongs to the life of the air,
with the light vapor which sets its azure haze around
the scattered branches, the slender trunks which space
themselves or assemble in clusters near the edge of the
deep forests, and the luminous glades away toward the
distance and the sky. The sound does not interrupt the
silence, but rather increases it. Barely, if at all, a
whispered echo reaches us from it. We do indeed see
the fingers wandering upon the strings; the laughter
and the phrases exchanged are to be guessed from busts
leaning over or thrown back, and from fans that tap on
hands—the actors in the charming drama are at a distance from their painter, and scattered to the depth of
the clearings which flee toward the horizon, whose blue
grows deeper, little by little. And the genius of painting
resolves into visual harmonies the sound of the instruments which hovers above the murmurs of the voices.
The green, the red, or the orange of the costumes of
comedy or of parade, and the dark and silky spots
made by the groups of people conversing, are mingled
with the diffused silver which trembles and unites the

tips of the near-by leaves with the sunny spaces which
stretch away among the dark trunks.

One suspects that he remained chaste, among these
assemblies of lovers whom he sees only from afar. One
guesses it from his statues of nude women, from his
nude women themselves, from his groups of actresses
and prattling ladies of high birth who have no other
concern than love and talk of love. His ardent
adoration of them al-
ways keeps him at a
distance. He fears to
hurt them, to penetrate
their mystery, to know
them from too near by,
to tear the aërial veil
which trembles between
them and him. He
caresses them only with
his wandering harmo-
nies, stolen here and
there—as would some
bee from the north, liv-
ing in the damp forests,
or under the lights of the
fête—with the powdered
gold of the hair, with the

Watteau.   Drawing (*Louvre*).

rose of the bodices, with blued and milky haze, with the
flowered moss on which rest skirts and mantles of satin,
with the nocturnal phosphorescence given to jewels and
velvets by the gleam of the moon and of waving torches.
It is the irised air which models the marble, which
quivers when it touches breasts or necks, and which carries the same poignant agitation to the sprightly faces,
to the fingers picking at the guitars, and to the delicate,
pure legs under the stockings of transparent silk. But
he never approaches; he is steeped in the breath of

nature, and its ardor consumes him, but the vision of nature which issues from him is as distant as an old dream. Observe it in its detail. The vast structure of the forms, solid, turning, and substantial, makes them appear to be on the plane of man; he builds his little personages as great as his desire; he paints with the breadth, the fire, and the freedom of Veronese, of Rubens, of Velasquez, or of Rembrandt. Move away from the picture. The harmony moves away also; man and the woods are no more than a passionate memory for this being who dies of phthisis, alone in his room, embittered, in pain, hating every one who approaches him, but loving from afar everything he has seen along his path, forgiving all for the pettiness of their minds because of the power of their instincts, and because of the splendor of the earth, peopled with leaves and waters.

This man who had sent forth over the world swarms of Amors to scatter roses through the azured mist that is touched with gold, who had seized in flight, from perfumes and from smiles, all that is subtlest and most secret in the confessions of low voices, and stolen all the transparent stones of rings and necklaces, to mingle them with the blood of the skin and the light of the eyes, had remained immersed through all his senses in the earthiest of existences. One divines in him the wandering poet of the street who spends an hour watching boxes nailed up, amuses himself at shop entrances with the coming and going of buyers, or, covered with mud, goes on to the near-by storehouse, to see a nag unharnessed there, soup being prepared, and straw being unloaded from carts, or a troop of soldiers, dripping with mud and water. The nature he paints is by no means "opera scenery." From the roots of the tree to the clouds in the sky, it trembles with the life which runs through it. No one had ever breathed with such intoxication the strong odor of the damp woods,

WATTEAU. The Luncheon (*Berlin*).

listened with so much surprise to the murmur of words in the silence of the great trees, or discovered with so much enchantment the gay spots formed by lovers, and people chatting among the dark trunks, and under the green shadow of the leaves. The "opera scenery" is only a

WATTEAU. Drawing (*Louvre*).

pretext calculated to bring about the acceptance of the man who comes to break it down. In reality, he reacts against everything which, at the time when he came into the world, brought about the success of the preachers, the style of the artists, and the fortune of the shopmen. The muzzled aristocracy which, in the preceding century, had consented to discipline its original roughness,

WATTEAU. Rustic pleasures (*Wallace collection, London*).

in order to give to the state that façade, straight and
bare, behind which politics and thought expressed
their desire to imprison the soul of France, had matured
rapidly in luxury, intrigue, and the exercises of the
mind. Feeling itself about to die, it unchained its instincts. And immediately, at the instant when it was
about to reach the height of an expansion of grace and
of intelligence on the other slope of which its decline
was forecast, it found, to represent it, a great artist who
preferred to die in a charity hospital rather than live
with it, but who found it adorable from afar. The clear
vision of La Rochefoucauld, the pain of Pascal, and the
bitterness of Molière excused in it two centuries of
hypocrisy and of baseness for the sake of that second
when a man of their race breathed its purest fragrance.
And Montaigne recognized the aptitude of France to
unite, in the same artistic expression, the most intimate
despair and the loftiest elegance of the mind.

II

Although Antoine Watteau gave his last days to
Pater, and a little of his nervous vivacity to Lancret,
it is neither Pater nor Lancret who will continue his
course, when he will no longer be there; they will not
follow in the very direction taken by that aristocracy
of birth and culture which seems to obey some order
coming from the living depths which it exploits, and
thereby determines its fall and hastens its dissolution.
On the contrary, it is, as always, the disciples of the
master who try to maintain intact the form he created,
around which they have not seen life breaking down and
moving. And yet almost everyone else is touched by
his grace; they alone live in the setting he discovered.
Watteau never ceased to hear the torrent of Rubens's
blood, the beat of his heart, and the air murmuring in

his breast, and so Rubens will, for a hundred years, breathe into the atmosphere of France a little of that fat and shining fluidity of northern painting the source of which the last painters of Louis XIV went to seek in Flanders and in England, forgetting the road to Rome, whence the School was returning, moreover, in full, though unconscious, revolt. Largillière is still alive. He often sets up his easel out of doors, under the trees, to paint his court people, and when they refuse to pose, one sees clearly, from their somewhat disordered appearance, that they are coming from him or are returning to him. Men like Coypel, Van Loo, de Troy, and a dozen artists around them who represent the School, will assume, in their mythological pictures and their state portraits, a careless elegance and a freedom of accent which indicate that people have been reading the "Lettres persanes," that Voltaire has returned from his journey to England, and that the bad King Louis XV is abandoning the good Queen Leczinska. The assembly of the gods is held in the boudoir of the favorites. All the good sculptors of the century, old Coyzevox first of all, in whom Puget is still felt, and already Clodion as well, then Lemoine, Pajou, Pigalle, Falconet, the brothers Adam, and Bouchardon, will not be quite themselves until they have introduced into the fashionable Olympus, chubby Eros or Venus at her toilette, like a lady of elegance well versed in matters of love. And Nattier will paint the princesses of the blood as rustic divinities, almost disrobed at times, their arms and their feet bare, and with flowers garlanded on their dresses, around their fingers, and in their hair. Rose bushes grow among the yews and the trimmed boxwood of Versailles.

Those roses, moreover, do not lose their petals as soon as they are picked. They will be applied all along the walls, they will encircle the sofas and the ladies who chat there, they will be around mirrors and chandeliers, and will be suspended from the canopies of the beds. Everyone, like Coypel and Caylus, for example, talks of "imitating nature." But upon condition that it submit to the caprice of the society least prepared to feel it living in man, and to experience its mystic intoxication, without which art loses the sole cause of its eternal

Hôtel Biron (1728).

character. Watteau is a king of the spirit whom the aristocracy of France will obey. But it will take its revenge, in its turn, by giving its orders to those who will succeed Watteau. "Nature" will reduce itself to a kind of *objet d'art* placed on a shelf, and destined for the usage of fashion set by those who possess favor and money, which, by the way, they employ with extreme elegance.

Watteau being dead, the eighteenth century is

æsthetically bankrupt of taste. The entire *élite* is furnished with an intense art education, which rises and broadens in it in the measure that creative force declines and shrinks in the souls of the artists, its servitors. It is drawing-room art, which does not pass the limits of the drawing-room (*salon*). The exhibitions of paintings are themselves "Salons." Painters, sculptors, engravers, jewelers, goldsmiths, cabinet-makers, hair-dressers, tailors, and bootmakers all contribute to surround the fine flower of a highly developed culture with this frail and creeping frame which brings out its splendor, but which tightens around it, gradually causes its natural origins to be lost to view, and exhausts itself in satisfying a spirit which is fading and dying of ingenuity and ennui. Everywhere, around the conversationalist and the coquette, in crystal, unglazed porcelain, marble, and tapestry, from the glass cabinet for bibelots to the tableware, from the carriage to the sedan chair, and from the antechamber to the alcove, this charming art repeats and reflects the words exchanged about love, about new-born science, about Persia, about China, about the spectacles of the day, and about the countryside seen from an opera box. A fashionable art, which uses up and completely drains the amiability of the artist, scatters it with the flights of the Amors and the flowers which are strewn about, disperses it through a thousand toilet articles, and debases it through those same surroundings.

François Boucher is its soul. Fashion insinuates itself and fixes itself around his easy fecundity, which everywhere, on ceilings, screens, carriage panels, and small friezes above doors, on caskets and fans, scatters its monotonous subjects—shepherdesses and pastorals. Charming in manner, generous, one who loved enjoyment and who is adored by men and women, ceaselessly exchanging with his century that which they both need

in order to love and be loved, he stands, with the
mistress of the king, at the center of his own revolving
circle of winged loves and of flowers woven in garlands,
which he is quite free—as artists of his race alone are—
to bring forth in greatest profusion and to hang up
wherever it pleases the alert and spontaneous fantasy
of his desire, which is ever in accord with his require-

BOUCHER. Girl bathing, red chalk (*Private collection*).

ments. In order to yield to the flexible grace of this
world, where philosophic and gallant conversation
flows on sinuous lines and makes delicate détours,
everything adapts itself without effort to the forms
imagined by the architect and the cabinet-maker of
society, forms tending constantly more toward the
circular. The fat, soft roundnesses turn with the wood-
work and the frames; there are chubby shepherds,
beribboned shepherdesses, and serving maids whom the

painter raises to the dignity of goddesses by disrobing them, to show their full-blooded young flesh, their smiles, their dimples, and the elastic and quickly swelling curve of their buttocks and their breasts. The plump children of Bouchardon, the sculptor, are swept into the dance. Fragonard is prefigured; and Boucher, through his savory master Lemoyne, through Watteau,

BOUCHER. Loves, detail (*Louvre*).

and through the world of decorators and artisans inspired by him, links the whole fragile setting of the French aristocracy with the supreme teaching of the Italian fête which Tiepolo, at the same time with him, is unfurling over the ceiling of Venetian bedchambers and drawing-rooms. Almost freed from form, the aërial harmonies sprinkle, with the rouge of cheeks and the powder from puffs, light skies, where the whirl of the clouds effaces itself little by little in the diffused rose and silver.

Unfortunately, the twisted and serpentine line prevents the decorator from making a complete escape into space and ever recalls him to labor for the tyrannous world of fashion, for which he was born. He remains the prisoner of the prince. For the first time, the artist is admitted to the drawing-room and the table,

BOUCHARDON. The Fountain of Grenelle, detail.

with the critic who dictates rules, the *littérateur* who explains, the scientist who diffuses knowledge, and the philosopher who destroys. It is the painter and the sculptor who lose most through these contacts; they are ill at ease between rationalistic analysis and sentimental abstraction; they forget, little by little, the life of the profound volumes and of the colors steeped in rain and in light, when they enter upon moral considerations, where they very quickly lose their way. The only one

La Tour. Portrait of J. Vernet (*Dijon*).

who gains is the newsmonger of plastics, who grows up
somewhere between the rhymer of epigrams and the indiscreet confidant—the engraver of anecdotes of gallantry and of spicy gossip, who pretends that he was
present, concealed behind a screen, at the disrobing of
the bride, at the consultation of the marquise, and at
the vicomte's or the abbé's capture by assault of the
chambermaid. The genius for gossip, rendered sharp
and subtle by a century of the life of fashion, overflows
the drawing-rooms, the suppers, and the teas in the
English style, and sweeps over everything that is expressed by pen, pencil, or modeling tool. Cochin,
Beaudoin, Moreau the younger, Eisen, Leprince, and
the Saint-Aubins create a chronicle of fashion peculiar
to this country and this period. Conversations are
carried on in exquisite style with a pastel crayon, a
luminous engraving, pretty as a blonde—that one
finds on turning the pages of a tale of gallantry or of
a classic tragedy, or in a delicate, powdered head on a
translucent medallion a quarter the size of one's hand.
Everything is conversation—letters to the ladies, the
article in the Encyclopédie, the short story by Voltaire,
and the critique by Diderot. A witty word shakes a
world, and a hundred thousand such words are struck
off every day.

III

The art of the century converses, which is what saves
it, while condemning it to a place below the great in-
tuitions that open the spirit to lyricism when it is freed
from the necessity for giving pleasure and for killing
time. These sharp images, in their thin language, with
a wrinkle at the corner of the mouth, or the dimple in a
chin, or dilated nostrils, or an upturned nose, succeed in
relating what is most furtive—but also most characteristic of the thing itself and of its time—in the inmost

soul of a prelate, or a writer, or a man of the court, or a woman of fashion; but there is nothing save their appearance in these images to relate them with the grandly sensual art of plastics, to which psychology makes but a weak appeal. But they bring us testimony of a singularly sincere exchange between him who listens and looks, and him who speaks and acts. Perronneau is not often a painter. But he is always a precise observer, clear and firm in his language, and abandoning nothing without first interrogating it. The faces of those around him pass from his eye to his hand as if his intelligence were a filter retaining everything that is not the expression of the intelligence. La Tour is not an artist. He is a mirror. He does not imagine a new form into which all the elements of the world, magnified, enter at a single bound and raise life to the level of a soul. Of the school of Voltaire, a friend of Voltaire, he criticizes, like Voltaire, with a line exact and dry. When, in his later years, he pretends telling more than he can and more than he knows how to tell, he comes to grief. Meeting the empty mask halfway, the mind is registered by crisp strokes. Under the mask, there is neither form nor matter. The mind stands alone, isolated from the heart, and reduced to the accurately fitted mechanism through which it dissects and classifies. There is nothing but the skin; the bones are lacking; but in the skin, shriveling and grimacing, there is a flash of lightning from the mouth and the eye. People think that this century is material. It is nothing but mind, dried-up mind that twists and consumes and corrodes. All there is of charm and of youth is burned in it, like a moth in the flame of a lamp.

It is mind, and its passion is entirely of the mind. It is a critic, which is why it is not a poet. It is sentimental, which is why it is not plastic. It is declamatory, which is why it is not lyrical. It is sensitive, which is why it is not sensual. It leads a double life. The one demonstrates, the other devotes itself to enjoyment. And when one does no more than demonstrate, one never goes to life to ask it to educate one's desire and make it fruitful. And when one devotes oneself merely

A. COYPEL. Young Girl, drawing (*Louvre*).

to enjoyment, one never turns to the mind to deepen and purify one's enjoyment. Watteau and Gluck apart, in whom love is mingled with tears, and lips never give themselves save with a deep sob, and an ecstasy of lamentation rises from laughter and song, this century has no love for love. He who loves ideas builds on ideas alone. He talks, and he paints ideas, in an intellectual idiom. He yields himself upon command. His emotion reveals itself only under such circumstances, and apropos of such sentiments. And he who loves women loves them only for the pleasure that he gets from them, forces this pleasure, falsifies it, and ends in aberration. There is no unity. The century analyzes itself to the point of splitting its fibers in

OLLIVIER. A Tea at the Palace of the Prince de Conti (*Louvre*).

two, and lives along two divergent lines, which separate more and more. And so, at about midway, it results in a deviation of sentiment and a monotonous debauch which find no common ground upon which to realize an equilibrium and to liberate from matter—loved in all its aspects and passionately enjoyed—the mind charged with love which is simply its whole essence. It seeks counsel of it in order to purify and ennoble its own self more and more.

Hence, we have on one side Greuze, and on the other Fragonard. The one, who might have expressed, demonstrates; the other, who might have loved, amuses himself. The one bores us a great deal; the other irritates us a little. Moreover, both deceive themselves. That is not nobility, and love is not that. Greuze, whom the good Diderot,[1] who nevertheless loved painting and even understood it, urges on to render moralizing dramas by means of painting, explores, as soon as he is not watched, the camisole of little girls; weighs with a shining and quickly averted glance the breasts heavy as fruits seen through the shadowy opening of bodices, and surrounds the eyes and the lips of the women with a moist and troubled atmosphere which veils his lubricity. Fragonard, who gives himself up to his work as a painter of bedrooms and boudoirs, and who applies himself to it unrestrainedly, sometimes grows tender at the sight of the soft roundnesses which he discovers, and, in a few triumphant sketches, gives rein to the healthiest sensuality. One forgets the excess of puffy skins, and of trees and rocks blown up like unhealthy flesh, for the sake of a round thigh perceived under a flying drapery, for an undulating and hollow back caressed by the moist penumbra, for a breast stretching and swelling under the arm that enfolds it. Clodion, the sculptor of bacchanales, whose work is associated discreetly with the decoration of the lovers' chamber, or finds a more intimate refuge in the dressing room, or even at the depths of a secret closet, has more of love, of health, of intoxicated freedom. After the flying huntresses and the naïads of Jean Goujon, between the beautiful nymphs of Versailles surprised at their bath by Girardon and the female fauns of Carpeaux, drawn forth from the woods to slip into the fêtes of the cities, to smile, to dance, and

[1] His *Essai sur la Peinture* is a masterpiece.

to disappear—Clodion's bibelot, caressed and whirling, affirms that woman, in this too-rascally and too-moral century, is not very different from her sister, the woman of all time, protectress of life, and made for natural love which she attracts and retains by her furtive mystery.

The century had misunderstood her. It had made of her now a philosopher, now a beast of pleasure.

AIX EN PROVINCE. Hôtel d'Albertas (1756).

One feels her to be superior to these two things in some of those portraits, so often anonymous, or escaping the intellectual emotion of Perronneau, of Drouais, of La Tour, or of Houdon especially, who have given her to us so worthy of being loved under the skepticism forced upon her and under her slightly sad smile. Her generosity takes the place of virtue, she makes tolerance a revolutionary weapon, and never seems more an aristocrat than when she comes out of the gutter. On these faces one sees hovering a native finesse which goes beyond intelligence, a winged nobility which has no need of morality, a living grace superior to beauty. These are the women who, after having read the *Nouvelle Héloise*, will all go toward Rousseau in a frenzy of eager adoration, to thank him for having restored them to their sex, for having understood that

CHARDIN. The Bun (*Louvre*).

they have a function of sentiment, and for having led them away from the privilege of philosophizing without emotion, and of loving without love. All those ironical pouts swell with loving tears. Why is Watteau no longer there? Gluck arrives, and at once he is understood. Yesterday, everything belonged to reason, everything to science. To-day everything belongs to sentiment. Or rather, rationalism becomes

a thing of sentiment and passion. In the name of
"nature," gradually recovered by newborn science, and
by criticism, which has turned around itself, morality
returns to fashion. The immoralist Diderot himself
sheds tears before all these beautiful sentiments, and
takes Greuze by the collar to drag him to them by
force. As happens so often in France, in a few months
there is a change of front. Exaggerated negation

CHARDIN.   Still-life (*Louvre*).

everywhere arouses the affirmations opposed to it.
"Nature" made man good; it is society that mars him.
Freed by knowledge of "nature" and of himself, he
need now do no more than efface himself, and consent to
the *Contrat Social*. The Protestant spirit, which had
been marching on underground since the time of the
Jansenists, of Bayle, and of Montesquieu's books, was
to burst forth into the daylight with the philosopher of
Geneva, and with it, England, her literature, her

economic science, and her naturalistic philosophy, enter among us. The French gardens are thrown into confusion so that winding roads may be traced among them, irregular lakes dug there, and trees planted at random on the great lawns. Everyone hastens to the fields, milks his cow in his cottage, grows sentimental over the mother suckling her last-born child, and raises temples to love. The great architecture of France, which, since Descartes, had been continuing on its straight road during those periods of pure abstraction, and was discreetly bathing its elegant logic in the life of fashion and the free grace of the time, gave forth, with the admirable Gabriel, its supreme blossom: buildings of medium size, never too large, almost always small, whose harmony, clear and measured as that of a cantata by Rameau, seems to call upon the trees, the clouds, and all the accidents of space and of the soil to yield to its equilibrium, not to spread themselves forth in too great disorder, not to listen to any excessive impulse, but to accept without constraint the proportion which man gives to all the beautiful things amid which he lives.

The last and, it must be said, one of the most admirable efforts of the collective genius of the race, it is through an apparent reversal of the habitual laws that it appears in this time of rising individualism, which still possesses, however, an impeccable workmanly tradition, and, within a political and moral philosophy held in common, makes its general effort in common. The art of building is the least sensual, the most intellectual, of all. Geometry and logic are profoundly cultivated; the style of ornament is pushed to its most extreme limits of refinement and research; taste is sure; luxury is fervent. Everything needed for the palace, the princely mansion, the pavilion, and the château is here: the last French architecture—by its impeccable measure, its discreet rhythm, its musical proportions, its nervous structure, at once slender and firm, under ornamentation the least apparent and the rarest, with its admirable decision to suppress decorative overloading of the big rooms, and to preserve for them great empty places, spacious as the intelligence, with tall, clear mirrors which raise them and broaden them again—is the essential art of this time. But it will come to an end, almost suddenly, and will make way, with all the accessories which accompany it, for a sentimental form of construction, still logically conceived, which will combat its first principle and entirely ruin it.

CHARDIN. The Marketer (*Louvre*)

At bottom, this is the end of a great aristocracy and the essay at the establishment of another. It was in vain for the one that was dying to deify Voltaire during his lifetime. If it was he who gave its meaning and value to its dissolution; it was also he who killed it, by breaking all the idols which guarded it from dissolution. The impartiality of Houdon penetrated the destroyer seated on the ruins, with his shriveled hands and his infernal laughter, as well as it comprehended the generosity or the obstinacy of the builders—Diderot, welcoming everything and making a confidant of life which flows forward and backward, and passes away, and constitutes itself anew; Rousseau testing all his materials with a suspicious and stubborn attention; and Buffon, with his powerful, round face which tells us of the germination of the myths of the future. The tender women of Trianon and of Versailles will do no more than follow a fashion, or else arrive, too late, at the sentiment of liberation. The palaces crumble, and the work of the artificial cottages does not sufficiently roughen the hands. The elements for the restoration of souls are in those blackest and most swarming quarters which behold the heaping up and the toiling of the men and women of Paris.

IV

Chardin proves it. He is the son of a carpenter. He does not leave his street. He paints signs. He exhibits in the open air, at the Place Dauphine. Later on, to be sure, he sends to the Salon. But he has no contact with the world of fashion, none with the court, and little with the artists, the critics, and the collectors. He is an honest fellow, a worthy man. His life is that of the lower middle class. He is a good workman. That is all. Since he knows his trade as well as it can be known, he is indulgent toward those who do not know it, for he understands its difficulties. He does not paint much, because he paints slowly, with a laborious and passionate application. He has no models. His wife, his children, a few familiar animals, the every-day tableware and cooking utensils; and then there are meat, vegetables, bread, and wine bought that same day from the butcher, the meat-roaster, the baker, and the vegetable seller. With that he writes the legend of domestic labor and the obscure life; his images speak to us after the manner of La Fontaine's words, and he is, with Watteau and Goya,

G. DE SAINT-AUBIN.   The Dotard (*Private collection*).

the greatest painter there is in Europe between the
death of Rembrandt and the maturity of Corot and
of Delacroix.

One must see how he lived, in the rooms of that
time where there was but little light, and where, for
a century, the family was organized and renewed amid
the same objects. From the moment when he arises,
while dressing, while at table, and in the little trips
from the pantry to the dining room, and from the yard
to the cellar, he looks, he meditates, and, to transport
that which he has seen into the intimate poem which
rises peacefully from his heart to his fingers, he need
do nothing but awaken the sonorities in the things
sleeping around him. Why should he take any other
background than the bare wall, or any other air than
the one he breathes with the remainder of his family?
Everything will get its accent through its exact shadings and its transparence; the apparent monotony
will concentrate in intimate silence the savor, the
secret spirit, and the expressive force of things. "One
uses colors, but it is with sentiment that one paints."
Yes, indeed. The whole splendor resides exclusively
in the voluptuousness of the act of painting which
no one, except Vermeer of Delft, to be sure, ever possessed to that degree. The good painter Chardin
performs his task with love, like a good carpenter, a
good mason, a good turner, or any good workman
who has reached the point of loving the material that
he works in and the tool which saves him from tiresome
uniformity, and which raises him to the dignity of
knowing his means. There is no more love expended
on the bare arm coming out of the rolled-up sleeve
than on the napkin that it holds, and on the leg of
mutton which fills the cloth and weighs down the fat,
pink hand. In the "Bénédicité," it is with the same
attention that he paints the little girl saying grace so

diligently, in order to get her soup more quickly, the mamma who is going to serve her and watches her with amusement, and the harmonies of the middle-class home which surround the group—the aprons, the woolen dresses, the blue stripe running through the

MOREAU THE YOUNGER. The Little Godparents, engraving.

tablecloth, the tureen, the varnished oak furniture, and the shadow which circles round everything and caresses everything. He knows that all of these things harmonize, that the life of objects depends on the moral life of people, and that the moral life of people receives the reflection of objects. Everything existing deserves his tender respect. In France, he is, with Watteau, the only religious painter in this century without religion.

He animates his material with an inner flame, which he never allows to flash forth, and which he locks up in the things at the very moment when they are about to issue forth from him. He knows them all so well! Here is the tureen from which, each day, he sees aris-

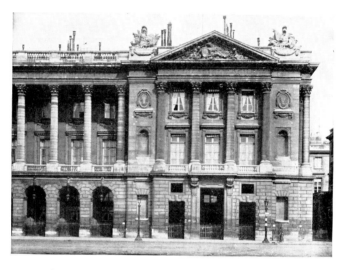

GABRIEL. The Ministry of the Marine, detail.

ing the odorous steam from the cabbages and carrots which his wife brought from the market. That fish covered with slime and blood has just been cleaned so that it may be eaten that evening with sauce, with leeks, bread rubbed with garlic, and wine. Here is his glass. Here is his spectacle case. Here are Madame Chardin's thimble, scissors, work-basket, and balls of wool and of thread. She has been wearing for a long time that good, plum-colored dress striped with mauve

and blue. By the way he has of placing that pipe on
the table, one guesses that he smokes it every day.
He expends so much application, love, and delicacy in
painting it, that he seems to be afraid of breaking it.
With that earthenware picture and with that milky
porcelain, he incorporates the flowers painted on them,
just as the sun and life mingle with fruits the color of
their juice, and with flesh the color of its blood. Everything, the sinkstone, the oak table, the three eggs
which have been deposited on it, the knife, and the

JOSEPH VERNET. Ponte Rotto, Rome (*Louvre*).

copper water urn on which a silver plate is awakened
by a reflection, take on, through his loverlike insistence, an appearance like that of fruit. One would
say that stone and wood were first reduced to a powder
in order to be mixed with that red liquor sleeping in
the crystal, with the gleaming blue of that blade, with
the varnished red or green of that apple which has
just rolled on the table between that glazed cup and
that ivory-toned chinaware, and then concentrated
and rendered denser by the fervor of the artist as
he caresses its grain. Mingled with blue, with rose, and
with gold, the whites of the earthenware and of the

table linen seem steeped in the light which bathes the palette and the brush. The sugar which autumn has condensed in the ripe fruits oozes from those heavy bunches of grapes and from those great pale peaches, and that hot bun, with the sprig of laurel on top of it, is fat with melted butter. That ivory top you see spinning, that pencil-holder halfway withdrawn from a bureau drawer, that white paper, and that goose quill seem a condensation of the material atmosphere. The pearly mist which composes it seems to thicken here and there into white feathers, into powdered hair, and into silk ribbons of vague color gently animating the motionless penumbra surrounding the inconceivable mystery of the form awakened by the mind and fashioned by the hand. In the limited space, all aquiver with gray dust, the merging reflections accumulate and reply to one another and come into accord so that, at a distance, they may create a harmony so measured that all its elements are effaced, and that it speaks with a single voice. Chardin paints each object with the combined reflections of all the other objects, foreseeing the living conquests of those who will come more than a century after he is gone, and he demonstrates, through the limpid purity of his

HOUDON.   Mme. Houdon (Louvre).

style, that melody can contain the richest polyphonic
tumult, as a single sentence spoken by a profound man
can express the whole intoxicating complexity of the
dramas he has lived.

All by himself he suffices to show that, by their
attentive mind, their conscious honesty, their faculty
of organization, and their combination of delicacy
and vigor, the lower middle-class artisans of France
are worthy to seize the power of the king. For the
artist of fashion, with his adorable ease, can no longer
build and preserve, any more than can the totally
decadent class which caresses and feeds him. A dozen
painters or engravers, Louis Gabriel Moreau, with his
luminous, clear-cut landscapes, Gabriel de Saint-
Aubin, with his savory chronicles, Lépicié, a good
craftsman in painting and in engraving, and Joseph
Vernet, though he feels the need of excusing his transparent and golden vision of space by a Roman frame
which cannot crush him, form, between Chardin and
the artists of fashion, a kind of continuing chain in
which one finds, to a greater or less extent and with all
the intermediary degrees, the solidity of substance of
the one, and the fugitive charm of the others. Ollivier,
who has his qualities of gray, tender, and meticulous
vision, seems indeed like a subtle emissary sent by
him into the drawing-rooms of fashion to give an
image of them which shall not be solely that of a
psychologist or of a decorator. Houdon, to be sure,
carries on, and far more visibly, the same fight as Chardin
when he represents, with his spontaneous penetration,
his subtle strength, and his ease, those who give to
the Tiers-État the instrument which it needs. He
entered far more deeply than Chardin into the intimate
mind of women, and even into acquaintance with the
adorable astonishment with which children look upon
life. And yet, of all, Chardin is the one who best repre-

sents, and most exclusively represents, the essential task of the century. Houdon floats, and loses flavor as soon as he tries to deal with the goddesses of the Olympus of Versailles. There is a timid and mannered quality in the others which has caused them to be too quickly forgotten after having been too quickly loved. And it is through Chardin that we see that if the abyss is near, all those who act and work will have the power to cross it.

V

But it will be without lyricism. Lyricism never comes when the conquest is being prepared, but is born of the conquest itself, when energy attains its summit and catches its glimpse of the future. The Tiers-État, whose average virtues were expressed by Chardin, imagines itself called upon to strain after effect on the eve of triumph, and to demonstrate its virtue. Rousseau, having dreamed of the absolute man, the successful contestant for political power, ingenuously proposes himself as the realization of that man, and around that idea he organizes his morality, his religion, and—unhappily—his æsthetics also. It should be said that everything tended to give him this rôle. He reacts against the dissolution of the class which he claims to dispossess. Although calling himself a follower of Diderot and Voltaire, he reacts against the skepticism of Voltaire and the philosophy of immorality of Diderot. Imagining himself to deal a blow against Christianity, he reacts, in the name of Christianity, against the irreligion of the *philosophes* and the natural mythology which Buffon and his pupils are preparing to take its place. In reality, what he is claiming to follow is that Cartesian rationalism which, after having organized everything, and then destroyed everything, aspired, when once it was rein-

forced by Jansenism and by English culture, to recon-
struct everything. Finally, the æsthetic and moral
decomposition of the century causes him to believe
that his victory can be obtained only by reversing its

HOUDON. Woman shivering (*Louvre*).

activity in every field. In monuments, furniture,
statues, and pictures, a straight bare line will replace
the sinuous and overladen line. And the incorruptible
man will oppose his rigidity of principle to the amiable
cynicism of the lordling of the antechamber and the
dilettante of government.

The new order is offered the tool which it demands. For a quarter of a century, Antiquity has been before the minds of men. That way lies Virtue, and there also is Beauty. André Chénier dedicates hymns to David, in whose works Robespierre recognizes the physical expression of that which he himself represents in the moral world; and it is to David that the Convention intrusts the work of organizing Republican æsthetics on the model of the austerity, the pomp, and the stoicism of Rome. His education as a painter and as a man has prepared him to become the Le Brun of the Revolution. As a winner of the Prix de Rome, he finds Rome filled with the fever of archæology. Less than twenty years before, there had occurred the discovery of the mummified cities, Herculaneum and Pompeii. Piranesi's engravings circulate everywhere and animate the ruins of Rome with a somber and living spirit. Hubert Robert haunts the crumbling walls there, the unequal colonnades, the broken vaults covered by ivy and grass, and all the fields of dead stones where the ground, as its level rises, still gives a glimpse, here and there, of half-buried gods. Joseph Vernet descends from the two emigrants of the great century, Claude and Poussin. Since the time when Vico created the philosophy of History, the very soil of Italy seems to awaken. The tragedies of Alfieri exalt the republican virtues, Beccaria wrests Crime and Punishment from the domination of mediæval theology. Canova will soon come, to resuscitate his stale heroes and to make a drawing-room propaganda for Davidian doctrines adjusted to the understanding of the ladies of easy virtue, of the diplomats, and the *littérateurs*. The Germans seek to found a science of æsthetics on the basis of a Greco-Latin archæology that is insufficiently understood. Winckelmann has just written his History,

Lessing publishes a whole volume on the tiresome Laocoön. In France, besides, where Montesquieu, by his *Grandeur et Décadence des Romains*, pointed the road long ago, where Soufflot is building the Panthéon, where the Encyclopédie has had to search the ancient world through and through, and where Caylus, a man of taste, to whom the artists lent a willing ear, is writ-

FRAGONARD. The disrobing (*Louvre*).

ing innumerable memoirs on the sculptured stones and the medals, Barthélemy and Volney are recovering from the earth the august cities and their customs; and the reading of Plutarch carves the statues of antiquity in the soul of the young men.

A nephew of Boucher, and loving Fragonard, issuing from them and retaining their imprint, Louis David sees clearly that if their century still kept some reflection of living life, it is to them that it owes it, to them who, after all, represent the direct descent from Watteau and from Rubens. It is in their name that he so harshly combats the Academy, which the Convention suppresses as soon as he demands it. But between them and him there is the distance between the conversationalists and the journalists who prepare the revolution and those who made it. They destroyed; he constructs. As he thinks to rediscover in the Roman marbles the discipline he needs in order to look truth in the face, he goes straight ahead to it, his head down, and his back turned on the men and the things of his time. He does not see that he is falling into the same error as the School which he execrates, and that, jealous of his authority,

GREUZE. Young girl (*Montpellier*).

he is substituting the dogma of the antique for the dogma of the Renaissance.

His whole life, thenceforward, will be a stubborn and laborious collaboration between his nature as an artist and his will as an æsthetician, between the needs of his being and the beliefs of his time. He is a painter, as much as anyone can be. In those of his scenes from history in which the external movement is most closely copied from the ancient statues, in those of his pictures of the ceremonies of his time which are most directly brought back, by their cold, stiff arrangement, to the basreliefs of Roman arches, a purple robe, a cushion of blue velvet, a golden embroidery, a plume, or a silk flag, everything connected with his immediate time, such as an accessory impossible to modify as to its material, is painted with the richest, densest, and most opaque splendor. Whenever he is not treating the nude body, the rigidity of the ensembles—always built up from

HUBERT ROBERT. Ruins (*Private collection*).

without and by the processes of a technique interpreted according to its appearances and never according to its spirit—is sometimes forgotten before the intensity of the harmonies and the splendor of matter, which by an act of his will he deprives of its fire. One thinks of some Spanish painter of the seventeenth century, Zurbarán, for example, whose monklike severity was no obstacle to his perceiving the thickness of fustian robes, the dense pallor of bread, the sonorous and hard grain of

L. G. MOREAU. The Slopes of Meudon (*Louvre*).

DAVID. Marat (*Brussels*).

earthen pots, and even a certain silvery palpitation of
the sky as it receded to the far horizon. And often he
makes us think of some story-teller of our France,
robust and truculent, by the way he paints a rosy-faced
church singer, or a fat-bellied canon, whom one must
search out patiently in the least visible corner of some
solemn canvas, but whom La Fontaine would find, and
whom Courbet did not fail to see. Almost always his
will outstrips his sensibility, but sometimes it is the

PRUD'HON.   Sleeping Venus, drawing (*Ecole des Beaux-Arts*).

latter which forces the former to retreat. How many
portraits he has left unfinished, intentionally perhaps,
the painter in him having been warned by his emotion
at the instant when they were attaining their highest
degree of power! Doubtless, he had, at such moments,
the courage, so rare, of being stronger than one's
principles and of halting in time. With their gray and
troubled backgrounds and their hesitating pigment,
with their expressive vigor and their fidelity, they seem
as if suspended between the diffused life in which man's
emotional existence begins, and consciousness in which

DAVID. Portraits of Pius VII and of Caprara (*Private collection*).

his intellectual empire begins. They live, and yet their
life remains between precise limits. They are built
like monuments, and yet their surface moves. They
breathe force and liberty at one and the same time. It
is before them that one understands fully David's
chagrin when, in 1816, he saw the marbles of the
Parthenon. He felt that his career was a long misunderstanding, a permanent confusion between the
truth which he encountered and the life which he had
believed himself to be seizing.

He is deserving of respect. To be sure, he did not
observe the terrible accent of the scenes in which he was
often one of the actors. He did not hear the rolling
sound of the wooden shoes as the women of the people
marched along the pavement, nor the cannon that were
defending the different sections of the city. He did
not look at the livid heads on the points of the pikes, nor
the red streams of blood. He did not listen to the storm
rumbling in the breast of Danton. A member of the
Convention, one would say that he did not live the
tragedy of the Assembly. He did not feel the grand
horror of war, nor shudder to have the archangel
before his eyes. No matter. He is deserving of respect.
He restored to painted matter the substantiality which
it had practically lost, and rehabilitated the religious
and passionate spirit with which an artist should approach form and consider structure. He is, like the
Revolution itself, practically intolerable in the letter,
admirable in its intentions and its spontaneous movements. In his presence, one has the sensation of a
people regaining control of itself. Everything before
him is talk, frivolity, and gossip. Introduced by
Rousseau into artistic activity as the Jacobin was introduced into political activity, he comes, stirs minds,
and tries to remake a world on the plane of the will.
Grace flees, alas, and the remainder of life which it was

DAVID. Mme. Récamier, detail (*Louvre*).

dragging with it; but here is strength appearing, and here we catch a glimpse of truth. An abstract truth, outside of space, outside of the movement and the exchanges of life, to be sure, and corresponding to the abstract man. His æsthetics, it is true, resemble those constitutions drawn from Montesquieu and from Rousseau, borrowed from Geneva, London, or Rome, which jostled one another and tumbled over upon one another for ten years, giving France a political support which neither her aptitudes nor her temperament had prepared her to receive. No matter. During those essays at theory, the spirit of the Revolution, the spirit of life, was spreading over Europe with its armies, and mounting in the sentiment of everyone who was noble and strong.

VI

Men saw it well. Kant turned aside from his road. Goethe stopped on his own for a moment. Beethoven took all the winds of heaven to breathe his hope into them. What matter if the France of this great, live century is occupied almost entirely with reason and but little with art! She had quite enough to do with the old myths that were to be beaten down, with the young myths that were to be anticipated, and with the terror and the love that had to be imposed with iron. She had had Montesquieu, Voltaire, Diderot, Jean-Jacques, and Vauvenargues. She had had Buffon, who recreated the earth. She had Laplace, who recreated the sky. She had Lavoisier, who recreated water and fire. She had Lamarck, who recreated life. Germany was offering her hymns to the multitudes and thereby unchaining their spirit.

Mysterious flux and reflux of souls! While an atrocious war was stifling Germany, the aristocratic

France of the seventeenth century was erecting the intellectual scaffolding of which German music was first to take possession, in order to give the support of the heroes to the voice of the people. Until Wagner, French rationalism will guide German music. Without the architect Descartes, Sebastian Bach would not have come; and Beethoven could not have introduced Rousseau into Occidental passion if Bach had not taught him how to give order to symphonic masses according to the intelligence, lifted up by doubt to a feeling of its reality. The peoples were communing over the heads of the Christian sects. And French thought, in order to vanquish the Catholic theocracy, was borrowing from Protestantism its preoccupation with morality, even as German music, in order to vanquish the Protestant theocracy, was borrowing from Catholicism its architectural genius.

It is doubtless in music that we must look for the pursuit and continuance in the souls of men of the moral upheaval which prepares the death of the ancient theocracies; and the French Revolution stands only as the tragic passage of that upheaval into fact and law. Music is the most universal and the vaguest voice, the one always used by men to rejoin one another when they are most dispersed. It appears in Italy like a despairing appeal when the Renaissance has broken open the sheaf of social energy. When architecture is dead, when sculpture is dying, and painting is reaching its full expansion, music is hardly more than born there. Here is Palestrina, with his great wave rising and descending like a breast, the long sob which does not die away, the swelling voices which call to others, and the more valiant and pitiful hearts which sustain the other hearts. A century passes. The dispersal becomes more pronounced, and only one voice arises: the melody of Monteverde has the quality

of the painter's arabesque; it unites into a line as hard
and continuous as a sculptured volume the contradictory sentiments of an anarchical crowd, which no
collective sentiment can bind together any longer.
Another century passes. The despairing eloquence of
Arcangelo Corelli is already broken into by strange
cries; his line, too tightly strung, breaks in places; he

feels that he is not
understood. With
Marcello, we no
longer hear more than
a voice of iron, and it
awakens no echo.
But in other places,
other crowds are stir-
ring. Lulli has al-
ready carried the
Italian soul into
France, where Gluck,
the German, will be
understood. Watteau,
the Frenchman of the
north, feels the cur-
rent of hope coming
out of Germany, and
through the German
of the south, Mozart,
an infant Hercules of

PRUD'HON.   Joséphine Bonaparte,
drawing (*Private collection*).

music who trails garlands of flowers through the tones
of concerts and balls, there opens to Italian passion
the formidable vessel which Bach has just constructed,
in which the voices of Händel and of Haydn awaken
multiple echoes, and in which there is already the dull
rumble of the cry of Beethoven.

Between the innermost circle of the *élite* and the
people, everything is effaced at that moment. The hero

of the spirit sings. The people acts. No halfway art
connects them, and none is necessary. All hearts beat
together. The passage from one world to another is
affirming itself irresistibly in the popular symphony
which is embodied by Danton within the country, and
which, later, is carried beyond it by Napoleon. But
perhaps there is not more than one artist in France who
feels that this passage is being accomplished in the
spirit of the masters of intelligence by the voice of
music alone. Prud'hon is a musician, even if he is unaware of it. In the art of this lover of form, everything
occurs with relation to form, in the warm shadow
which causes it to recede and which accentuates its
depth. If the Revolution manifests itself in David
through the stiff tenseness with which he draws himself up as he stands at the brink of the abyss, before the
radical overturning of the horizon, it is felt in Prud'hon
through the insensible progression with which the luminous surfaces emerge from the obscurity. From the
superficial harmonies which Boucher and Fragonard,
following Tiepolo and Lemoyne, associated in space by
a slight brushing together of the paint, he penetrates to
volumes modeled right in the material, and it is in the
complicity of his penumbra, where the transition takes
place, that Romanticism in painting appears for the
first time. Prud'hon has read the *Confessions*, and the
Nouvelle Héloise also, it is certain, and even *Paul et
Virginie*, which he illustrates, but which his insinuating
and sensual art dominates with all the force of a passion
drawn from sources infinitely more pure than the sentimental wordiness of the *salons* of fashion. He loves the
sculptured form which steals away and turns gently,
pursued by the moving shadow. As he has the secret
of making bosoms breathe, of caressing trembling
breasts, and round limbs as they emerge from a kind of
twilight, it is his right to give to them, as a frame, the

dark woodlands full of brooks, and their murmuring
leaves, and their black and slanting trunks. Certainly,
he tries to obey David, whom he esteems; and Rome,
where he passed several years, watches over him. But

PRUD'HON.   Abundance (*Private collection*).

it does not touch him. And then he has seen Greuze.
And above all he is Prud'hon. The severe profiles are
softened by sensual languor, the attitudes of the statues
sink as if under a weight, until they become tender
gestures and loving abandon. The bosoms of the
vestals bear down the folds of the antique robes, and

the arms of the tragic muses are heavy with voluptuousness. The necks of all the women continually
swell with the sighs which he seizes on their warm lips;
and their eyelids know the pain of waiting for happiness or of seeing it pass. His women have the maternal
abandon of those who love deeply and for whom man is
always the child. Gluck is still very near to him. And
the tender Prud'hon is the last evening of the dream of
pleasure, of nostalgia, and of music which Watteau had
begun, and which is on the threshold of a dawn bathed
in a bloody mist.

FRAGONARD

LANDSCAPE

Chapter VI. ENGLAND

I

THE fortress having disappeared—the fortress which is always beautiful, because
it is built with a positive end in view—
England has no longer an architecture.
England has no sculpture: there is too
much rain and too much fog, the profiles
of the earth are soaked in water, clogged by fields, and
clothed with woods and with heather. England has
only one century of painting, and the Puritan spirit
and the practical spirit are repelled by it and, when it
comes, turn it away from its goal.

Here are mighty trees, cascades, granite cliffs,
eternal mist, a wild sea everywhere, summer nights
like an hallucination when the light of the moon, appearing for a moment among the clouds, bathes ruins and
lakes, where the sob of the nightingales rises above
the murmur of the leaves, where the ponds reflect

the trembling phantom of the branches. . . . The Celt is sensual and mystical, the Saxon dreams out loud. Here were born, from Shakespeare to Byron, from Milton to Shelley, the greatest poets of the world. When aërial space is not sufficiently subtle, and the planet is not sufficiently pronounced in aspect to impose beyond all else the love of colors and of forms, when the world of colors and forms is rich and mysterious, and lacking in that ungrateful and monotonous quality which drives the spirit back to the inner domains of sonorous symbols, and when, added to all this, the crowd possesses a force of accent, and such energy for life and for conquest as it has nowhere else, man's faculty of words is unchained and seizes kingly command. Here is Shakespeare, all the voices of the tempest and of the dawn, the treasures rolled by the sea, the palaces built in the heavens with the tissue of stars offering themselves to the soul to interpret a confession of love, or the anguish of an irresolute man, the terror of a murderer, or the wrath of a king. Here is Milton taking, for the first time since the biblical poems and Michael Angelo, the wild gardens, the flesh of fruits, the flesh of women, and the dust of flowers to express to consciousness the tyranny of God. Here is Byron, raising the damned from their abyss to fire the stars with their fever, and to cradle it upon the ocean. Here is Shelley, each beat of whose heart sends harmonies streaming, like a river whose waters trail the reflections of the Milky Way, and the tremor of plumes and leaves which it has swept along in its course through the woods.

The English soul consoles itself for the too practical activity of Englishmen by constantly widening the spread of its wings. Even English science cannot resign itself to building its monuments impartially. It has to rise higher than the eagle, or else it applies

HOGARTH. The Shrimp Girl (*National Gallery*).

itself to satisfying the material needs of man, and often the man of England. The supreme idea of Newton is a mystic intuition. Beyond the solar system, whose frontiers are not crossed by Copernicus, Kepler, or Galileo, it extends to infinitude the power of reason, and, passing over contradictions of detail which might cause it to stumble, it realizes its harmony with the immutable order of the world. . . . But Bacon assigns to consciousness an immediate and practical purpose; Hobbes builds up his social determinism like a geometer. The merchants organized their material Republic without pity. The Roundheads impose laws of iron upon their moral Republic. There must be expiation for the lyric orgy by which the great sixteenth century, in the Occident, burst the theocratic armor from within, and caused the passion for freedom to rise in the hearts of men. There is only one book— the Bible—as later, for the Jacobins of France, there will be only one example—that of Rome. The theater of Marlowe, of Shakespeare, and of Ben Jonson will be closed. The image will be driven from the cult and swept from the mind. An easy matter. No one understood Holbein when he came here to earn his bread. No one looked at Rubens's dazzling ceilings at Whitehall. Here, anyone who is great must take refuge within his inner life or else outside the country. The imaginary world of Shakespeare permits him to satisfy his whole soul and re-create it each day. Milton is blind, Byron and Shelley, later on, will flee the virtue, the fog, and the cities. When van Dyck arrives, he will work for a king whose head is to be cut off, and for an aristocracy which is to be deposed from power. The crowd does not understand him, the theologian curses him. Charles II must bring back from France easy morals, ordered literature, and improvident politics before painting can appear without effort, as one of the wheels of the new system, and as one of the profound and irrepressible needs of the English people.

And yet the Puritan imprint has sunk in so sharply and the English people is so strong, that the first in date of its painters, the one from whom all the others will come, is the most English of all, and, though he himself is unaware of it, the most Puritan of all. The morals of William Hogarth are not irreproachable, perhaps, but his satire is virtuous. He is a contemporary of the first novelists of the manners and customs of England, and regulates his pace by theirs. Swift encourages him. Fielding congratulates him on following "the cause of righteousness," and considers that his engravings "have their appointed place in every well-kept household." He undertakes sprightly crusades against debauchery, gambling,

REYNOLDS. Little Girl
(*Wallace collection*).

drunkenness, and the politics of elections, and for the protection of animals. He desires the "happiness of mankind." And his work shows the effects of it. It is encumbered and confused, orchestrated in almost a haphazard manner. One thinks first of the subject, and if there is on the canvas a passage of savory painting, one perceives it only after having had a good laugh. But he has the raciness of the people. He knows London to its depths. He comes out of them, and he goes back to them. He is an Englishman, and despises everyone who is not an Englishman. The fencing-master, and the grotesque swaggerer, and the ceremonious freak must, of course, be Frenchmen. He has the atrocious raillery and the sad clearness of vision which are the backbone and the atmosphere of the comic genius of his nation. He laughs with violence, in the same way that men get angry. His healthiness will not suffer anyone around him to be in ill health.

Can one say of a painter that he missed his career as a painter when he has, for once in that career, looked on the world as a great painter does? If all English caricature, from Rowlandson to the humorous illustrators of the magazines and of popular prints, comes from him, he painted—doubtless in a few hours—a thing that contains the whole spirit and the whole flower of all English painting. In the splendor of the laugh and of the teeth and of the clear eyes and of the dimples of a girl of the people, her flesh tingling with the health that comes of milk, the juice of meats, of air, and of water—he seized, one day, all the wandering harmonies of this country of moist landscape, and of its cool ocean. The picture is a sudden flash which lights up, which will grow pale, from one painter to another, and then burn out, after the poets of landscape have picked up its silvery trace in the fog and in the heavens.

II

A single flash. Before him, no one in England suspected that manner of painting. There had been only van Dyck, and those who succeed Hogarth, with their ease and their careless grace, as if they were representing the climax of a long effort, will not often give

REYNOLDS. The Two Waldegraves (*Chantilly*).

expression to any such fancies, but will rather follow the Fleming. He is easier to understand, more soft and empty, and far less a master of character. He is the master needed by a group evolving outside the essential genius of its race. Here are noble faces, each one a little bit similar to the others, and interchangeable hands emerging from fine clothes. An enriched and distant aristocracy, ignorant of the people, without intellectual connection with the lofty national thought which burned out a hundred years before, are well adapted to love and patronize such an art. They are narrowly practical in their purposes, and meet their need for an ideal with the foreign culture enthroned by the Restoration in its effort to combat the Puritan. They are touched by French fashions

GAINSBOROUGH. Portrait of a Child, detail (*National Gallery*).

and ideas, and when a kind of moral beauty comes to them with the perpetual war, with the continual and brutal expansion in distant lands and on the sea, Reynolds and Gainsborough will have formed the generation of painters needed for their great, comfortable luxury. The whole of English painting gravitates around the peerage, and is created for it, for its women, and for its gardens. Born at the moment when the lords gather the fruits of their allegiance and of their privileges, it is only one of its fruits. It resembles the lords, it models itself from them. It does not have to bend to their caprice, it forms a part of their domain, outside of which it would not exist. It is not annexed to them for an hour, it is determined by their needs. The English painter is not, as in France, an artisan still retaining his traditions, but domesticated for a time by the double tyranny of money and of fashion. In France, the painter is a workman of art at the service of the man of society. In England, the painter is a society man who practices painting as an amateur.

And that brings about its inferiority, even to the French painting of the same period—of a secondary order, though it was. It was in England, perhaps, that this century, so little of an artist—save for the music of the Germans—shows itself to be most devoid of creative force. There is not a Watteau, not a Chardin, not a Goya, not even a Tiepolo, perhaps, or a Canaletto. Not only is the intellectual atmosphere, here as in other places, unfavorable to painting, since here, as in other places, everything tends toward criticism, journalism, society correspondence, the literature of information, scientific essays, and moralizing novels, but here, in addition, man is not a painter, or rather he is so in too narrow a sense. When his eye is satisfied, the English painter stops. Not one passes beyond the expression of the superficial harmonies quickly revealed to him by the study of Flemish and Venetian painting, and of which he quite easily finds confirmation in his beautiful, well-washed landscapes and his skies laden with vapor; not one attains the expression of the profound, turning volumes which lead us, little by little, to discover the architecture of the world, and thus the architecture of the mind. In the course of his travels on the Continent,

Reynolds was not able to see, in Rembrandt, whom he
pillages, and in the Venetians, whom he treats loftily in
his Discourses, anything but a creamy and triturated
paste, melting tones, and lights with warm shadows, in
which reddened gold plays over the thick whites. He
treats his admirable gifts as a painter like frippery to
crumple with the tips of the fingers. Under that crust
of painting, the form is soft and spongy, like a fruit
swollen with water. The material of the flesh and the
structure of the bones are similar to those of the
dresses. And as soon as one has pierced the artificial
patina, the work sounds hollow.

After him, all the painters resemble one another.
A little more charming or a little more disdainful, a
little more animated or a little more cold, a little more
savory or a little more insipid, a little more graceful or
more awkward, all are empty and facile; and the
delicate gray harmonies which some, like Raeburn,
harmonize with the dresses and the neckcloths of
taffeta, of silk, or of muslin, with space, and with
powdered hair, cannot cause us to forget a wearisome
monotony of attitudes, a quality of pigment like paste-
board or like plaster, and form without a skeleton,
without muscles, and without density. The fall is as
rapid as the effort to rise was easy in appearance and
factitious in reality. The charming color engraving
everywhere current at that time is perhaps the thing
which best interprets the spirit of English plastics,
which, after all, sees color only as a means of giving its
bloom to the home, and of there transforming into cool
and comfortable harmonies the woods, the fields, and
the skies of the country, its tall, elegant women, their
beautiful horses, their hunting dogs and pet dogs, all
bathed in clear light and the open air. But all the
portrait painters, Romney, Raeburn, Hoppner, and
Opie, sink, step by step, when one thinks of the initiators,

GAINSBOROUGH. Portrait of Mrs. Mordey and her Children
(*Dulwich*).

Reynolds, Hogarth, and van Dyck. Lawrence, the last to arrive, is, as soon as he gets past his sketch, which is sometimes charming, only a dispenser of cold syrups. In this group, Gainsborough alone retains a certain bearing. His psychological sense of the portrait, which the study of the French painters of his time has permitted him to affirm and to extend, makes of him a nobler amateur, one who lives in the provinces, apart from the others; he is a man who loves his art. If there is, in this England of the eighteenth century, rebellious within and conquering abroad, carrying on, along the same front, the satire of Swift when it lifts its mirror to its face, and the practical epic of Defoe when its eye follows its sailors and its traders, if there is some aristocratic retreat for noble modesty and for pride, it is in him that we must seek it. Whether the lord leads the soldiers of the oligarchy to the Continent, or, in Parliament, enters the practical debates of the merchants and the legists, his wife remains an object of luxury which he keeps for himself in the majestic frame of the castles and the parks. Blue of the thickets, gray of the clouds, and space of humid silver, all the delicate and distant beings who cross the monotonous backgrounds which you form have really the air of belonging to a race unknown before him, and which no one will see again when he shall have ceased to be. If those ethereal robes were torn, if the dulled tones of the crossed neckcloths, the high, powdered coiffures, the laces, the blue ribbons, and the scarfs of pink pearl were to mingle their impalpable dust with the ashes of the airy harmonies which always accompany them, we should doubtless see, appearing for a second and instantly fleeing beneath the trees, tall, chaste huntresses who would not reappear. For the first and the last time in England, where all music and all painting pass through the heart of the lyric poets before reaching us, a little

JOHN HOPPNER. Lady with a Coral Necklace
(*Metropolitan Museum, New York*).

undefined music passes into painting itself. Gainsborough seems to be the only one really to have heard,
resounding in England, the sonorous poem that Händel
had brought there from Germany and which cradled
his contemplative life. In his melancholy, there is a
little of the grand solemnity, and in the gentle and
delicate honesty of his vision, a certain echo of the
mystic positivism of the old musician.

Unfortunately, the quality of his meditation on
nature is not on the same height as his instincts and his
intentions as an artist. Like the others, he is forced to
obey the suggestions of his country, to which its living
verdure, its limpid coolness of tone, its long undulations
covered by grasslands and by trees too well nourished,
perhaps, too richly endowed, give neither the firmness
of geological construction nor the infinite movement of
the air which are both necessary to the formation of the
great painter. He is forced to follow the suggestions of
his epoch, the one least spontaneously English in the
whole history of the English, with its universal criticism,
its negation of all that is most distinctly English in the
English soul (the writer imitates France, and Garrick
corrects Shakespeare), and the systematic sensualism
of its philosophers, which cuts one of the wings of
lyricism and condemns plastics never to go beyond
sensation. He is forced to yield to the temperament of
his race, which, as soon as it abandons itself to poetic
flight, transposes all the matter borrowed from the vast
world, to realms of sentiment in the mind, where the
word reigns as master but where the architecture of
form lacks a base, and where sculpture and painting
vacillate and whirl, like a tuft of smoke at the mouth of
a volcano.

Thus English painting dies of that which causes the
English poet to live and reign in the imagination of men.
If the English novel of manners and customs justifies the

OLD CROME. The Windmill (*National Gallery*).

enthusiasm of Diderot, the English people, through its love for Greuze, shows that it understood painting as badly as did Diderot—who understood it so well as soon as he consented to consider it according to the painters. English sentimentalism disheartens itself by borrowing the language of painting, in which reverie and tears have no place. Reynolds could pass for a great painter —thanks to his portraits of men especially, sometimes sturdy and broad enough to give a living idea of the soldier, the sailor, or the despot of letters of that time— were his soul not that of a shopgirl grown insipid by foolish dreaming. Hence his cats and dogs bedecked with ribbons, his chubby little girls with cherries at their ears; hence the eyes he paints swimming with tears, the clasped hands, and the faces pink with shame hidden under round and pretty arms. It is a painting that causes old ladies to weep and young girls to sigh; impotent, ambiguous, and perverse, it trails the mantle of Rembrandt through streams of perfumery and of caramel sauce.

III

What remains of all those elegant painters who spent almost as much time in writing about painting—with much competence, distinction, and sagacity, it is true—as in trying to attain the profound purpose of painting, like those whom they imitated, men who had never written about it—Rubens, Rembrandt, Titian, Veronese, and Velasquez? There remains the superficial, but sincere and clear-sighted love for color of a century during which, since Watteau, not a painter in western Europe, save Chardin, Goya, and the last of the Venetians understood the voluptuousness of color. There remains an effort, insufficient but unanimous, to bring the art of painting back to its sources, which are space, light, shadow, and the tangle and play of reflections on

forms in movement. There is a progressive reconciliation with the real trees, the real flowers, the real grasses
of the country, and the real clouds in the sky, at the
hour when all the littérateurs, all the artists, and all the
philosophers of the Continent, caught in the current of
fashionable and ideological scene-painting, no longer

CONSTABLE.   Landscape (*Private collection*).

saw anything but artificial, weak, and sentimental
symbols.

The lordly castles, which the painter follows as his
model, are buried under ivy and ampelopsis at the
center of those great parks which William Kent, during
the first third of the century, was designing as a reaction against the fashion for Italian or French gardens.
The dryness of southern Europe, the canalizations
which it necessitates, the basins, the jets of water,
the thinness, the well-determined form of the cypresses
and the umbrella-shaped pines, the aloes, and all the

somber plants which grow in the sun and the dust, impose on the mind a clear and sharply cut image which French rationalism was to carry to its highest point of stylization and arrangement. Here, on the contrary, there is almost eternal rain, a soil into which the roots burrow deeply to carry nourishment to the luxuriant masses of leaves; and here is the forest, its dense leafage gathering every drop of water that comes with the fog; here are wide-spreading boughs dividing into many branches; here are enormous black trunks covered with moss and lichens. Disorder imposes itself, and savage strength, and verdure, heavy with water. Amid smooth lawns, as lustrous as a deep velvet, the majestic trees seem to absorb the silence. The majority of them are isolated in groups, like peaceful giants. Some of them trail their mantle of branches upon the ground. Leaves fall on the greensward, and the birds that drink and go marauding there whirl by in swarms. Flower beds appear like carpets cast here and there to affirm, amid the pantheistic disorder and the impassable vigor of the world, the presence of calm and of will. Man imposes nothing on Nature; he takes care that she shall follow, with his aid, the hints which she gives him. From winter to summer, he enhances the effect of the obedient multitude of the plants and the brooks which await the decisions of the wind and the sun in order to change their appearances.

Milton, in "Paradise Lost," sings of the natural garden. The natural garden is the most powerful expression of the domestic style of the English. In France and in Italy it expresses an artistic aristocracy, in their cult of intellect and of design, and within these limits it stops short. In England it originated with a practical aristocracy, which extends, by way of the collective wealth of the country, to all the men of the city, even to the poor, for whom the garden remains

CONSTABLE. Weymouth Bay (*Louvre*).

open and for whom its lawns are accessible; it submits to daily contact with herds of sheep and oxen, whose wool and whose meat clothe and feed the nation. Outside the flights of imagination expressed in its lyric power over words, far from its violent trading and its practical destiny, England carries its effort for æsthetic organization into everything which assures comfort and repose to man—the garden, the house with its furnishing, its clean and almost bare rooms where nothing useless is dragged in, its definite solid furniture, its flowered windows, and its walls of red brick or of white painted wood. With the work of art among other peoples, political and domestic styles are to be renewed incessantly, but like the work of art again, they preserve, through revolutions and conquest, a traditional character. There is little or nothing for the mind. Everything is for the body and the soul, and their health and their well-being. Morals, sport, religion, and business are in complete agreement.

The art of the English landscape was born of that indifference of almost all Englishmen to that which is not virginal nature, suppleness of muscles, and rectitude of morals. It already appears in the gardens which Gainsborough opens wide behind his somewhat distant apparitions of great ladies and of blond children. Indeed, he has often seen a romantic landscape, suns setting over pools, and rays of light piercing the clouds after summer rains. At the decline of the most skeptical century in history, the English soul finds itself even by the aid of painting, which expresses it insufficiently. It waxes enthusiastic over the novelists of poverty, and over peasant poets. It has such a need of nature and of reverie that it listens with exaltation to a literary impostor because he claims to have rediscovered the barbaric poems of the first men of its fjords and its mountains in their struggle with the voices and the phantoms of the ocean, of the storm, and of the fog. The Revolution in France arouses those who are falling asleep, and renders feverish those who awaken. Byron and Shelley flee England out of hatred for her commercial and bigoted positivism. Wordsworth takes refuge on the shores of a solitary lake, where he will no longer hear anything but the fall of the rain and the

TURNER. The Fighting Téméraire (*National Gallery*).

cry of the water birds, where he will no longer see anything but the forest on the hill slope, the mist in the hollows, and the universal awakening of silent life at each return of the springtime.

It is at this moment that the English painters, leaving Lawrence, the most mediocre among them, to continue their tradition of fashion into the heart of the nineteenth century, scaled the walls of the parks to explore the countryside and to consider the sky at their

ease. Old Crome, whose father was a weaver, never
even left the part of the country where he was born,
and, like Burns, alone, without guide and without companion, crossed the threshold of the mystery of the
world. The broad English land, with its covering of
damp earth, its soil kneaded of clay and water, is
contained entire in each one of his visions. With earth
on the soles of his shoes and a stick in his hand, he goes
over it like a peasant who loves it for the difficulties it
gives him and for the bread that he knows how to get
from it; the blood comes to the surface of his shaven
cheeks, as the mist enters his nostrils. That is all; his
painting expresses nothing more; but at that moment,
when the Hollanders are silent, when the French and
the Italians—Vernet, Moreau, Hubert Robert, Canaletto, and Guardi—are writing their careful pages about
cities and stylized ruins, and mythological countries
illumined by a pale reflection from the sun of Claude
Lorrain, when Wilson, himself an Englishman, cannot
tear himself from their seductive domination, this is a
revolution. The odors of the earth, all its aspects
determined by the weather and the season, the shadows
which the rain clouds carry across it, and the darkening
caused by the wind blowing over the earth and by the
approach of evening, all of that together enters human
sentiment, with Crome.

A landscape when it is painted contains no transposition, especially when imagination adds nothing to
its effects. One must look at it. One cannot describe
it. The greatest achievement of English landscape, in
the work of Old Crome, Cotman, Bonington, and
Constable, above all, furnishes Delacroix with certain of
the technical elements of the lyricism which animated
French painting for eighty years and which has not
yet died out. When Delacroix saw Constable's landscapes, the year when he was painting the "Massacre of

Scio," he repainted his immense canvas in four days. He discovered in them a principle, that of the division of colors, almost realized by instinct by Veronese, by Vermeer of Delft, and by Chardin, but whose fecundity Constable, with the severity and the thoroughness of the Englishman, consciously demonstrated in his works. Near by one sees reds, oranges, greens, blues, and yellows, a confused mingling of juxtaposed colors, without apparent relationship with the distant coloration which they claim to imitate in nature, and the well-defined form which they try to evoke. From afar, one sees the great sky, washed and limpid, where the pearly clouds sail like ships; one sees the watery veil ever suspended and trembling above the plain; one sees the blue haze growing denser and stretching away to the distance. Here is the infinite countryside, in England so rich and green after the rain, that it seems as if spread out on a giant palette, pearly with drops of water. Everything, the thick greensward, the deep mass of the oaks, the red and white houses appearing amid green copses, space with its azure and silver, and the flowers sprinkled with dew, everything shines and trembles and scintillates, like a world rising into the daylight at the coolest and the most transparent of the hours. To Constable the scenes of his country spoke the words, "I am the resurrection and the life." And his soul plunged into these scenes as the fairest woman's body plunges into the water.

It is when Constable arrives at that transparence that he touches great painting most nearly, and perhaps he is a greater painter when he works with watercolor than when he tries to render, by means of the oil so lavishly used by Reynolds and his group, the moist and glistening splendor of English landscape. Watercolor, by its slightness of body, its liquid freshness, and its incapacity for rendering oversubtle shades, is the material best suited to the Englishmen. Constable owes to it his most luminous notes, Turner his most translucent jewels, and Bonington uses it with such mastery that he reaches the point of incorporating with his oil painting—blond, ambered, and accented by reds and greens which seem to die out, little by little as if under a layer of water—something of its gleam, and to offer a reflection of it to the flaming and funereal color of Delacroix. Oil-paints, on the contrary, are almost always dangerous for the English painters. The uniform splendor of their atmosphere does not harmonize well with that complex material, of a profundity so rich and agitated. They become victims of it. They desperately insist upon rendering with it their sky laden with vapors and, at the same time, the transparence of the air so frequently revealed to them by the sun after the rain. They triturate it, they thicken it, deprive it of its savor by trying to make it too savory, and by becoming exclusively absorbed in the study of it, get caught in its creamy mud, and confuse the pearl and the silver which they have gathered from the air. English landscape, even with Constable, often sinks into the heavy cookery in which Reynolds left almost all his gifts.

IV

Turner is the last victim, and the most illustrious, of this need to force the language of painting, to which Rembrandt and Velasquez give wings and a soul by permitting painting to follow their objective vision, and to unite that vision with their imaginary world. His desire certainly goes beyond, and far beyond, the equanimity of sentiment and the pacific positivism of the other English painters. He was almost the only one to see the sulphur sun shining at the depth of the

TURNER.   Ulysses Deriding Polyphemus (*National Gallery*).

mist. It was for him alone that the livid river showed itself through the trailing smoke. He surprised great phantoms in the fog and the rain, towers of brick and of old stone, ships, black chimneys, and red lanterns piercing the confused darkness, as a muffled cry issues from a great murmur, only to go back into it the instant afterward. He felt the sea and the light of the tropics enter the somber city with the tarred hulls and the sails of the vessels, with the wandering flight of the sea gulls, and with the phosphorescent slime, and mingled with their vanished wake, the indistinct echoes of receding streets, of docks, of sinister places, and of parks bathed in emerald, full of trees and of herds. And by an incredibly gallant lyric effort he tried to transpose this turbid and splendid material to an imaginary world where he mounted so high that the rarefied air could not sustain his flight.

He seems like a bird wheeling about in the lightning, intoxicated by electric storms and blinded by the flashes. Wherever he is on the planet and in history, whether he voyages with Shakespeare across ancient and Romanesque Italy, whether he plunges with van Goyen into the illuminated mist, or whether he visits, with Homer, the old heroic universe where the flame of the volcanoes and the song of the sirens lead Ulysses in his wanderings over the ocean, whether, suffocated by the wind, and drenched in salt and spray, he joins in the rescue of men shipwrecked on a fishing boat, or whether he accompanies Nelson amid the thunder of the cannon and the smoke, with the flags flying and the great sails torn, everywhere that sea water, and the water of heaven, and the sun mingle, he saw, in a land of supernatural legend, an aërial palace borne by the clouds, reddening in twilights and dawns which he confronted, flooded with bloody shadows and with corruscations of opals, sapphires, and rubies. One day he fixed his eyes on the setting sun of Claude. And thenceforward he cared to see no one else. The solid architectures have become translucent specters behind the fantastic fog, which permits the English country to show through only as furtive apparitions, supernatural at times, when the moon rises, or when the evening light, piercing the watery veil, where it is

TURNER. The Snowstorm (*London*).

partly torn, shows the top of a tower suspended in the clouds, the turning beam of a searchlight, or the dark and flaming globe that sinks little by little. Everything becomes unreal and distant, like that water where Claude's sun, before disappearing, leaves its trail of liquid purple. It alone reigns from dawn to darkness, filling the world and filling history, bursting and scattering over them in explosions of blood and flame.

The superficial harmonies on which the English painters, since the time of van Dyck, had been expending their virtuosity, were to find their consummation in that strange art of Turner's, which marks the definitive separation of form from color, and the flight of painting into space alone, isolated from all material support, from every visible volume, from every deep bond with the universe of the senses. In reality, that sky and that water, confusedly mingling and seething in the incandescent flame, conceal an obvious coldness of the senses, a complete impotence to understand and supply an equivalent for the trunk and the intermediate branches which forever connect and render sensible, for one another and through one another, the roots of mankind and the perfume of its spirit. Turner masks the indigence of his color under fireworks. The light blinds him. He no longer sees anything but the light. Everything that it illuminates has disappeared. By itself, miracle that it is, it avenges the forgotten earth and the misunderstood heaven. The great harmonic unity of the world crumbles in places and wavers everywhere. Veiled by these gems, broken by these reflections of imaginary fires, the soil loses its consistency, the air thickens, that which is hard becomes fluid, that which is fluid becomes compact, the planes go flying, the values are jumbled, and the disunited universe floats like a luminous smoke torn to shreds by the wind. The poetic emotion and sentiment, superior, doubtless, to the means of expression, evaporate almost entirely, and no longer impress any save those who have not learned to understand the language of painting. Turner demonstrates both the lyric grandeur of the English soul and the impotence of English painting to communicate it.

v

This whole art from van Dyck, its initiator, to the pre-Raphaelites, moves between two reefs, which it

COTMAN. Fishing Boats (*National Gallery*).

strikes against alternately, without ever succeeding in avoiding both completely: the insufficiency of the form and the tenacity of a poetic sentiment which words alone could express. With Reynolds, with Gainsborough, with Raeburn, with Hoppner, and with Opie, the richness of the color manages to conceal the void which it covers, and makes us forget the poverty of the sentiment in which English lyricism, when turned aside from its path, is swallowed up. But Ruskin arrives, and tears contemporary painters from their worldly courses, to cast himself, with them, upon the primitives of Italy, and to exhaust himself in resuscitating a dead soul— succeeding only in scattering upon its tomb the artificial flowers of a poetic sentiment which still fails to comprehend its means. An incredible misunderstanding! He preaches ingenuousness, and is followed only by liars. This time the repulse is far more complete and far more manifest than at the time of Reynolds, the virtuoso. When the English were following the Venetians or the Flemings, who are painters above all, their gift of color, at least, could expand. When they follow the Florentines, they forget their gift of color, and try researches in line, for which they are not fitted. The reasons for the check sustained by English painting are all to be found in that impotence to construct in depth, which drives it either to the false step of wrecking itself against form, or that of seeking in color and in literature its development and its purpose.

The English soul is not plastic. Painting demands a faculty for objective generalization which is not called forth either by the activities characteristic of Englishmen or by their surroundings. That power of meticulous and direct observation which distinguishes them and which renders their novelists, their actors, and their clowns incomparable, raises the obstacle between great painting and themselves which is most difficult to

overcome. If the Anglo-Saxons are the foremost illustrators and caricaturists of the world, it is precisely
because their observation of detail, of action, and of
character excludes the faculty of embracing, in their
ensemble, the great expressive surfaces and the essential
volumes. The peoples of painters and of sculptors have
neither the gift of illustrating books, nor that of gather-

BONINGTON. The Park of Versailles (*Louvre*).

ing up into a stroke or a point the detail which fixes the
dominant note of a race, of a profession, of a gesture, or a
temperament. Among such peoples the Japanese alone
possess the gift, and their whole art, precisely, has been,
since archaic times, leaning toward the spirit of caricature, and flowing into it.

That faculty, which the Englishman has for observing
and describing, is transported entire into the external
characteristics of his painting, which, at bottom, has

never been, except for Constable, more than imitation. It is in part responsible for that museum art which, for more than a century, has raged over Europe, and which consists in giving to fresh paint the appearance of the smoked and rancid paint of the great masters of oils, an error into which Reynolds was forever falling, although he pointed out its gravity to his pupils, and against which the French, from Delacroix to the Impressionists, will not cease to struggle. A picture by Rembrandt must have flamed like a tropical landscape— with fruits of dark gold, flowers of scarlet, and birds of topaz and of fire—perceived through a silvery haze, or through the russet light in some poor home. A canvas by Veronese, if we were to see it again in its original freshness, would doubtless make the boldest colorist seem timid and sad. When new, it streamed with flame. Even in the shadow, it must have been resplendent and have illuminated everything.

WHISTLER. Battersea Bridge
(*Tate Gallery*).

The English artist, one must confess, imitates with such perfection, and produces work of such close resemblance—the cathedral in the Middle Ages, and painting, for the last two hundred years—that it is capable of giving the illusion of original force. Never

WHISTLER. Thomas Carlyle (*Glasgow*).

were noncreators "artistic" to this point. Never have counterfeit masterpieces been produced with equal skill. Reynolds draws upon the Venetians and Rembrandt, Gainsborough upon van Dyck, the early Turner upon Claude Lorrain, and the result of their study of the earlier masters is something incomparably better than a servile copy or a successful imitation. They resemble those virtuosi of the piano, the violin, and the violoncello who conjure forth from silence the soul of the masters of music, and with it the acclamations of the public. Later, it is true—and I have said why—Ruskin's disciples fail. Burne-Jones is only a sentimental Mantegna entangled with a Botticelli infected by Puritanism. Rossetti shelters his chlorosis under the ægis of the Platonic æsthetes. Watts produces a learned but cold mingling of Michael Angelo, Sodoma, and Titian with the precursors of Raphael. Stevens in turn enters with perfect ease into the garments of Michael Angelo, and breathes the tempest of the Last Judgment and of the Creation into an English hunting horn. The last to arrive of the Anglo-Saxon painters, who moreover violently reacts against pre-Raphaelism, Whistler, in his irresolute flights from the Japanese to Velasquez, and from Courbet to the Impressionists, succeeds at least in keeping the virtuosity of his race away from the danger of form, in bathing subtle harmonies in mystery and fog, and in surprising phantoms in them, and trembling lights. He is the prince of amateurs. He "arranges" with sagacity his grays, his blacks, and his pinks. One step more and the art of Veronese and of Rubens will empty into the modern print and into the desire to please the milliners and dressmakers.

No matter. The intention of English art and the effort made by its painters to express their too narrow vision has resounded over all the great painting which

has come after them. Constable, the least incomplete
of them, transmitted to Delacroix a part of his science;
Turner, the most enterprising of them, liberated through
his revolt, the successors of Delacroix. Later on,
Ruskin, despite his incapacity for loving the forces of
the present day, saw that the machine was crushing
the workman, the artist of the people, that utilitarian
liberalism was rendering life ugly, and that the critical
and scientific mind was killing living sensation. And if
French romanticism attained, through sculpture and
painting, one of the essential moments of the spirit, it
owes it as much to the poets and painters of England
as to German music, and to the idealistic and warlike
expansion of the Revolution.

ROMNEY. The Parson's Daughter
(*National Gallery*).

PARIS

Chapter VII. ROMANTICISM AND MATERI-ALISM

I

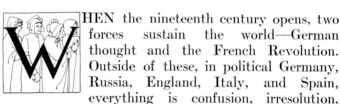

HEN the nineteenth century opens, two forces sustain the world—German thought and the French Revolution. Outside of these, in political Germany, Russia, England, Italy, and Spain, everything is confusion, irresolution, sordid interest, stammering, stagnation, or half-sleep. And in France itself, the activity is too powerful for a dawn of the spirit. With the voice of Lamarck stifled, there is, in the Occident, but one thought, that of Kant; one word, that of Goethe; one cry, that of Beethoven. The only man who replies to them, the only one whose imagination is sufficiently vast to give to action the grand face of the dream, the inner order sufficiently master of itself to assemble into a living symphony all hearts—which are happy in their obedience, the mind sufficiently imperious and rapid to stamp strategic marches and the movements of armies with the continuity of line and the harmonious grouping of mass which define a picture, effaces all, in France, who around him attempt to exist by themselves, and makes demi-gods of all who, by habit, are the most humble of men. Moreover, Beethoven is vexed but admires, Goethe understands and acquiesces, Byron flies in the wake of the lightning, Goya grinds his teeth under the hot iron, but, to gain his victory, rises still higher. The rumblings of the thunder will not die down for a century; they will unite the fragments of the peoples, will break the last bonds of the Middle Ages, and will plunge into the soul of the great pessimists of Europe, Chateaubriand, Stendhal, Schopenhauer, Delacroix, Wagner, Dostoievski, and Nietzsche, the image of the only power, since the power of Christ, capable of giving direction to the world. Napoleon the poet, leading the aroused crowds, determines the character of the century, and, if he drains the peoples of their blood, he injects such a ferment into their souls that they seem to date from him.

A romanticist through his original culture, his love for Rousseau, for Goethe, and for the Ossianic poems, through his need to turn his eyes toward the Orient, toward Egypt, toward India—the whole Empire of the sun, a romanticist through his great, pitiless dream, which handles multitudes and souls like lights and shadows on a surface to be sculptured, through his violent lyricism which precipitates conquest on the heels of desire, and through his vision of the final nothingness, which causes him to go through life with passion alone as his object, and fatality as his law, he unchains romanticism. The mothers curse him. But their womb trembles from the moment when he appears

on the horizon. Every man who will be great in France,
during the century—Corot, Vigny, Delacroix, Michelet,
Balzac, Hugo, Berlioz, and Daumier—to speak only
of artists, and who is there that counts between such a
man and the artists?—is born, and grows up between
the Italian Iliad of 1796 and the hour when he reaches
his summit.

When they attain maturity, the sentimentalism of
Rousseau has ripened in all hearts; Chateaubriand
brings into literature
the art of the Middle
Ages, the Orient, the
forest, the virgin rivers,
and legendary Christi-
anity; Madame de
Staël brings the un-
known soul of the
north, with its meta-
physical torment, and
with its vertiginous
need for color, for the
exception, and for the
vague intoxication of
religion; and the whole
of literature rushes
upon its course of
lyric passion, along
which the individual,
indifferent to every-
thing which is not himself, surrenders himself to the
torrent of the forces and of the eternal images of the
universe and of love. The stamp of Catholicism, and
the reaction of form and of desire against the abstract
rationalism of the preceding century are of but little
importance. By its capacity for passion, by hurling
itself with its wild exaltation into the conquest of the

GROS. Bonaparte at Arcola
(*Louvre*).

GROS. Eylau, detail (*Louvre*).

earth, of history, of the light, and of death, romanticism contributes to break the ancient forms of religion and of the law, which science, with its slower, stealthier step, attacks at the same time. France, who for two centuries had been a reasoner, suddenly becomes an artist again, and launches forth wildly toward life, which reveals its new rhythms, and bursts the old molds. In the domain of sensation she equals the effort which the preceding age had made in the direction of war and liberty. The philosophical investigation of the French, the metaphysical analysis of the Germans, and the impotence for action after the greatest moment of action in history have produced intellectual despair, and also the sensation that it is increased by its indifference to the moral problem; but again there is consolation for that in the endless splendor which has been achieved. France has inundated the world, which flows back from everywhere. Here is the whole terrestrial universe, and all the skies and all the oceans, all the adventures of the men of the olden time and of to-day, all the ancient or distant myths of the sun and of the mist, the Inferno of Dante, the pitiless, clear sight of Goethe, and the immense reverie, enchanted and poignant, of Shakespeare. Sebastian Bach, Mozart, Gluck, and the last to come, Beethoven, contribute, to the troubled depths of existence the tumult of the great harmonies of nature, which turn confusedly into new elements expressive of the delirium of the intelligence and of the tragedy in men's hearts.

Painting offers itself to the artist. It is music in its power of expressing the form of sentiment, by color, by its multiple reflections which answer one another, by its gradations, its passages, its immense keyboard, from black or colored shadow at the bottom of the abyss, to the brilliant summits of the most strongly marked projections. The sensation of sonority and the sensation of color merge in it, the tempest of the orchestra unchains in it a rhythmed tumult of subtle sense impressions in which one perceives clamors, moans, cries of anger, and sighs of voluptuousness, even as one sees grand architectures arising, and forms

RUDE. Portrait of Monge, marble (*Louvre*).

mounting and descending like a sea when the power of an orchestra forces one to close one's eyes. In this century, the poets will be painters. The whole surface of the world breaks up and vibrates and moves in the work of Hugo; and in the work of Baudelaire, the whole burning spirit of matter, of perfumes, and of colors pours forth from the heart, like a lava of blood,

following each throb of the arteries. In the music of
Berlioz, the face of nature appears like a violent drawing, in which decisive strokes cross their flames, or
crawl like reptiles, leaving a wake of fire. But painting
is an object in itself, an object which France has kept
under her eyes constantly for three hundred years,
while Germany, who never really loved it, has, for two
hundred years, no longer had the vision for it, while
in Italy it is falling to dust, and while Spain no longer
perceives it save in the glare of a single flash of lightning.
The dictatorship of David bears its fruits at once.
While the Academy claims to follow him, in order to
drag on for two generations more its insolent and servile
poverty, everything strong and green turns to David
to seek the structure which Delacroix will break in
places, will brutally twist, and will combine in a hundred
fashions, in order to sustain the burning flesh and the
movement of his fever, and which Ingres will purify
and vivify, little by little, in order to inclose in it the
concrete and definite object of his desire. Down to
Courbet—and including the time of Courbet—David
will hold the regency of painting. Under him the
sculptor Rude studied the anatomical nude and learned
how to set a violent body in equilibrium on legs which
seem to hold to the ground like trunks of oak trees,
and how to hurl into the stone his democratic enthusiasm—a trifle hollow, but living—which sets up a
vibration on the face of the walls. The "Raft of the
Medusa" of Géricault, the "Barricade" of Delacroix,
and the first plates of Daumier bear the traces,
quite as manifestly, of the lessons of the old regicide,
who would have recognized his spirit in their moun-
tainous modeling, which throws the muscles and the
skeleton into relief, and so brings these masters nearer
to him than Ingres ever was. And it is from him
that Gros will borrow, for his military poems, the

solid, but too stiff and too fixed, architecture which will end by paralyzing their movement and stifling their flame.

It is certain that the man was born a great painter. Whereas the fire of Watteau was no longer giving forth more than a few intermittent gleams in the painting of Greuze and of Fragonard, whereas Davidian discipline concentrated itself entire upon the rendering of brute matter and upon following the contours of Roman sculptures, Gros felt the warrior energy of his time burning in his veins. Rubens, the man who launched his own life like a great river into all future time, had dazzled him. He had followed Bonaparte on foot, from the Alps to the Tyrol, lived in the tumultuous crowd of the camps and of the marches that struck like thunderbolts, seen the slender boy with the eyes of fever seizing a flag amid the bullets and pass through death, in order to gain possession of the right to command men and to subjugate the future. There is no abstraction in his desire. He painted war horses with open nostrils, bloody eyes, and hair matted by blood and dust, while their breath and sweat mingle with the reddened haze of smoke of the northern battlefields. He copied cadavers in the blood-stained snow. While Bonaparte was annexing to the moral domain of Europe the desert peopled with sphinxes and with tombs, and the oldest adventure of the world, Gros experienced the chagrin of remaining exiled in France, imagining the burning sand, the leaden expanse of the mirages, the storm of the horsemen with the wind whipping their bernouses, and, in the damp, ill-smelling shadow of some mosque where the lamps have burned out, where the dulled glaze of tiles is soiled by disease, the dying men who crawl there, their faces turning green, and their bandages spotted with black blood around open sores. With the blue steel of the cuirasses, the

cloth and the velvet of the multicolored uniforms, with
the flashes of the firing, and with bits of sky seen amid
flying manes, he had acquired the power of organizing
dramas full of the color and movement of war; in them
life was exalted by war, whose brutal movement was
carried into the young and lyrical souls which were
opening up everywhere.

Had Gros already possessed the mastery needed to

RAFFET.   Nocturnal Procession, etching (*Lille*).

project outside himself his furious gestures and his
powerful harmonies, as a free and unified symbol of
the storms of his heart, romanticist painting would
have been finished at a single blow. But he hesitated.
He hesitated between the object too closely pursued
and the magisterial doctrine to which he gave too
servile attention. The two things clashed. A too
direct realism enchained the tragedy. The overtense
drawing of the School arrested the living sentiment

which was ready to bound from the soul, paralyzing its flight in a tangle of bizarre and factitious forms. Gros's work stands as a passage full of anguish between the immobility of David and the tumult of Delacroix. He kept on stubbornly till the end, and even seemed to comprehend the situation less and less. While around him, with Géricault, and soon with Delacroix, the flame of revolt was rising, he made it his point of honor to defend the School of the old master, exiled in Brussels by the Restoration. But the old master was, in his letters at this very time, confessing to him his admiration for Rubens. Against the young men who were taking him as a point of departure, almost against David, and, above all, against himself, Gros remained obstinate in establishing his art at the antipodes of his being. Upon a certain day, in despair at the oblivion into which he was sinking, bleeding from all the wounds which the art he had revealed was inflicting upon him at each new exhibition, incapable of breaking the matrix which was hardening around his genius and was crushing him little by little, he killed himself. He died a romanticist, at the very moment when, through Hugo, through Berlioz, and through Delacroix, Romanticism was affirming itself.

II

The death and the life of all beings are linked one with the other. An invincible harmony reigns in the destiny of men, and even after their days. In complete triumph, but misunderstood and alone, Delacroix, like a sick lion, vomits his blood in the depths of his cave. An old eagle whose feathers have been torn out, Berlioz, preparatory to his death, retires to the high aërie where the ice and the sun of the peaks complete the burning out of men's nerves after they have delighted in love too much. Hugo, a giant demagogue, emperor of words and of the boards, expires, lulled by the murmur of an immense people, which tries to retain him. Baudelaire ends as a wreck, poisoned by the perfume of his great venomous flowers, and mingling his sublime putrefaction with the fermentation of the sensual universe. When his mystic dream of society crumbles in the conflagrations of the Commune, the arteries break in Michelet's brain. Wagner, at the center of the city ardent in its setting and in its painting, falls to sleep in the arms of Isolde, between sea and sky. Vigny dies without speaking. Corot takes the pipe from his mouth, and draws his last breath amid a few good friends. Musset, the man drunk with sentiment, dies of drunkenness. Dostoievski is taken away to the cemetery by a noisy mob of prostitutes princes, priests, and convicts. Tolstoy, in order that he may live according to the last dictates of his heart, dies of cold on the threshold of a poor cabin.

The life and the end of Géricault symbolize romanticism. They possess its violent and absolute spirit of conquest, irreparably, without thought of the morrow, its indifference to morals, and its bitter taste of death. He is in the vanguard, coming from Prud'hon, as he says of himself, and standing between Gros, whose weapons he gathers up to combat David, and Delacroix, who will take possession of his passionate movement, to inject into it more of flame and of mystery, by causing to enter into it his tide of ardent matter and of moving color. Too much black. Too many nude statues, but a modeling accentuated by the tragic shadow; the dead lying everywhere, a heap of livid cadavers tossed by the ocean; he is possessed by a mad passion for invading the world of sensation through all the senses. When his brief task is ended, and his young friend Delacroix has exhibited

GÉRICAULT. The Race, lithograph.

the "Bark of Dante" and begun the "Massacre of Scio"—the war cry of romanticism—he dies, consumed by phthisis and by dissipation, through having fallen from a savage horse. Delacroix will not complete that task, for he is too powerful ever to accept frontiers between life, which is ever incomplete, and his work, which is ever rising; but when he dis-

DELACROIX. Women of Algiers (*Louvre*).

appears, the world will find itself in the presence of a new mystery. A man will have possessed, in a state of incessant germination, the silent pride of Vigny, the endless plastic wealth of Hugo, the eternal sensual vibration of Baudelaire, a tormented aspiration similar in its profundity to Shakespeare's, and, in a heart throbbing with fever, the harmony of will gained by his constant frequentation of Racine and of Poussin. The strongest and greatest painter-soul since Rembrandt.

DELACROIX. The Taking of Constantinople, detail (*Louvre*).

A few hours had sufficed him, while the exhibition was being organized behind official doors, to repaint the "Massacre of Scio" after having seen Constable's canvases which taught him the luminosity to be drawn from divided tones. English painting, so superficial, but of so rich a surface, and unknown in France during forty years, because of the incessant wars, entered his mind at the right moment, both by the authority of the masters and by the insistence of a friend, Bonington having confided to him his gifts and his dreams, while working near him. Almost at once, he acquires his technique, which he will go on perfecting until the end. He made for himself a chromatic frame, on which the colors are disposed according to the diametrical oppositions, which are reunited with one another by their intermediary tones.[1] Already one sees violently heightened tones, transparent glazes over long passages of distinct cross-hatching employed to make the painting vibrate; one sees the colored transparence of shadows, and the use of pure colors and of separate touches in order to banish neutral tones and gray. But what trifles all these things are! His lean, small hand brandishes, as if it were an arrow, this instrument which is so heavy for those who are alarmed by the weight of the weapon they are to raise. He reads Dante. He reads Shakespeare. He reads Faust, and illustrates it, and the old Goethe is startled at being understood by such a boy. He listens to Gluck and to Mozart. He writes much, almost always for himself alone, and his metaphysical torment often makes one think of Pascal. He meditates and trembles

[1] Reported, in his *Artistes Français*, by Th. Sylvestre, the only writer, after Baudelaire, to have the sense of great painting in the nineteenth century. Fromentin, a little painter and an eminent littérateur, understands it less, and hypnotizes himself—sagaciously, indeed—upon questions of technique. He is, and must remain, the idol of the grammarians of painting.

DELACROIX. Medea (*Louvre*).

with fever before Michael Angelo. He reaps a harvest from Veronese, and with full hands. The power of Rubens fills him with its great continuous wave. His external life is dignified and somewhat aloof, with an impeccable varnish of fashion, under which rumbles the volcano. In the street, he observes the walk of women, the roll of their hips, the tremble of their breasts, and the dull splendor of their necks, as solid as a column; he loves horses, trees, the great sky when cloudy or when it has its aspect of twilight, and the coming of night. There are his elements, there is his language, even if he is to sharpen it, and render it more supple, more firm, and more direct. It serves him to carry outside himself the symbols of his thought, as the gesture of an orchestra-leader wrests from the silence of wood- and wind-instruments which had been sleeping, the song of all the nightingales of the forest, mingled with the voices of all the rivers, and all the words of men which are swept along by all the winds.

For of all the musicians of painting, he is perhaps the most complex and the most poignant. He often causes one to think of Beethoven, often of Wagner, sometimes of Berlioz. In poor health and nervous, with the face of a sick lion, he has the drawn features, the burning eyes, and the pale complexion of men in whose tense heart dwells a symphonic, chaotic, and contradictory storm, but who have the mute strength to impose upon it the order and mastery of the mind. A singular discord reigns between his temperament and his culture, but if he takes the brush in his hand, everything obeys at the very instant, and the cries of passion roll under the dull harmony, like those boiling jets of water through which submarine eruptions lift up, in places, the somber surface of the sea. His soul is bound to the universe by the luminous vibrations which his eye alone perceives, and which have the sonority, the mystery, and the infiniteness of music. All space resounds, like an immense lyre, with the colorations and the lights which place it in the region of his own inner drama.

Of what importance are his subjects, those of all the men of his time—history, sometimes myth, the tragedies of the dramatists of the north, the Orient which

DELACROIX. The Massacre of Scio, detail
(*Private collection*).

is being opened by conquest and by travel, and which a long excursion that he himself makes to Morocco reveals to him with its scorching sadness, its color of blood and of tragedy, its men and its animals, indolent and convulsive, the antique fatalism, and the implacable, nomadic spirit which continue and prolong themselves in its cunning immobility, its silence, and its cruelty? That which he paints is the agitation of a hallucinated soul, which a great harmony, piercing but accepted, dominates from the regions of the invisible, of which he has a presentiment. Everything expresses movement: the distant and narrow streets of a city, twisting like masses of serpents, the clouds and the smoke carried along by the same wind in which the pennants flap, the waving flames of torches, oak trees gashed in the track of the lightning, the ascending and centripetal gallop of the horses who draw the chariot of the sun, or the twist of trunks and limbs which a central tragedy hurls around the same point or distributes from one end of the canvas to the other, according to the bounding rhythms of flight, of attack, of defense, or of voluptuousness.

That which he expresses is rather the spirit than the form of movement. Or rather, his own spirit determines the movement. He draws from the object, but the moment that he takes up his brush he shuts himself up all alone; without a model, he attacks his picture from all sides at once, hastens his whole march toward the horizon of his desire, sees surrounding life like a sphere, full and confused, and goes to it to demand the expression of the accidentals of its surface from the spiritual density of its secret depths. Here is hunger, monstrous paws clutching torn arms and bleeding breasts, muzzles drawn back from teeth, eyes like hot coals, and wild boars covered with blood as they tear through lungs. Here is anger, here are the bare shoulders, breasts, and arms of mothers stung to fury, the child hanging from their fierce embrace, and a dagger in their hand. Here is war, blood as red as the sky and the conflagration, eyes consumed by weeping, black or red hair twisted like vipers, the arms of a cadaver stretched out over the knees of a dying woman, and here are horses who scent death. Here is love, with the tragic meaning it assumes with anyone who has greatness, the somber flowers in the depth of the

DELACROIX. Andromeda (*Private collection*).

perfumed shadow, the necklaces chinking on the burning skin, the ambered bellies which recede into the
shadow of the hidden thighs, the terrific attraction of
the deep fruits in which the strong man finds strength,
from which the weak man drinks poison, but before
which no man knows in advance whether he is weak or
whether he is strong. Here is death, the lips of children
feeling around breasts hardened by the cold swelling
of the putrefaction soon to come, and the waves, under
low clouds, rolling decomposed cadavers, stiffened
arms, white mouths, and lips turning back over teeth.
The form and the color are a thought in action. One
can no longer speak of them, but of a continuous rhyth-
mic bounding, in which the imagination of the painter,
a prey to the ordered lyricism of those who absorb the
world in order to give it the form of their skull and the
movement of their heart, liberates and fuses his sensations, his ideas, and his sentiments. What does the
word "drawing" mean in these moving surfaces which
the drama twists, convulses, and embosses from within,
so that it may bring the expression of the spirit to
certain dominant projections, which cause the color
to roar, sigh, laugh, or sing? The color itself moves.
It vibrates, it hesitates or sinks down, and rises and
descends like the sea. The local tone, the reflection,
the passage, and the value are the very actors of the
drama. That red which sinks and grows somber in the
carnage sends forth a continuing clamor, that pink
laughs in sinister fashion amid that dark hair, that blue
sends into revolting hearts the mirage of paradise
that one thinks to be within reach of one's hand, that
gold and that carmine undulate and burn in the ener-
vating warmth of a room of voluptuousness, and that
livid green is taken from seas of storm and from flesh
in putrefaction, to express the passage or the empire of
death. The tone which is born and dies and is reborn

DELACROIX. George Sand (*Private collection*).

under the eyes of men sixty years after the death of the painter, interprets the profound movement of his dramatic emotion, which the breathless line pursues in order to inclose it in the actual. And whatever the energy of this line, which bounds and rebounds under the repeated burning touches of the creative flame, the tragedy of the color seems to escape from it, to outstrip it, and to drag it along in its torment, as it hurries to reach the mystic depths where the universe seems to unite its confused force with the soul of greatly inspired men. Delacroix is probably the only man who, without ever being vanquished, has constantly gone to seek outside the eternal symbols of the Greek myth and of the Bible, in literature and in modern history, pretexts for manifesting his passion. This overflowing, one over the other, of the languages of faith, music, poetry, and painting, is a new phenomenon, one in which romanticism usually strikes against its reef, but also, with two or three men, Delacroix, Baudelaire, Wagner, sometimes Hugo, sometimes Berlioz, the summit whence it can claim to reach the invisible region where all forms of faith dwell and are confused in the highest symbolism. Of all, it is certainly the painter who runs most dangers, for if he, for a second, loses sight of the object—the plastic architecture of the earth and of heaven, the sinking of the volumes into the depth of the planes, the gamut of the values, and the solidarity of the lines—the whole world of sentiment in which literature moves at ease entangles him, steals his savor, submerges him, and misleads his mind, taking it away from the region of the concrete, where his imagination must seek all its food. Reality, for the painter, is surely the inner vision of the universe which he possesses. But all vision whose material roots do not plunge everywhere into the unlimited substance of the sense life of the painter, does not belong to painting. The English pre-Raphaelites, the German didactic painters, Boecklin the Swiss, and Gustave Moreau the Frenchman, will learn this to their cost, and not at the cost of painting, which is in no way concerned with them. Because his eyes possessed the secret of sight, he is, then, the only one on this peak who possesses such mastery that his literary emotions, his metaphysical tortures, his aspirations of sentiment, and the confused visions which music arouses in him, are transposed into the real world of colors and of forms which thereby is extended as if by a god. Here, then, is the history of men and its fatality, which we name love, or will, and its pitiless serenity, which we call cruelty. Here are the faces of ecstasy or of sorrow under which the march of events goes its indifferent way. Here is Faust, the doctor. Here is exact knowledge arrived at the brink of nothingness and leaning, appalled, over its abyss, where the void and night plunge from a bed of flowers. Here is the reverie of Hamlet. Here is the invincible mystery, the boundless immensity of space and of feeling which was contained entire in a box of bone for less time than the life of a plant, and which disappeared thence forever in the space of a lightning flash. And here is the only image for the possession of which it is important that we should live: the one which a great soul realizes in order to test the value of its enthusiasm, and which is found to correspond to so many undecided, stammering indications in the fleeting objects of our love, that, little by little, it becomes for us more real than the world, and affords us a faith which has greater youth after each one of our crises of despair.

"What is most real in me are the Illusions which I create. . . ." Yes. And by these Illusions which he creates, Eugène Delacroix converses, as Baudelaire expresses it, with the "supernatural." His religion is a burning and inexhaustible hearth, fed by all the dramas, all the faces of nature, and everything that is tragic and that is charming in the brief human adventure; and on this hearth he pours his fire. With Rembrandt, Rubens, and Michael Angelo, he is perhaps the man who has labored most and best in painting to wrest the great mystery from the domain of theology, and to install it in the deepest recess of the human heart,

DELACROIX. The Chariot of the Sun, drawing (*Louvre*).

which is forever borrowing it from the impassable immensity of the universe, in order to give it humanity's confused animation, and return the mystery to the universe, increased by the immensity of the heart.

III

Not one among those who were, doubtless, the greatest among the great painters, not one, it seems, equals him—Rembrandt excepted—in profundity, and in force of sentiment; not one—Rubens excepted—in

DAUMIER. The Burden (*Private collection*).

the torrent-like power of expressive movement; not one—Michael Angelo excepted—in capacity for transporting into painting that which seems to belong to the domain of abstract meditation and of the moral prophet. But perhaps there is sometimes lacking in him, that which is never lacking in any of them—the faculty of suppressing and of selecting. There is order in his brain, and even a kind of impressive calm beneath the apparent agitation, but it is not always in his heart. He feels too much, he wants to say too much; and if the ensemble is always living, it sometimes is too much alive, it reels, as if it could not bear the weight of silence. The romanticists construct organically, their point of departure is the inner impulse, and they spread forth their expressive surfaces with so much haste and violence that too often the movement appears confused and overloaded. The contemplation of the object intoxicates the individual to such an extent that the object becomes as living as the individual himself, but its lines waver and the core of the expression bursts forth alone, brilliant, hallucinating, and radiant with strength and love. Hugo abounds in holes, in empty places full of smoke and wind. Wagner is often loose and prolix, and his giant breast suffocates under the flowers he heaps up. The grandiose melody of Berlioz soars for a moment, its two great wings spreading, and then it falls headlong, in a crash of vulgar noises and deafening cries. Delacroix, who, most of all, retains mastery over his power, bounds out of his own rhythm at times, and gets out of breath in racing to regain it. Rodin, the last of all in point of time, has a colossal power of expressing the profound life of the object by the vibrations of its surface. But it is at the expense of his equilibrium and of his relations with those who surround him; there is not one monumental ensemble which holds together from top to bottom.

That is the ransom, doubtless, of every too excep-
tionally expressive force, necessarily as far from the
great architectural calm as the reasons of the heart
are distant from reason. Since the painters of the
coffins of Christian Egypt, the Hindus, Rabelais, Tintoretto, and Shakespeare, no one has possessed, in the
same degree as the great romanticists, the power of
expressing that which is most irresistible and most
intoxicating in the inner movement of life. The process scarcely changes, but what renders it all-powerful
and impossible to imitate is that it is not a process
but a way of seeing, a way of acting, a way of living.
The romantic painter, or sculptor, or poet finds in the
object, with a certitude like that of a thunderbolt,
the summit of his expression. Then he surrounds this
summit with his creative fever, and, from every point,
all things are swept toward it. He is born within the
object, he lifts it up, he guides it from one side only,
he breaks open its surface. He bursts forth to meet
the light, casting behind him into vagueness or the
night everything hostile, secondary, or merely indifferent. Hugo, whether he writes or draws, carries
his tyrannical desire to the point of diametrical oppositions: the ruins on the promontories, the storm, the
ocean, the mountain, everything that is unmeasured
and everything that is fateful is indicated and violently
modeled by the conflict of antitheses—of light and
shadow. Raffet creates a straight line of aigrettes in
swift movement, walls of steel, long flowing manes,
and a thousand silent hoofs—the whole thing is a single
block—and the rumble of destiny is heard in the darkness. Baudelaire accumulates in the center of his
vision all the scattered sense impressions which a
fanatical and consuming sensibility has permitted him
to gather up from a hundred thousand similar objects.
Constantin Guys lengthens the painted eyes of the

courtesans, accentuates the blood-red note of their
mouths, weighs down their hard breasts, makes their
jewels heavier and more sonorous, masses higher on
their necks the coils of dark hair with its combs and its
flowers— and at once the odor of love fills the ballrooms
and the shows, prowls the length of the hot streets,
enervates the summer evenings and the anxious waiting of the night. Barye concentrates the whole spirit

DAUMIER. The Soup, drawing (*Private collection*).

of attack and of defense in the big paws of his wild
beasts, in the bunches of muscles of their shoulders,
and in the vibrant, tight-strung planes of their thighs
and of their backs. Daumier seizes the heart of the
drama, and ties tight around it all the expressive knots
which a grand and intuitive science of form in action
reveals to him incessantly.

He would suffice to define that aspiration, held in
common by all the romanticists, for concentrating the

DAUMIER.   The Bath (*Private collection*).

whole expression in some sudden projection to which all the lines and all the lights flock from every side, enthusiastic and obedient like so many units of energy moving toward a central force which is to be manifested. Millet, at the same time, is attempting this, and sometimes almost realizes it, when he lays down his brush for the pen or the pencil. But the form, which he seeks to keep simple and naïve, defined by a few bare planes, almost always remains empty. Later, at the other extremity of romanticism, but with the same means, Carrière expresses not so much a desire for the qualities of plastic art as he does his need for sentiment.

With Daumier, on the contrary, the form, which an arabesque of light sculptures, describes, and directs, by its gradations, its surface progressions, and its flowing into depth, turns and twists, as full as a living bronze, knotting and distending itself under the impulsion of effort, of desire, or of hunger, like intertwined vine- and ivy-stems, which draw from the heart of the earth their nourishment and their support. In considering him, one always thinks of several of the masters who have best rendered the pathos of the human form in action. This simple, direct man is the natural fruit of an intense European culture which has not yet left its orbit, and all the old classics recognize themselves in him. He is of the south and of the north. Born in Marseilles, where the shadow and the sun sculpture mountains and shores into broad planes, as expressive and as solid as a structure of bare bone, he lives in the Paris street, in the seething center of everyday tragedy and comedy, which one perceives as soon as one suspends one's automatic pace in order to let one's glance rest for a moment on the scene. He lives in the Paris street. He certainly knows Rembrandt, Rubens, Tintoretto, and Michael Angelo. But he does not think of them when, with the living daylight, which Rembrandt used at will, he illuminates men and women whose action is revealed by projecting volumes which Michael Angleo would have recognized, and by tangles of limbs in which Rubens and Tintoretto would have seen their power of making all the movements of life find their echo in the continuity of lines and the receding of planes.

One would say that he paints with burning clay. It is a sculpture of our drama in which the bones and the muscles collect the entire spirit of the drama, whose penumbra takes back little by little or suddenly the past or present incidents which are not its real point of connection or its spiritual sense. A sublime expression of sentiment arises from the plastic means exclusively, and if he is as good as a saint is, it is because he is as strong as a hero. The drawn shoulder and arm of that woman carrying a basket who is followed by the toddling steps of the child that clutches at her with its little fist, express the effort of a lever too weak to raise a heavy weight. But from the depths of the centuries, pity wells up to accompany those passing figures. The enormous swelling breast from which a little being is drinking, the head and the muscular neck leaning over the soup which the iron spoon carries to the outstretched lips, all express, doubtless, a double meal. But the tragedy of hunger rumbles there like a storm. That powerful woman who presses between her arms and her bosom those beautiful nude children expresses physical health and strength in repose. But the spirit of revolt hovers over her in majesty. That little ass crushed under the weight of that fat peasant, and that skeletonlike horse which could carry no more weight than that of the thin knight, express physical poverty and vulgarity crossing a desert of ashes. But the inner spirit of man marches forth there to wrestle with God.

There is the artist. And there is the work. It is useless to recount the paradox of his career. Regarded as a caricaturist, he died very poor, very celebrated, and wholly unknown. He was a caricaturist, and that is not a serious matter. Delacroix was prudent enough to get himself elected—with difficulty—to the Institute in order to go and dine in society and wear evening dress. And Corot had the luck to be the son of prosperous tradespeople. But this man lived between the barricade, his garret, and the editorial rooms of small radical papers. He was content to possess the street and to conquer the future. They say he was unconscious of it. I doubt that. The mark of a powerful man is to be aware of his power. When one has that fine forehead, those piercing eyes, that courageous mouth, and that face, full and broad like that of Rabelais, and when one kneads the form as one pleases with that good thumb, one is not ignorant of the fact that one is a king. And if one is silent about it, and if one even reaches the point of allowing no one to imagine such a thing, it is because there is a sufficient recompense in modeling life into a resemblance to oneself. The whole dark stream of men obeyed his first call. He reigned over the street, he felt himself the sole master of it, from the moment that he set foot there. Nothing that moved in the street was foreign to him, and into this formidable disorder he introduced the despotic order which all the movements and the passions of the street organized in his mental life. The epic vision of things is only a superb submission of sensation and of the mind to the living strength of everything which the weaklings of sensation and the pontiffs of the mind neglect as inferior to their abstract or mechanical life. He stopped each time that an eloquent gesture pierced the confused uniformity of the crowd in action. He knew the broad streets where the strong man of

DAUMIER.   The Towman   (*Private collection*).

the fairs lifts iron weights and harangues an attentive circle. At the hour when the workshops pour their dramatic flood over the greasy pavement, he mingled with the passionate groups forming around the street singer and the barrel organ, and joining in on the last verses, in which popular idealism expresses its revolt or

INGRES. Portrait, drawing
(*Private collection*).

its hope. One would see him in the first row, in the fairs of the quarter, when the drummer beat his drum and the glorious barker made his speech. He loved those powerful creatures who stir the soul of the people, simple as they are, and as he is himself. The athlete folds his arm over his gigantic chest muscles, a peaceful demigod of strength and righteousness. The man singing has the fateful countenance of the first poets of heroic deeds in whose mouth

the primitive religions affirm their victory from their first cry. And that clown with the painted face and the great living gesture has something about him resembling an archangel opening and shutting the gates of paradise and of hell. . . . It was in a similar spirit that Michael Angelo traced the biblical symbols on the ceilings of the Vatican. Daumier, if he lives in less torment, is probably as grave, and if, in his raci-

ness, he thunders in the language of the rough neigh-
borhoods, there is, each time that his bolt illuminates
or strikes, prophetic lightning which carries and
anounces the shock.

For he is a man of justice, a man of truth. The law
is a small matter to him, and the law courts even less.
He is a just man. He has the mighty gayety of such a
one, the irresistible strength, the indulgence, the
measure, and the charity. Fines and imprisonment
renew his virulence. In his prints, to which a few
poor hovels in some corner, a few bare trunks on a
bank, a sky where the wind blows, or a strong suggestion
of the country or of the city, give the grandeur of a
fresco, the blacks and the whites have the velvety and
profound sonority whereby his avenging pity takes
the love of the living world as a pretext through which
to pour itself forth. Everywhere that a man is unde-
servedly vanquished, or a poor person is humiliated,
everywhere that a weak man cries for help, everywhere
that vulgarity and baseness triumph, he is there, by himself, to cover the one who seeks protection, and alone to
face the one who is not willing to understand. He is present in the court room, where, with a magnificent laugh,
his whip lash flays the unjust judge and the lying lawyer.
From the top benches, he models with fierce strokes
the faces, the knees, and the bellies of the legislators.
He brings cartridges to the wretched dwellings of the
workmen where the last visitor had spilled blood on
the ground and brains on the wall. He fires his rifle
with the army of the miserable, from their heap of
paving stones. This simple man has in his heart all
the innocent forces which, through the insurrections of
the serfs and of the Communes, through the cathedral,
the war of the Fronde, and the revolutionary days of
1789 and of 1830, opened to the dregs of society the
roads of the future. The Pharisee and the hypocrite

hide when he passes by, the bad rich man grinds his teeth, and the bad shepherd goes white. And since, in his time, it is the middle class that reigns, he lashes out at the middle class.

IV

This hatred against the bourgeois is a phenomenon of romanticism, excessive, like all romanticist phenomena, but very healthy. Berlioz proclaims it with fury in his memoirs. One finds the trace of it in Delacroix's journal, though he is of too high a caste for public negation or invective. The exodus of the landscapists to Fontainebleau is an active manifestation of it. Gautier and Baudelaire wear its insignia on their clothing. A little later, Flaubert will seek in it the pretext, and Zola one of the oftenest repeated subjects of their arts. Almost the whole æsthetics of Ruskin starts with a protest of sentiment against the social order imposed by the middle class. Ibsen contrasts the muddy valleys where it reigns through the submission of the crowd, with the solitude of the peaks in their ice and their sunlight. Such unanimity as this has its necessary reasons. He who loves protests against him who profits, he who has enthusiasm rises against him who knows only interest. Balzac alone sees the beauty of conquest, but, alas! in activities of the lowest order. Not content to sing of business, he engages in business. The "get rich" of Guizot, and the narrow, domineering ferocity of Thiers are not merely objective phenomena to be described with passionate interest, but objects of admiration before which his strength abases itself. Not one of all those—neither the one who admires, nor one of all who protest—not one is capable of feeling that which there is of vigor and of grandeur in this taking possession of the wealth of the

INGRES. Portrait of the Painter Granet
(*Museum of Aix-en-Provence*).

planet by a class which had reached political freedom, at the time when they were seizing upon freedom of sensation.

It is men a little older than they, born in the prosperous families of the bourgeoisie approaching its triumph, and reared, consequently, for the practical

INGRES.   La belle Zélie (*Rouen*).

man's conquest of freedom of action, not men carried along by victory as they were, who represent, in the domain of the mind, the beauty of that conquest. They are southern men, moreover, as far from the idealism of sentiment, wherein the art of the north finds all its pretexts, as the realistic soldiers of the south, loving war for its terrible intoxication and its immediate advantages, were distant from the idealistic warriors of the north, accepting war only in order to deliver, through it, the oppressed peoples of Europe. Among them, certainly, are the connecting links, Bonaparte, Berlioz, and Daumier, among whom the melody of southern line, and its lightning flash enter the material of the north to model it profoundly, like a colored clay. But Berlioz, at Rome, turns with disgust from Stendhal, whose only offense was that he had been born twenty years earlier, at an hour when there was less enthusiasm, and in the same part of the country. And when Ingres, arriving from Rome, enters the thick of the romanticist battle, everyone who is mildly or strongly tinged with romanticism instinctively opposes him; and all the mediocrities shocked by romanticism, which stood alone at that time in its fight for the life and the freedom of passion, group themselves around him who, through weakness and vanity, permits his hands to be tied. The romanticist and the bourgeois hated or praised in Stendhal and Ingres only the dryness of their line, their apparent coldness before the object, and their narrow and direct application to rendering it as it is. The tottering academic spirit seeks in the purity of Ingres's line the justification for the Davidian doctrines upon which it is propping up its exhausted classicism as well as it could. And despite the effacement of Stendhal, and the crying paradox of the career of Ingres—who hates the School and the juries and who is made head of the School and president of the juries, who proclaims his disgust with anatomy and whose anatomical drawing is opposed to the disconnected form of Delacroix—the same error is made with regard to both, and made by all, friends and enemies alike: no one perceives, at this moment, the flame under the ice, and the ferment of revolt and the implacable pessimism under the colorless form and the traditional calm.

Ingres is a bourgeois of his time, throwing himself into the conquest of form, like the notary or the banker into the conquest of money. But he is a great bourgeois. He has the precise intelligence, rigorous and limited, the brutal idea of authority, and the specialized probity of those strong conquerors who, with an eye to lucre and to practical domination, dug canals, laid out roads, covered Europe with railways, launched fleets, and exchanged paper for gold over their counters. And so he could make, of these men, portraits which seemed to be cast in bronze and hollowed out with steel. It is because he closely corresponds with those who are of his epoch and of his class, that he is the last in France to trace with a pencil as sharp and hard as steel, those clear-cut psychological images which leave nothing of the inner character in the shadow, and which suppress every detail which does not emphasize this character of the man and of the woman who belong so intimately to this country. The continuity of these images is scarcely interrupted from Foucquet and the Clouets to himself, passing through Lagneau, Sébastien Bourdon, Coyzevox, Le Brun, Perronneau, La Tour, Drouais, Houdon, and twenty others; and, from Montaigne to Stendhal, all the French moralists, La Rochefoucauld, La Bruyère, Saint-Simon, Voltaire, and Chamfort, bring to them the support of their clearsighted testimony. The Frenchman is a born psychologist; he is lyrical by fits and starts when, in the thirteenth or the nineteenth century, some great social event—the Commune or the Revolution—occurs, to agitate, with a sound of storm, the sources of his sentiment. Stendhal and Ingres, at the hour when the poem was being reborn in the heart of the writers, of the musicians, and of the painters, had inevitably to remain unknown or misunderstood, the one finding no publishers, the other selling for twenty francs those

INGRES. Drawing for Raphael and La Fornarina (*Lyons*).

penetrating drawings, as grand as a Chinese portrait, as pure as a melody, and as close to the mind and to life as a letter or a story of the century toward whose apogee he was born.

He is a realist by force of will who, in a country of very subtle and delicately shaded realism, contributes nothing new save a form renewed and made firm once

BARYE. Tiger sleeping, bronze (*Louvre*).

more by a contact, passionately sought, with the antique and with the Italians. Before Delacroix was born, he is already in the atelier of David, studying Roman statues and bas-reliefs at the command of the despot, keeping secret his enthusiasm for the drawings of the English sculptor Flaxman, which revealed to him the engravings after Greek vases in the language of his time, and unable to do other than admire his master's portraits, solid, authoritative, full of love, even though it is so controlled, in which the respect for the inner structure is affirmed in order to lend its support to the whole rising century. It is in Italy that Ingres will pass almost all of the first half of that century, where his ardent study of Hellenic antiquity, of the Italian Gothic, and of Raphael will very soon make him conscious of the continuing thrill of life in fresco and in marble, which appears to him like the

BARYE. Lions near their cavern (*Louvre*).

face of a woman under a half-raised veil; and it is Italy that will deliver him almost entirely from the paraphernalia of archæology and from the narrow dogmatism against which romanticism itself is struggling. Two victories, of which neither Delacroix nor himself will admit the solidarity, and which will precipitate their reconciled influences into the forms of the future.

He came near to seizing the soul of antiquity at its

sources, and while Delacroix is bringing to men freedom of sentiment in movement and color, he is preparing for them, with freedom of form, the revelation
of true Greek thought which set itself to embrace the
living block in its ensemble and to express it, without
preoccupation with picturesque detail, through the
roundness and the plenitude of the contour. It does
not matter that his color, from which the reflection is
voluntarily exiled, is oftenest only an attribute applied
to the form, although, in most of his portraits, discreet
harmonies of deep blacks, the blued and slatey grays
of the backgrounds with their slight undulation, and
the fineness of his whites touched with pearl, with
blue, and with gold, assure him a place between Chardin
and Corot. The music is in his line, in which Gluck
and Mozart and Beethoven, for whom he has an uncompromising love, would recognize their melody, which
is not yet drawn toward the romantic maelstrom, to be
swept along by Berlioz, and submerged by Wagner in
the orchestral storm of the symphony.

The music is in his line. According to the formula of
the School, according to David even, he "draws badly."
In his work, men constantly find that the feet are weak,
the hands are badly placed, that the necks have goiter,
joints are disconnected, and arms and legs a third too
long or too short. But it is always to the advantage of
the expressive power of the line, which insinuates itself,
launches forth, or bends back, in order to give the total
feeling awakened in him by his model. He gives a
tapering quality to fingers, rounds the limbs, hollows
the small of the back, thickens the lips, lengthens the
eyes, or accentuates their angle. Drawing, portrait,
large picture or small—everything is linear melody,
naïvely following the form in its continuous undulation, but, when it receives the shock of the idea sug-
gested by the form, swelling, or prolonging, or caressing,

BARYE. Jaguar devouring a hare (*Louvre*).

or restraining that undulation in order to impose its meaning. One might here surprise the trace of the romanticist deformation, were it not that he first considered the ensemble, not from the point of view of a dramatic impression to be rendered, but from the point of view of a general idea, objective and pagan, to which his Latin soul and his culture, formed on the antique, have led him. A woman's arm on the back of a chair, a beautiful drooping hand, crossed knees, or a sinuous torso, melting away or coming forward, are never isolated as they attract his eyes; they are only summits of a firm and progressive wave, all of whose contours respond to the sensation which he seeks voluntarily, and finds in the heart of every object.

He is haunted by the desire for the feminine body, round, full, and swelling with strength, like a world. It is in him that we find the affirmation of that hymn to woman of which the painters of the eighteenth century had given the outline with more verve than love, but which will assume, in the nineteenth, through Delacroix, through Chassériau, through Corot, Courbet, Carpeaux, Puvis, Renoir, and Rodin, a character of ardor, sometimes adorable and sometimes tragic. One hears it rumbling everywhere in his work, in which, because he has more will power than lyric power, it is clothed with a definitely erotic, and almost animal, meaning. If he were more spontaneously a painter, one would think of Goya. Here, above all, his bourgeois soul breaks forth, with its appetite unrestrained and without inner struggle; neither laces covering the skin, nor trinkets and chains around the necks, nor ample dresses around the waists and the legs, nor subjects drawn from religion or mythology, succeed in concealing this. His Blessed Virgins were first painted nude, and when they have their hands crossed over their heart, one still sees the bending curve of the breast, and the line that grows round on the maturing abdomen. Certainly, before his finished drawings and his allegorical pictures, one might think, and people have thought, that what is called ideal form is the only one that interests him. But his real nature is shown by his thousands of sketches, and it is in these that he is great. In them one sees furrowed torsos and drooping breasts, one sees broad flanks with folds as deep as the bark of a tree, and heavy and burning as fruit. And when he casts his eyes on some illustrious sitter, however austere the costume is intended to be, the person is already disrobed. As man is defined for him by wealth, woman is defined by love. He weighs the bellies of the bourgeois and the bosoms of their wives. How many beautiful heavy arms, emerging from their shawls, with fat hands, and the fingers spreading as if full of sap, which the rings press to the finger tips! How many dewy glances under heavy eyelids, how many moist mouths where voluptuousness trembles! How much warm flesh satisfied under the cold velvet, the stiff satin, and the inert scarf of gauze which does not succeed in masking the languid droop of the trunk, the fat waist, and the neck full of murmurs and of restrained sobs! Some of his large painted sketches draw to the surface of the skin the warmth exhaled by the breasts, and the echo of profound sighs.

Isolated, these portraits and these studies are among the finest things which France has produced. But if he tries to imagine, to compose, to seize the trumpet of heroism, and rise higher than his nature, he is seen as that which he would always have been, if his sensual genius were not there to save his soul: a spirit rather common, or perhaps even one of a slightly low order. As soon as he ventures upon the great symbols and the great myths, he is icy or ridiculous. As soon as

he attempts to force them, even in their own direction, to create—with an assembly of women of the
harem or with amorous divinities—the poem of voluptuousness realized by his slightest study, his feasts of
flesh are without nobility. All he does is to pile up
meat. All those fat sides, all those elastic breasts, all
those well-rounded thighs, make up a heap of trembling
things like swarming larvæ. If one does not isolate a

COROT.   The Colosseum (*Private collection*).

fragment of the picture, there is nothing to connect
them with the spirit.

Here again, in this narrowness of a nature which is
very audacious, certainly, very powerful and honest,
but limited, he is bourgeois. He represents eighteenth-
century rationalism which has come into power and is
determined to hold it, even if it must do so by brute
strength, and by regarding the lyricism of the romanticists as a kind of canker, caused by demagogues and
revolutionaries, which must be extirpated at any price,

COROT.   The Isola Sacra at Rome (*Private collection*).

even by making use of institutions and of formulas which he makes no secret of despising. He represents artistic positivism, practically a contemporary of philosophic and scientific positivism, and as restricted in scope and as necessary as they are. It will soon bear its fruits, and will even assume toward the reason of the bourgeois as well as toward the imagination of the romanticist, a rôle of socialistic, anarchistic, anti-Christian opposition by the rabble, in its blind slavery to the religion of "facts."

V

But that will not be without resistance. France has two faces, whose differences and contrasts are attenuated when one looks at them from afar. It is in the very bosom of this positivist rationalism that we find the source of the current which will unite with itself the vast sense-contribution of romanticism, in order to demand that pure science open up to it the world of brute matter. And it is from this rationalism that there descends the current which will separate from pure science or will ignore it totally, in order to continue demanding of structures scarcely the work of the imagination, well balanced, very solid, and very convincing structures, that they express that French idealism which adheres so closely to real things, and differs from them only by the insensible shades of a continual transposition, which spiritualizes them without seeming to touch them. Taine and Renan issue from the same sources, contribute to what is really the same work, but seem to incarnate the antagonism of the two tendencies of the mind. We shall see Courbet and Puvis, the one with his eyes ever on the ground, the other looking ever toward the line of the horizon, revealing to the France of their period her plastic soul, and to such a degree that if one of them had not been born, she would not know herself. It is thus that between Ingres and Delacroix, between the dominating, conquering bourgeoisie and the prophetic transport of a people whose desire always outstrips the realization due to the idealism of preceding generations, Corot appears as the truest and purest representative of their movement. He shows us neither the enthusiasm of victory nor the powerful egoism of practical results. The desire of the spirit, which brought him into existence, is still clarifying itself in certain men. In him France continues on a broader wing after his flight, but remaining in the straight line that she followed to Chardin, ever since Poussin and Claude Lorrain offered, to the charming and penetrating soul of Foucquet, the architecture of method. Without being aware of it, perhaps, he retains their historic landscape, or rather he renders it vaguely, as a frame to his idylls, ingenuous and anachronistic, without symbols and without pretension. Through Chardin himself, his trail is easy to follow in Vernet, in Ollivier, in Louis Gabriel Moreau, and in all those delicate Little Masters of the century at the end of which he was born. In him, their strength and their charm are to be multiplied a hundredfold, by all the living growth of that century's great events. He experiences the same joy that they had in watching the houses and the trees trembling in the water, the wooded slopes limiting a calm plain, and light clouds in one of those pink skies touched with amber and silver in which northern France recognizes the smile of the light in the grace of her watercourses and the freshness of her fields. Sometimes, the most subtle spirit of the most delicate romanticism haunts the breaking day that he perceives coming through the black stems of the trees, bursts forth through their pure branches which twist like

flames, and circulates in their bushy mass, as it hums
with light and air and birds. Like Delacroix and like
Ingres, he loves music, and the same music as they, but
it is especially from Gluck that he will ask the proportion
and measure which music can offer to the mind, and to
the heart, that which is most pure and touching. Like
Chardin, a Parisian also, and a son of lower middle-class

people, and like La
Fontaine, he will be a
grown-up child, in his
enjoyment, through-
out his life, without
close association with
the writers and the
artists—the good and
sublime Daumier ex-
cepted—faithful in his
family ties, not fond
of talking painting,
and each evening
under the lamp, till
he was nearly sixty
years old, continuing
in the society of his
old father and his old
mother. He wanders
over the French prov-
inces, where, in each

COROT. Torso (*Private collection*).

place he has modest friends whose names are now
unknown; he stays for weeks with them, not troubling
anybody, since, except at the hour of the good meals,
he is out all day, with his easel and his pipe. He is
regularly received at the Salons, for nothing shocks
the public, nor attracts it in this purity without brilliance, this firmness without violence, and this apparent
impersonality, which continues and crowns the old

COROT.   Reverle (*Louvre*).

French classicism. He is fairly ignorant, but of an exquisite judgment, simple, open of hand and of purse, without rancor, without bitterness, and without envy, of great finesse, and unnoticed as he passes. As he works on his little canvases, he sings, like a house painter. The storms of his heart—and he had some—do not descend into his fingers. He loves, and he admires, but he never makes any outcry, and if, for example, Delacroix is spoken of in his presence, that man who, at the time, represented the loftiest plastic genius of his race, he says with the kind smile on his clean-shaven face, good-natured, broad, and powerful: "He is an eagle, and I am only a skylark. I sing little songs in my gray clouds."

And so he did. He arose at dawn to study the fields, for "the sun extinguishes everything." As soon as the morning mist had fallen, the values asserted themselves in the transparence of the air with their maximum of exactitude, of fineness, and of purity. The morning light, rosy, and so subtle in that Ile-de-France where an impalpable vapor persists, until the golden twilight, making of all space a prism which gives the delicate shades and affording a blond glow as it hangs over everything, flooded the sky and the landscape and streamed over the waters. With the moment which precedes the fall of evening, it is the hour when the air seems to condense its fruity color on trees and stones, to penetrate the trembling firmness of walls, and to marry the tone of the light clouds with that of the soil. The eye of Corot was like a liquid mirror, which reflected faithfully the poetry of those luminous and calm days of France when the rivers, silvered under the silver rain of poplar and willow leaves, the serene air, and the barely undulating line of the hills, seem a crystallization of imponderable harmonies, which the slightest lyric outburst, or the slightest

mystic intoxication would shatter. He copied what he
saw, but the quality of his vision was divine. It is
the halfway meeting place of the objective world in
its most unanimously accepted aspects, and of a soul
attentively receiving the discreetest and rarest teachings of that world. If the lens of the photographer
—by your leave, O Corot!—were endowed with a
heart, it is thus that it would doubtless see the world.
The world is, indeed, rendered in close likeness; the
painter seems to have added nothing to it and taken
nothing from it. It seems. . . . For the miracle is
precisely the invisible work of the mind transposing
the elements of the object to the canvas with so much
tact and measure that they do not appear to be modified
either in their material, or in their local tone, or in
their proportions and their relations. His imagination
evolves no new schemes, but in the delicate centers
of an exquisite intelligence, the purest revelations of
sensibility are associated.

He had made three long journeys to Italy, and no
one ever made better use of his time there. Before
a too hasty production, immoderately sought for
toward the autumn of his career, caused him to forget
the lesson of its limpid landscapes and produce too
many cottony trees and misty ponds, he had understood how well the structure of the land of Italy and
of its cities, as precise, as compact, as trenchant, and
as clear as a theorem, could serve him when he should
be ready to hold the gentleness, the peaceful coolness,
and opalescent light of the French landscape within
lines firm enough to reveal it to the mind. He had
drawn the denuded vertebræ of Italy, the abrupt
contours of its promontories, its trees, straight or
twisted, but pure as swords, the straight outlines of
the houses and of the citadels, and the continuous crest
of the mountains of marble, silhouetted by the fire of

the sky. He had meditated before the visions of Canaletto and of Guardi, which move one by their profound
purity quite as the strain of a violoncello does. On
his journeys, each time that at Fontainebleau, at
Ville-d'Avray, at Mantes-la-Jolie, at La Rochelle, at
Avignon, at Douai, at Rouen, at Arras, or Chartres,

COROT. Maternity
(*Private collection*).

or in the Basque
country, he found the
close and mysterious
union of the line with-
out accidentals, of the
impeccable value, and
of the tone at once
the most exact, the
most veiled, and the
most rare, he remem-
bered. At every place
where a street goes
down between two
huts, where red tiles
show at the edge of a
wood, where a firm
road runs between
two rows of young
elms, where an old
city outlines its ga-
bles and its chimneys
against the sky, or where the spires of a cathedral
point up through the silvered mist, he remembered
the terraces where the houses and the towers roll like
amber beads, he remembered the immobility of the
stones under the incandescent flame of the light, the
spread of the pines above roofs and cupolas, and the
ruins gilded by the evening. The intimate poetry of
things entered the clearness and the force of his memory.
I verily believe that he forgets neither a crevice on a

COROT. The Road *(Private collection)*.

scaling façade, nor a round window under a drain
pipe, nor the last cluster of leaves which trembles on
the last branch; but the crevice or the façade establishes
a plane, the window appears as a necessary spot, bluish
or pearly, in the mauve or the gold of an old wall, and
the leaves suspended between sky and water define
the immensity of space. The grays and the blues, the
golden reds and the pinks, penetrate one another and
reply to one another, in a tremble like mother-of-pearl,
as they ripen this fruit of France, whose harmony
inscribes itself among waves of melody as limpid as
the notes of a flute of crystal.

From this admirable and gentle song to the tone of
the idyll of antiquity, the distance is quickly traversed.
Here are nymphs under the branches and divine silhouettes leaning over the darkened lakes where the
branches which spring forth are seen in reverse with
the first or the last star, and the cupola of the sky.
How many immortal figures he has met near the springs,
and under the wide trees laden with drops of water,
with aërial murmurs, with twittering and the sounds
of wings! How lightly he stepped that he might look
at them at ease, as they dreamed or danced, the lyre
or the thyrsus in their hand! And with what mute
adoration he contemplated their slumber or their games
when he surprised them nude, behind some bush hum-
ming with bees, or at the edge of some stream wont
to reflect heads crowned with flowers in its pure
waters! Since Watteau, there had not been in painting a being so profoundly enamored of the touching
grace that emanates from the firm flesh of women,
whom he painted from afar, like the older master, and
with a troubled reserve, seeking, in the undulation of
the volume, and in the arabesque without projections,
limbs and bodies in which the blood mingles with the
pulp of fruits, and which gleam with the caress of

COROT. The Bridge of Mantes (*Louvre*).

amber and of silver. A hymn as chaste as love, where desire takes on a sacred form. The ardent gravity of the lands of the south here again renders the face of woman dark or calm when she is before him, crosses her beautiful hands at her girdle, and gives to the breast and the neck the firmness of marble columns and of round shields. Under the homespun skirt and the crossed neckcloth of the Italian peasant woman, under the gray dress touched with dull reds and pale blues of the young French woman, in all those little pictures which haunt the memory like veiled and merging sounds of violins, oboes, and harps, the form of the antique is divined, in the embrace of the modern soul, reanimated and all atremble at having been surprised once more.

VI

There, then, is French idealism in its most concrete, but also in its most spiritual, expression. To attain this expression, it is useless to spurn as unworthy the desire for matter and the possession of it. To prevent its irresistible rejuvenation, it is useless for this form to hurl itself upon matter, closing its soul and its heart to its loftiest precepts. It is, however, these two simultaneous and parallel movements to which, at the moment when Delacroix and Corot became mature, but also at the moment when scientific civilization affirms itself, the writers and the artists will yield. In England, for example, the protest of the painters against science and its industrial aspects will, under the influence of Ruskin, assume an abstract and literary character, which will cause it to misunderstand and forget painting. In France, the century is fortunately too strong in its painting to stumble in its path. At most, when we approach the final development of what is claimed to be French symbolism, so stammering, so poor, and so submerged under the plastic power of the century, a fragile work will appear, the supreme flower of a culture which no longer possesses anything living or human, and lacks the faculty of revelation and the power of renewal: like so many men of the tragic periods when the mind oscillates between two faiths, Odilon Redon will have every quality of a great painter—and of a great man, nothing. The others accept life and do not go seeking the mystery outside of it, aware that knowledge thrusts back its frontiers and extends it. Corot, who maintains, high and pure, the flame of the spirit in the matter regained and solicited by the spirit, was very glad, I imagine, to make use of the railway in order to reach his painting-ground more quickly. Courbet will not be wrong when he laughs heavily if people talk to him about the soul: but just the same, there will be more "soul" in a square centimeter of the most materialistic of Courbet's paintings than in all the works of the English pre-Raphaelites, of Gustave Moreau, and of Boecklin, put together. When Puvis gathered inspiration from Greek and mediæval legends of the ideal world, as he did, he was not frightened at the sight of telegraph poles.

And so Puvis, amid the current which sends painting to the positivist philosophy of the time, and soon to science itself, to ask for a technique after having asked for moral support, Puvis remains the only one who with a sufficient plastic intelligence maintains French idealism in his means and in his results. To tell the truth, he is far less of a painter than Corot, who unites him, through Poussin, with French tradition. His master, Delacroix, did not transmit to him the sense of pathos and the sense of the mystical in painting, doubtless because that sense is the most personal and the most living of all. Movement and harmony do not

flow as a unit and from within; in his painting, the
unity of the work is external and of the will; his high
culture, alone, among the elements of his vision,
creates solidarity, one that is sufficient to satisfy taste,
but insufficient to subjugate it. But there is not, in

CHASSÉRIAU. The Vintage, detail, decoration of the Cour
des Comptes (*Louvre*).

the whole work, a suspicion of literary or symbolical
intention foreign to the sentiments which the language
of plastics is capable of expressing. And if the instinct
of the painter is less vast than his mind, his feeling for
decoration lends him a moral force which the Gothic
men of Italy seemed to have exhausted.

CHASSÉRIAU.   History, decoration of the Cour des Comptes (*Louvre*).

He could not concern himself long with Courbet, his elder by a few years, and whose effort at its beginnings, when he left the atelier of Delacroix, interested him, and always commanded his respect. This somewhat beast-like power must even have revealed to him, by contrast, the secret of his desire. Another painter besides, of the same age as Courbet, revealed to him, at the decisive hour, the great decorative style. Fiery, sensual, intoxicated with love and with painting, the creole Chassériau, celebrated when twenty years old and lacking only, perhaps, a longer life in order to become the greatest painter of his century, was in the very center of the whirlwind in which the wild lyricism of Delacroix and the determined style of Ingres were clashing, influencing all the artists, shaking Chassériau himself and tossing him about without respite, until his death, which came when he had attained the age of Raphael and of Watteau. A life too short, especially if one thinks of its grandiose ambitions, the frescoes in which human forms marry their undulations, like those of rivers or of flowers swaying, with the flowers them-selves, with the rivers, with the seaweed, with the branches, with the vines, and with the sheaves, the French poem of Goujon, of Poussin, of Girardon, and of Watteau, unfolding under the burning shadow of the tropical forest, and under the romantic frenzy of death and voluptuousness. A life too frail, a health too precarious for the unforeseen robustness of a plastic intelligence capable of forcing upon the intoxication of his century structural discipline and the heroic grace of the Greco-Latin genius. A life too passionate, per-haps, from which there escaped a fire which returned upon it, and burned it, and permitted to surge up from its fallen ashes the immense splendor of those corollas which grow on some flaming rock, and which one per-ceives from a long distance, strange, hallucinating, and

solitary. When he disappeared, a few ardent compositions, full of the meaning of the great natural symbols
—broad flanks, splendor of arms and of knees, the
tinkling of jewels and medals, women like some great
fruits of the tropics, heavy, ripe, swelling with odorous
sap, and giant trees with the wide expanse of their
trunks, and their branches like twisting flames—had,

PUVIS DE CHAVANNES. The Poor Fisherman (*Luxembourg*).

at all events, outlined the reconciliation, possible only
in a spiritual organism as new and strong as his own,
between the two hostile masters in whom the century
might have found its decorative expression. Ingres,
indeed, from the time of his return from Rome had,
with his misunderstanding of reflections, his local
tones, his unbroken backgrounds, and his linear
rhythms, initiated a type of mural painting which

neither he nor his pupils ever brought to realization. Delacroix was too much of a painter, too much of a musician, too much enamored of subtle shades and of lightninglike passages, to subordinate his great epic frescoes to the solemn unity and the austere tone of the walls.

Puvis de Chavannes, with far less genius, but perhaps with more patience and, in any case, with more time than Chassériau had, at least attempted the miracle which no one, since Giotto, has wrought completely. With a little more of sensual intoxication in the color, which is held in too close subjection to the bareness of the stone, a little more of plenitude of life, and of accent, in the grand lines which attempted to bring form and gesture back to the simplest architectural rhythm, he would, through the synthesis of his landscapes and through the pale perfection of his well-controlled harmonies, have touched the highest accord to be attained between painting with its life and the monument with its idea. The noble spirit is practically alone on its peak, where a few pale flowers are strewn and where the sounds of the world become tenuous before they reach him. This ruddy Burgundian, sensual but an aristocrat, who loved women, the country, and good wine, ever rises to imaginary constructions which summarize our universe in majestic forms and chastened melodies. There is no surrender to the sensation of the moment. Everything is masterly evocation of the spiritual aspects of the event and of the place. The moon rises at its hour to lend its glow to the saint who watches over the sleeping roofs. The sea is dead for the poor man whom it feeds, and the shore discloses to him only the anæmic flowers of hope and of memory. When he wills it, all the departed or dying civilizations rise from the oceans they have ransacked, in order to tender their submission to the modern world. The angels

PUVIS DE CHAVANNES.   Summer (*Hôtel de Ville of Paris*).

fly in a heaven conquered by the industry of men. Let us accept everything, in order to understand everything, he seems to say, and let us spread our two great wings above the miserable quarrels of doubt and of negation. . . . . The trees, isolated and straight, with their open leaves, the bare plains, the calm rivers, the foam and the azure of the sea, the skies which dawn or evening slowly illuminate or darken, the motionless herds waiting for night, and the groups dispersed by labor, games, study, and war, have the grandeur of a prayer offered by an unbeliever to universal life, to thank it for loving him. It is Renan between the Church and atheism, the double and serene protest, of a nature somewhat too voluntarily spiritual, against excessive literary abstraction, and against encroaching sensualism. He has not the faith, but he understands it, and he expresses it. And then he has a noble vision of things, which is also a faith. And the intellectual epic of France, with its calm harmonies, its measured architecture, and its limpid idealism, is unrolled on all these walls between lines of white muses bearing the sword and the lyre, and somber laurel woods.

At the other extremity of the universal movement which sweeps French painting onward toward the renewal of its means, Courbet accepts the name of "realist," which is given him in derision. He shouts the word like a challenge, with his drawling voice. Every time that people speak of the ideal, or of imagination, or of beauty, or of poetry, or of mystery, he shrugs his heavy shoulders, picks up his brush and paints a manure heap. He is right. Only, he is too right. He has almost no general culture, he has known no fervent apprenticeship under a master of his profession. At the Louvre, he copies those in whom he finds the direct qualities, which are the only ones he understands, and which he seeks to carry further than they—the Venetians, the

Flemings, and the Spaniards. Anarchistic and self-taught, he of course founds a School, which is to say, a religion. He calls himself the free man, free from the prejudice of æsthetic education, even while he himself is in search of culture and of government. And he reproduces the faults and the blemishes of

COURBET. Baudelaire (*Montpellier*).

cultures and governments in their decay. He copies the pictures of the masters as faithfully as he thinks to copy nature, and carries over into his art the blackened backgrounds of the canvases in the museum, their opaque shadows, and all the foreign substances that age and dirt have deposited on their surface.

By good fortune, his craftsmanship is tremendous. He copies the splendor of flesh, the great gray skies, the brooks under the leaves, the vast trees, the foggy sea and its breaking waves, with as much application, exactitude, and force as he does the bitumen and the rancid oil of the masterpieces which he ill understands. He does not compose, he does not transpose; with black, white, blood, a little gold and clay, his trowel plasters the object under his broad eyes, those of a somnolent, sensual animal ruminating slowly, with a few obscure ideas, and with powerful sensations. He has a gluttonous delight in mixing his thick paste, and the stories he builds up are rudimentary—a country burial, drinkers around a table, stone breakers, or women sifting wheat—which leave a remembrance, dull, very tenacious, however, and sometimes very moving. He believes himself to be bringing romanticism to a brutal close, and he uncompromisingly preserves its antithesis, by opposing blacks and whites, a process easy to conceive and difficult to execute, but with which he plays with a grandiose breadth, as no one had since Frans Hals. Sometimes he thereby reaches depths which extend in veiled and heavy sonorities to the center of the eternal and simple feelings of the heart, like the lowest and purest notes wherein the violoncello and the human voice unite their passion. He knows how to make a drama, direct, present, and of a bare and somber gravity, with the handkerchief which a widow's hand holds to her face as she weeps, and which makes a white spot against her black veil. He knows how to unite there with great livid clouds, a low gray cliff, a few powerful reds, and a few mortuary emblems which carry into the mournful provincial gathering the sumptuous echo of the mystic symbols and of the death-feasts of love and of memory. He does not do this purposely, I should say. He copies. But perhaps, on that day, he writes—with nothing but dark garments, a little white linen, a few women

COURBET. The Burial at Ornans, detail (*Louvre*).

weeping and with bowed heads, some ordinary spectators, a grave digger, a grave in the clay, and a sad and leaden landscape—the most powerful epic of the family in the history of painting.

Such is the man, knowing no fine distinctions, almost coarse, though he has strange flashes, and—his portraits of Proud'hon, of Berlioz, of Baudelaire, and of Vallès are witness to this—though he is attracted toward the mind, like a big woodland insect that flies in, with a buzz of wings, through the open window into lighted rooms. Such is this magnificent painter. Everything that is animal, close to the earth, and the earth itself, in its torpid and obscure life, he recounts with a single and certain power which will not stir. A joy that is sensual and vulgar, but a thousand times stronger than grace, stronger than taste, and stronger than the sense of shame, weighs upon the work, often reaching a point of stifling the air in it till it cannot be breathed, and sometimes deadening the very paint and rendering it crude, heavy, and with no more reflection than comes from lead. The leaves of the trees are almost always without a tremor, and the trunks without nourishing humidity, but around their thick-set robustness heavy shadows are spread, in which the heat of the day collects over the motionless springs and the little sleeping beasts. The oxen plunge into the burning grasses, their eyes half closed, beautiful women stretched on the ground have big folds of moist flesh at their wrists and at their white necks which disappear into the opening of the bodice, and powerful legs under the dress which is sometimes turned up to the knee. When the woman is quite nude, he is uplifted by a kind of massive and radiant lyricism. He pursues her firm curves and the light and shadow, to make of them a single block, solid and full as a living marble. The splendid bellies and the hard breasts breathe in it, between the white arms and the loosened red hair, with the calm of a mountain plain stretched out in slumber. Other creatures of love seek, under the dense boughs, the water known to the creatures of the woods, in which to soak their skin, whose fat luster placidly attracts the eye of the male. The poem of matter marches on, heavy and slow as a plow. Courbet will drive it along to the end of his one broad furrow, whose dark gleam is like that of a damp and heated soil. In his passing, he will have mowed down the whole romanticist Illusion which had been lived through by two or three great painters, but which sinks to earth as soon as they die, because it was not supported by a sufficient mass of reality. The reality which he brings to replace it will go down with him, because it did not take sufficient account of Illusion, and when he has exhausted his reality, art disappears.

The prisoner of another Illusion, the materialist Illusion, Courbet constantly confused realism of language—which belongs to all the masters capable of remodeling the world in their minds in order to project it beyond them as its living symbol—with the realism of the subject. And in order not to become the slave of the Ideal, he became "the slave of the model."[1]

This atheist, with an asceticism which, to be sure, troubled him but little, because it was natural, interdicted transposition, which liberates the creative genius and causes it to enter the plane of the universe. He did not know that reality resides far more in the nature of the artist than in the nature of his subject. He did not know that life resides not only in the epoch, but also in the faculty of incorporating with memory, with the imagination, and with knowledge, the characteristics of the epoch. He did not know that life is not in the object alone, but in all the sensible rela-

[1] Th. Sylvestre, *loc. cit.*

COURBET. Woman sleeping, study (*Private collection*).

tionships of all the objects among themselves, and in their intuitive relationships with him who contemplates them. He did not know that it is from this precisely that painting derives its lyrical character, or, as Baudelaire calls it, its "supernatural character." But by that very ignorance, he assured the fecundity of the future.

VII

Science had been advancing for half a century. The "fact" itself had been left behind. Progress of a profound nature was being made in the analysis of matter, and each day brought forth some practical miracle. The mind carries on all its elements together, in a block. The science and the art of a given period are never more than particular modes of expression, distinct in their characteristics, but, through their spirit, belonging in common to all the men of that period. The unexpected results of the application to industry and to social life of the discoveries of chemistry, of electricity, and of mechanics were making an impression upon the mobile imaginations of the artists before all the others, and although by habit they are far removed from the utilitarian movement of the century, they showed themselves this time strongly disposed to accept its guidance. The literary men meet at the lectures of Claude Bernard. The painters interest themselves in the discoveries of Chevreul, who really does no more than prove that which had already been guessed by Titian, Tintoretto, Veronese, Greco, Rubens, Rembrandt, Velasquez, Watteau, Chardin, Reynolds, and Goya, that which was known by Constable and Delacroix, but which, when rigorously demonstrated, will enchant the French mind, enamored, even in the domain of the creative imagination, of clear reasons and of visible truths. The literary constraint to which the

Courbet. Woman bathing (*Private collection*).

romanticists submitted yields, after Courbet, to scientific constraint, and the artist passes almost without transition from the prison of the subject into the prison of the object.

This attempt to return to sources had nothing new about it save its scientific method, which, indeed, was

MILLET.   Haymaking (*Louvre*).

what rendered it decisive. At the very time of the antagonistic triumphs of Ingres and of Delacroix, the painters had left the studios and the Schools to return to "nature," in an outburst of sentiment, whose first origin must be sought in the influence of the *Nouvelle Héloïse*, the *Confessions*, and the *Contrat Social*. The city was a place of perdition for the man of sensibility. He could renew the innocence of his vision only by contact with the earth itself, source of the eternal youth of forms in metamorphosis, and of the heart, to which it gives back calmness and purity. An excess—the opposite of the abuse of the Museum and of the creative excitation of the cities—it was an ascetic assent to keep turning in the same circle, to see nothing of the desires and the urge of one's epoch, and to drug oneself slowly with the opiate of a personal formula, and with the increasing shadow of habit and forgetfulness. Delacroix is far more solitary at the center of the brutal cities which he forces to gravitate around his own mind, than are these romantic peasants, exiling themselves in the solitude of the woods, and in the stifling desert of a sentiment which dries up in advance the springs that the fever of living would open up in them each day. A landscapist—Michel—is so solitary that his very life is almost unknown, although the soul of Rembrandt sometimes crosses his path. Two painters remain at Barbizon throughout their lives. Rousseau, so moving at times, when he uses only his pen and notes his direct impressions, those that one keeps for oneself—measured, balanced, clear cut, musical, and composed like all those which the French masters of drawing have left us, from Claude and Poussin to Vernet and Corot—Rousseau falls asleep at the edge of his eternal marshes, whose color, of an uncertain violet, he finds again in the solitary oaks and the moist twilights where his sadness seeks a poetic intoxication, ending in ennui. Millet believes—or rather people believe since the time of Millet—that the reading of the Bible suffices to give them the sense of the world, and that poverty, simply and stoically borne, will render him worthy to sing of the existence of the lowly among whom he lives. A double error, from which there will be no escape, either in his feeling for the country—now epic, now Virgilian, or in his cult of

MILLET. Women bathing (*Louvre*).

Michael Angelo and of Poussin, or in his admiration for Delacroix, or in his friendship for Daumier, who comes alone from Paris, from time to time, to brandish the flame of his genius over Millet's obstinate habits. It is true that he plowed, when a boy, and that he went about in a blouse and in wooden shoes, but that is of no importance to us. It is true that during a journey in Auvergne, that arid and austere country, stained like an old cloak, he scrupulously studies the inner structure of the earth, and produced some admirable images, as pure as a Japanese drawing, as firm as a German drawing. It is true that in his peasant Georgics, there are reapers bending with the same movement, sowers with their lengthening shadow, men driving their spades into the ground, and all those simple figures of the noble, sad fatefulness of labor, with the feeling of sculptural expression in the forms, which exist in space solely through their broad surfaces and their expressive planes. But with him, this feeling is more poetic than plastic, and too often, when we descend beneath the plane of the idea, the form sounds hollow. And if his drawing is always sober and sometimes decisive, his painting—save for a few superb exceptions, the "Rainbow," the "Church," the "Harrow," and two or three splendid portraits—is muddy and dull. Of all those herds under the moonlight, of all that smoke of half-hidden villages, of all those muffled voices heard at the level of the furrows, and of all those distant murmurs of the "Angelus" and of faint bells, perhaps there will remain one day no more than a few broad flashes, caught by four strokes of the pen, and the memory of a power misled by being put at the service of a sensibility which we must respect, and of the artist's touching character.

If Daubigny, a good landscapist, had not gone to initiate himself in the beauties of the country close to

Rousseau and Millet, they would have exercised no influence upon the painters whose art was born at the meeting place of Courbet with scientific and literary materialism. And again, that influence is more moral than sensuous. The men who decide to turn their backs upon the School and the studio, in order to wipe from their eyes the soot of the museums and to ask of outdoor light the secrets of harmony, could not fail to hear that long protest against doctrinaire painting which was arising from the entire century, from Ingres, from Daumier, from Delacroix, and from Courbet, but which the pure landscapists expressed with more ingenuousness, if not with more force, than the others. Pissarro, enamored of theories and of systems, first of all follows Corot and Millet, and it is because he will set up his easel in a furrow, before a plowman with his plow, or before a herd of cattle, that he gradually discovers the nature of light and the quality of shadow, and on these discoveries builds the painting of the morrow.

The studio, the room where one paints, or even the falsified light of the street, all mask the object. The external world alone exists, man excepted, and only outdoor light reveals it as it is. Delacroix, to be sure, is a master; he rediscovered the laws of contrast and of association of colors which had almost been lost, but his imagination whirls him too high and too far, and carries his painting to a point where it is merely a symbolic expression—a step further, and it will be a literary expression—of the universe. And then he paints in the studio, and from memory. Courbet also, although he gets the facts, at least, and expresses them without commentaries. Millet and Rousseau certainly go to the open fields to seek their subjects, and in full daylight, but they limit themselves to making sketches, and then they come home and in the sad light of a

cottage or under a lamp, they plaster away at their
Christian Georgics and their idealized oaks.   Paul
Huet sees the fields, the forest, and the sky only through
a voluntarily dramatic feeling, whose majestic and
grandiloquent melancholy exasperates the young men,
who have been brought up in the idolatry of the naked
truth and in the increasing noise of the victory of

ROUSSEAU.   The tree, drawing

science over mystery, over doubt, over subjective
lyricism, and even over lyricism as a whole.   Corot,
to be sure, has a passionate sentiment for space and for
light, but even he paints from pencil- or pen-sketches,
which he combines at home; besides, one sees very
little of his painting; he keeps the best of it in his
studio, the remainder goes to the dealer.   And then
all have habits from which even the greatest have not

been able to rid themselves, and which nature, when directly interrogated, only rarely justifies, save under artificial illuminations and confined atmospheres: they oppose shadow to light everywhere, and connect all their tones by a gamut of intermediate semitones which are not to be derived from daylight.

Pissarro, who is becoming more and more unwilling to paint anywhere but in the open air, and who carries

CARPEAUX. Flora, high relief (*Tuileries*).

with him certain friends[1]—Claude Monet, Renoir, Sisley, and later Cézanne—discovers a young painter, Edouard Manet, who does not always paint out of doors, but who is the first man in Europe to have the audacity to lay one light color on another light color, to reduce the semitones to their minimum, or even to ignore them, and almost to suppress modeling by

[1] About 1862.

juxtaposing or superimposing strokes bound by a line, which is very firm, but which detaches from a background purged of shadows that might serve as adjuncts. It is primitive painting in one sense, with brutal illumination from in front, a sheet of diffused light falling straight down and revealing the objects in brilliant silhouettes placed one on another, or one beside the other, like big pieces of cardboard or of cloth, and cut out clear in the full light.

It is a downright, violent, uncompromising painting, that runs counter to the whole of the routine education which, since the Renaissance, has been given to the eye by the smoke and flame of the museums, and every time that it appears in public it creates an uproar. It is a revolutionary painting which, in order to return to the sources, in order to temper the art of painting in them once more, dares to suppress certain of its profoundest acquisitions for the purpose of establishing it on fresher ground and of strengthening the tradition.

A Parisian of Paris, and belonging to a family of the old middle class, a pupil of Thomas Couture (a painter without intelligence, but gifted, and sometimes powerful) fed on Ingres and Delacroix and saluted by them in his initial efforts, he was perfectly acquainted with the masters; but he had gone instinctively toward those in whom he found anticipated the justification of his boldness, the Spaniards, the Flemings, and Frans Hals above all, who merely for the joy of the eye, without any pretext to anecdote, or the picturesque, or literature, combined colors with the swift movements and the infallible sureness of a woman assembling flowers, or sorting out materials for a dress or a hat. He studies Goya also, the magician who, in a second, by the combination of a few limpid tones, brings out of the void a hand, an arm, a look, a flower, or a violent hallucination. Manet goes to see their work in the

C. Guys. Woman seated, water-color (*Private collection*).

place where it was done, and after that he knows his way. Rose on rose, white on white, in strokes that live—the whole thing shimmers like a bouquet; everything sings, nothing marks out the form as projecting, because nothing opposes it among the clear tones in the space surrounding it or grading off behind it in the backgrounds. The picture sings rather loud at times, but it never sings false.

This almost complete suppression of the passage, of the intimate echoing of one tone in the neighboring tone, this vision, pure and cruel, which presents the world like a sheaf of living flowers, gives to Manet's painting a certain lack of continuity, a sense of clashing like a broad piece of light-colored material, in which different pieces, one as light as another, had been sewn in, here and there. The flesh, even that which contains the mouth and the eyes, is of no more importance to him than the pink of the cravat standing out against the black coat, the red slash made by the book whose blood color contrasts with the yellow carpet, the bed sheet with its blue reflections, and the reflections he sets trembling in the mirror of the glasses and of the knives. It is an immense still-life, a trifle scattered, a trifle disjointed, but of such power that, forty years afterward, it is still the channel for the invasion of painting by color and, behind color, the incursion of all the audacities, all the splendors, all the shining and fierce brilliance of the Orient.

And then, of the great painters, since the all too rare essays of Watteau and of Chardin (for Debucourt is only a chronicler, penetrating, witty, and tart, and Boilly is only a spinner of tales of every-day life, with all his simple good humor and all his fine shades), he is the first to seek in the street itself, in the cafés, and in the public gardens the plastic and living emotion which he will interpret directly. And since he is stroll-

ing about for three quarters of the day and working
the other quarter, like a good, improvising, inquisitive
Parisian, he is finding, at every moment, things he was
not even looking for. By no means is this any longer
the dramatic street that Daumier evokes so powerfully
in the burning mud in which he sculptures; it is the
street without transposition, with its diffused light, its
lively colors, the shimmering mosaic of its flags and of

JONGKIND. Marine, water-color (*Private collection*).

its show windows; it is the café with its tables and its
plate glass, its smokers, and its rouged women, and
the garden with its groups under the trees, clamorous
spots in which the garments, the hands, the hair, and
the faces break and re-establish the harmony in a
vigorous disorder. Eugène Lami, to be sure, is a fine
painter of the movements of the streets, of the race
tracks, and of the gardens, but the pomp and the setting overpower his style. Constantin Guys is the only
one at that period who knows also how to see forms

passing through the dust, as in a dream, the quiver of the sunlight, and the scintillation of jewels and of lamps, and who has left eternal images of the instant caught in its flight. But the art of Manet, which has less of profundity, less of style, and less of mystery, has more of singularity and more of innovating audacity, and it exerts infinitely more influence on its time. And then this is not a matter of sketches in an album; this is a question of great painting. Limpid painting, washed in like a water-color, as hard and cool as a faïence, as full of diversity as a basket full of woolen yarns, as living as a field of flowers, and as firm and pure in form as a Japanese lacquer.

VIII

Manet reveals to Pissarro the secret of painting frankly and without shadows; Pissarro, in turn, carries Manet with him to the fields, and shows him by his example, and especially by that of the virtuoso of the group, Claude Monet, that the open air suppresses not only modeling, but the very contour of the forms, and substitutes for local tone an infinite interchange of dancing reflections, tangled and indivisible, wherein the form hesitates and is submerged in the tide of the universe. Manet, following his new friends, will, after that, paint but little save in the open air. There shall be no more studies combined in the studio, whose attenuated and mournful light stifles the vibrations of open space, changes the color relations, renders pronounced the fixity of forms to the detriment of their moving surfaces, and condemns the eye to return, little by little, to its old habits of progressive gradations from the too artificial light to the too gloomy darkness. Now you plant your easel right out in the fields, and carve out a section of nature for the picture, which shall be painted all out of doors. Here is the woodland of Courbet, with its green penumbra and its dark leaves spreading over pebbles and brooks. But the sun pierces

MONTICELLI. A woman (*Private collection*).

the branches, sends upon earth and flesh bright, moving spots, and the shadow vanishes. Then the eye of the painter, at first dazzled by the sun's illumination, becomes steadier, insists, gradually recovers its vision, and distinguishes a phantom of shadow where at first it could no longer see anything. The shadow itself is light, it is transparent, it is airy, and the colors of the prism, according to the thousand tones standing next to one another, and according to the angle of the light, are decomposed in the shadow and transmuted there into gamuts of ever subtler shades which no one had ever observed before. Soon the object no longer has its personal color; the play of sun and shadow, all the wandering reflections in their network, and the variations of the season, of the hour, and of the second, impressed by the passing of the wind or the interposition of a cloud, sweep over the surface of the object a thousand changing and mobile tones which turn the husk of the world into a vast moving drama.

When the young men will have seen Boudin's paintings, in which the sea air holds in its meshes rigging and sails, and trembles with the vapor and the spray, when they have studied the water-colors of Jongkind, the Hollander, in which air, water, ice, and clouds are one liquid gulf, as deep as the ocean and as transparent as the sky, when Claude Monet and Pissarro have discovered, in London, the dancing fairyland of the wedding of the sun, of the twilight, of the mist, and of the sea, with which Turner's canvases dazzle the eyes, the renewal of painting will have been effected in their instinct. While Pissarro is striving to formulate principles, and recommends choosing the spectrum colors alone, proscribing any mixing of them, and advising that they be juxtaposed or crossed in separate, comma-like spots, Sisley, Claude Monet, Renoir, and Cézanne practice their eye upon the discovery of the incessant movement on the surface of life, and its changes from minute to minute, depending on the march of the sun and of the infinite and trembling

gulf of subtle passages, of complex reflections, of lights
in their interchange, and of the fleeting colorations
for which the universe of the air is forever the theater.

Pissarro continues his apostleship into the inhabited
landscape. Painting the red roofs, half-seen behind
the apple trees, and the low hills edged by the curtain
of the poplars and by the river, he demonstrates that

MANET. The Bar of the Folies-Bergères (*Private collection*).

even when, by means of a severe technique, one ob-
tains the maximum of aërial vibration and of luminous
splendor, one may remain the most discreet poet of
the intimacy of things, the friend of poor houses, a man
who knows that the trees have a thousand admirable
adventures between their winter poverty and their
summer wealth, a man who tenderly unfurls the humble movement of the plants grown on the hill slopes,
and their spontaneous and mobile harmony, always

MANET. The Luncheon on the Lawn, detail (*Louvre*).
(Le déjeuner sur l'herbe.)

in keeping with the light and the weather. Later on, when he sees all this less distinctly, he selects some high place from which to paint the great cities, the façades behind the leaves, where a thousand lively and subtle tones quiver in the diffused silver, the golden vapor on the river, and the distant swarming on street and sidewalk. Renoir delights in decomposing the grayest atmosphere and the most neutral light into opalescent prisms, in which the carmines, the strong reds, the pinks, the blues, and the violets of the jeweler, and the gems reduced to powder play, with the sun, over nude flesh, in order to pursue its contours into the transparent shadows, and to rediscover, little by little, and with increasingly startled emotion, its profound volumes. Sisley tells the tale of fêtes on the water, of flaky skies where the storm is collecting, of the vast shudder of the air and of the rivers around masts from which pennants fly, of suburban regattas, of the light wind blowing through the leaves and the grasses on the bank, and of the tremble of the particles in space, uniform and gray. Claude Monet is intoxicated by the light and at a distance of two centuries replies, through his lyricism under the excitement of free expanses, to the lyricism of Claude Lorrain inclosed in the rigorous architecture of the will and of reason.

He perceives the sun before all the others, even when it has not yet risen, and even when the sky is covered. Piercing the clouds, or from beyond the curve of the earth, the sun floods the universe with a powdery rain of rays which his eye alone sees. The sheet of light spread by the sun over the world is for him like an innumerable crowd, through which there wander, along intricately crossing paths, a hundred thousand colored atoms, which other men see in a block. He distinguishes the winter sun from the summer sun, and the sun of springtime from the sun of autumn. The sun at dawn and the sun at twilight are not the same sun as that which shone during the ten or fifteen hours elapsed between its rising and its setting. From minute to minute, he follows its appearance, its waxing and waning, its sudden eclipses, and its abrupt returns to the immense surface of the life

PISSARRO. Rouen, damp weather (*Private collection*).

whose character and pitch and accent are changed by each season, each month, each week, and by the wind, and the rain, and the dust, and the snow, and the ice. Here are a hundred images of the same water, a hundred images of the same trees, and they are like the laugh, and the smile, and the suffering, and the hope, and the disquietude, and the terror, on the same human face, according to whether full daylight or broad

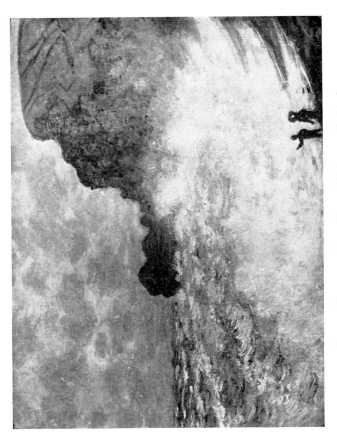

CLAUDE MONET.　The Wave (*Private collection*).

shadow reigns, according to all the gradations which separate broad shadow from full daylight. The form is still there, certainly, but it flees and steals away like that of those faces so mobile that the expression of their eyes and of their lips seems to float before them. In the work of this man, so much alive, what part does theory play? None. It adapts itself closely to the need of the moment and, in order to justify the form of art which, with Pissarro, for example, it presumes to govern, it utilizes the scientific systems in vogue at that moment. But what matter? The thing before us is water, sky, and an immense and changing light, in which there appear vaguely palaces, bridges, trees, cliffs, and towers, which tremble in the sea and in the river in a universal exchange, subtle, and dancing with reflections all tinted by other reflections, by moving and transparent shadows, and by sudden, unexpected bits of darkness and of light. Here are stretches of sea, here are sails, here are clouds floating between sky and water. Here are gloomy depths and illumined foam, and here are phantoms of flowers under the surface of the ponds. Here is the shadow of flowers mingling, in lively brooks, with the undulation of water plants. Here is everything that passes and trembles, that no one before him could arrest, and that continues to pass and to tremble when he arrests it. Here is the fog. Here are rime and frost. Here is the trailing smoke from trains and from boats. Here is the odor of burnt grasses, of flowering grasses, and of damp grasses. Here is the sudden cold vibration with which the wind freezes the colors of the world. When he paints the stones of the façades, the play of the sun and of the shadow and of the mist and of the seasons causes them to move like the surface of the trees, like the clouds of the air, and like the face of the water. He is the painter of the waters, the

CLAUDE MONET.   London (*Private collection*).

painter of the air, the painter of the reflections of the air and the water, of the water in the air, and of everything that floats, oscillates, hovers, hesitates, and comes and goes between the air and the water. A shadow passes, and deep in it one sees only the palpitation of a vague gleam, a distant spire, or the crest of a small wave; the light reappears, and everything comes back with it for a second, only to dissociate itself immediately and be bathed in the sun. Here Venice is his subject, here London, here some river of France, some canal of Holland, here the sea in Normandy, and everywhere the limitless empire of the air, of the light, of the dusk, and of the water.

Certainly, Claude Monet saw the Japanese prints, which Ingres had sought already, and whose influence, manifest in Manet, in Guys, in Whistler, in Degas, in Redon, and in Lautrec, increases from year to year in Europe, from about the middle of the century until toward its end. Like them, it tends to express the play of feature on the face of the earth, and the reflections of space in its eyes, which are the river and the sea. But whereas Hiroshige or Hokusai collects into a single image a hundred thousand impressions, scattered over his days from one end to the other, Claude Monet, in the impression of a second, gives a hundred thousand possible images of the season and of the hour when that second occurred. And the Oriental convention and the Occidental analysis arrive at the same result.

For the first and only time, doubtless, in the history of painting, the name given to this movement[1] is well applied, at least, if one limits it to the works of Claude Monet and of Sisley, to the larger part of Pissarro's

---

[1] In 1874, the public itself, in its indignation, spontaneously created the word Impressionism, from the title of one of Claude Monet's studies, "An Impression."

works, and to the first efforts of Cézanne and Renoir. It is the flashing visual sensation of the Instant, which a long and patient analysis of the quality of light and of the elements of color, in their infinite and changing complexity, permitted three or four men to seize. It neglects the form of things; it loses from sight, in its search for the exchanges of the universe, the line which limits them and the tone which defines them. It no longer sees anything but the luminous and colorful vibration of the husk of nature. But when it subsides and is transformed, it has cleansed the eye of the painters, enriched their senses by an enormous treasure of direct sensations which no one, previously, had known to be so subtle, so complex, and so living; had endowed their technique with a firm and new instrument; and, by its very refusal to compromise, had worked for the future liberation of the imagination which, until then, had been the prisoner of a plastic idealism and of a literary constraint whose fruits had all been gathered in the four or five hundred years before.

IX

This is an immense thing. And for that reason, all eyes have been fixed upon it for thirty years. While the Impressionists, in the face of the blindest and most commercial resistance, were pursuing their conquest of the light, the movements preceding their own, or parallelling it, were ending, or continuing, or outlining beside them, or within themselves, without anyone's perceiving that fact. This was the irresistible consequence of the social dissociation which was advancing with the same pace that they were. Between the solid construction of the artists who came forth from the Revolution and from its expression in romanticism, and the infinite fragmentation of the researches which were now being attempted, there was the same distance which separates the moral ideal of the triumph of the middle class from the new-born needs which it had itself delivered. At a time when Corot, Daumier, Millet, Courbet, and Puvis de Chavannes were still alive, it seemed as if they had been dead for years. Everything that was new, everything that was unexpected or personal, was called Impressionism, to ex-

SISLEY. The mills, winter (*Private collection*).

press people's hate for it, or love for it. Lépine, so classical in his delicate and clear-cut notations of the general aspects of nature, and who was indeed influenced by the group, was confused with it. Even after the final evolution of Cézanne and Renoir, people remained obstinate in classing them with Impressionism. Its visions of the sun and its analyses of the light were confused with the obscure symphonies and the analyses of darkness of Whistler, the American, an adroit

DEGAS. Women ironing (*Private collection*).

and subtle amateur, enamored of mystery and of
gleams in the shadows, but deriving, as Impressionism
did, from Delacroix, from Courbet, from Manet, and
from the landscapists of Japan. At its edges, and announcing it in advance by a few years, were the brief
and confused jets of flame of Monticelli, which few
saw moving in the penumbra. Under its banner were
ranged Degas and Toulouse-Lautrec who, the former
especially, had practically nothing in common with it.
However, these confusions explain themselves. The
naturalism of the last schools of the century, of which
Courbet is the apparent initiator, of which the scientific movement is the positive pretext, but of which
one can discover the manifold origins and the secret
course in all the social dreams and all the plastic
realizations which, since the Revolution, stirred the
sources of sentiment and of action, presents itself, in
its ensemble, as a violent struggle to acquire the elements of reality. But under the husk of the theories
and the systems, under the undulating surface of adventures and of manners and customs, that which persists is the temperament of man, the mode in which,
as he traverses the life of his epoch, he takes possession
of the spirit which circulates through the forms of the
universe and fixes itself in them. Naturalism, to be
sure, will know no more than the object, will submit to
its domination more and more closely for thirty years,
and will forbid itself to transpose, to imagine, to compose, to invent, and to ask myth and history for their
subjects; it will no longer be willing to do more than
open the window, copy the street and the people who
cross it, the sky, the trees, the markets, the assemblies,
and that which comes to pass, and that which passes.
But we shall see one man seizing, in this concrete
world, upon matter itself and the density, the savor,
and the evident external nature of the object. An-

other man will seize its color, the reflections which it welcomes and sends back, and the combinations of shadow and sunlight on its shaded surface. Still another seizes its form, the line which describes it and isolates it, its character, and its accent. And in the strong naturalistic unity which will deliver painting from the ball and chain of recipes and dogmas, and

DEGAS. Ballet girls (*Private collection*).

from the iron collar of the abstract ideal, this one will follow the indications of Ingres, that one of Delacroix, the other of Daumier or of Corot, and this other of Courbet, and all of them the ardent movement toward living color and form which characterizes painting since David.

This is what gives to the later movements of naturalism that appearance of being dissociated from one another, an appearance of analysis in its directions and its researches, and of lyricism in its sentiment, as always occurs, when men take possession of something of the unknown. From Delacroix to Seurat, Signac, and H. E. Cross, by way of the Impressionists, there is no interruption. But while joy seems to mount and broaden in the measure that the conquest of the sun approaches, with the vibration of the landscapes of the south carried to its apogee of violence, brilliance, and of light in its teeming movement, dissociation becomes more pronounced and, from one analysis to another, ends in the blind alley of a pictorial technique whence it cannot escape.[1] There is no deviation of direction and of influence from Ingres to Toulouse-Lautrec and, through Manet and Degas, to Seurat, the powerful, musical, and grave initiator of pointillism, the poet of the silent forms which wander in the quiver of the air and at the edge of sunny waters; and with his successors also there is no deviation. But the passionate and sensual realism of Ingres, and Manet's realism with its preoccupation with color and with plastics, tends, with Degas, toward documentation, grazes the anecdote with Toulouse-Lautrec, and turns, with their successors, to illustration, to a record of daily events, and even to caricature.

At least, it is in that direction that the study of the form in movement, and of gesture, in the street, the studio, the café, the theater, the race course, and the dance hall, has attained the sharpest rendering of immediate truth and of concrete character. There is no voluptuousness, none of the intoxication of arriving, beyond the form and the object, at wandering space, the infinite domain of the communion, like that of music, in which intuition causes all lines, all volumes, the whole succession of the planes, all relationships, and all the echoes of harmony to converge. Instead,

[1] See Appendix, (a), p. 497.

there is, with Degas, dried-up will-power, and a line that cuts like a knife. Whether his subject is a laundress with bare shoulders and arms, pressing down on her iron with both hands, or a group of dancing girls in the theater, in training to loosen their joints, or long race horses coming across the green to return to their stable, the gesture is so exact, although the muscle is not visible, that it seems to be followed and dissected by a steel point running with the current that throws it into relief. In the diffused light, everything appears livid, everything takes on the deadly aspect of the accessories of glass and of metal which modern life imposes on those who seek to forget it in the pleasures of the machine. The faces seem lit by the wan reflections from café tables, from spoons, saucers, and the absinthe on the counter. The angular and flabby bodies squatting in the pale metal of the tub with its splashing water, render hygiene as sad as a hidden vice. He shows us meager forms with protrusive bones, a poor aspect, harsh and distorted, of the animal machine when it is seen from too near by, without love, with the single pitiless desire to describe it in its precise action, unrestrained by any sense of shame, and without the quality of heroism which might have been given to the all too clear eyes by a lyrical impulse. There is loftiness of bearing in the vision without innocence which has rid itself of all desire to please, and which is eager to know in order to describe, and to describe in order to know. There is a constant sacrifice to the expression of the gesture, which is tenaciously followed in the most precise acts of the toilet, in the movement of climbing out of a bathtub, of raising the arms to twist or comb the hair, and of pressing the towel or the sponge on the breasts. As soon as his sharp eyes surprise the thinness of elbows, the disjointed appearance of shoulders, the broken appearance of thighs, and the

flattening of hips, he tells of all this without pity. And
yet it is strange that this Occidental, enamored of the
most disinterested truth, should often make us think
of some Oriental painter seeking to drown the disenchantment of his spirit in the richest and rarest tones,
broken at every moment, glistening, dying, and being

Toulouse-Lautrec.   The Moorish dance (*Private collection*).

reborn. It is a cruel art, rendered more cruel by the
flames and shadows carried across the flesh by the fires
of the footlights, which bring out the hollows and the
projections, but in which, at times, when the pastel
catches fire and flares up, there shines a poetic flash,
evoking, with the ballet girls swept along by the
whirlwind of the dance, with their glittering gauze and

make-up, some too brief dream in which the soul of some Watteau touched with acid, returning to wander under the artificial lights, might see phosphorescent butterflies flying up to them and breaking their wings.

With Toulouse-Lautrec, this dry flash is as if extinguished. The cruelty persists, turns to sadism, draws blood from the tarnished mouths, drags down the eyelids, oils the poor, flat hair, and renders more thin and wan the miserable flesh which is bought and sold in the market. Blanched drinkers, pale females, the dead glow of zinc bars, the sad, weary round of the café concerts and the dance halls, the moldiness beneath them, and the odors of pharmacies and pomades—everything that a strong century drags behind its conquering army in the shape of worn-out creatures of love, existing to console the wounded and the sick for having to live—all is violently evoked by Toulouse-Lautrec, with the leap of his line, the acid of his color, and the disjointed rhythm of his composition. It is the sinister face of pleasure, a last instinctive protest of agonizing Christianity against the rising intoxication of a universe accepted.

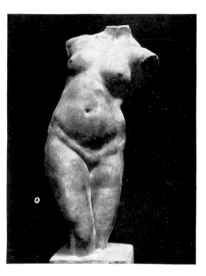

DALOU. Woman's torso, study.

X

And so it is finally to this acrid, over-sharpened work that the analysis comes. Romanticist pessimism, with its lyrical power, proud of its suffering, exalts voluptuousness. But since it depends too much upon its bitter conclusions, it leads straight to those images, after which there will be no more hope, save in a new Illusion. Here is Renoir, here is Cézanne, who are preparing an unknown world. One would think, though they are but little younger than the hard Manet and the cruel Degas, and but little older than the sinister Lautrec,—one would think that they belong, Renoir especially, to a new century. The world accepted in its indifferent strength, its sensual joy regained—all that which is contemporary with these clear-cut and somber works of art—will not mature in the mind until twenty or thirty years later. Fatigued by a hundred years of one of the most powerful efforts in history, the French soul of their period, penetrated by the tragic disenchantment of Schopenhauer, by the sensual Christianity of Wagner, and by the immense despairing murmur of the Russian novel, feels that what is nearest to it are the final and sudden awakenings of romanticist suffering, whose bitterness increases upon contact with the clear-eyed realism developing beside it and offering it new food. Even when it knows and reasons, perhaps then above all, the heart loves the Illusion. While the writers and painters of the document are pursuing their investigation, in solitude and without pity, the romanticism of Carrière and of Rodin absorbs into the sound of its lyric flight the voice of the truth which they know, and makes a heroic passage between consciousness, into which their time is sinking and carrying on its insistent effort, and the intoxication of the future which they feel to be growing up in them.

EUGÈNE CARRIÈRE. Portrait of the artist (*Private collection*).

At their beginnings, Carrière and Rodin are exact realists, the one rather hesitating, a little too moral and soft, the other penetrated by the double current of the sober practice of the stonecutter, and of an academic education which he is not sufficiently prepared to fathom or to reject. And here are the first collective portraits of the family and of childhood, and we see in them the traces left by Whistler's technique, doubtless, that of Courbet probably, certainly that of the good painter Fantin-Latour, and especially that of Renoir, whose mothers and nude children with the uncertain outlines of their soft flesh have been seen by Carrière; and here is the young "Age of Bronze," erect upon the threshold of the new time, like an antique image barely touched by its enervated disquietude. Then, with the sculptor's rising spirit and broadening knowledge, there grows up a lyrical movement which will burst the earlier form, so that new rhythms may be liberated. With the painter we find once more the sentimental thought which Millet started on its course and which, after having been rendered firm in the sculptural mind of Daumier, will finally result, after traversing the social idealism of the century, in the forms, sometimes epic, but almost always theatrical and hollow, of the Belgian sculptor Constantin Meunier. But with Carrière it takes on a didactic and metaphysical accent which will cause it to be accepted too quickly by the *littérateurs*, and too quickly forgotten by the painters. He knows, through Daumier and through Rodin, the power of the expressive volumes on which all the light falls; he has discovered the spirit which circulates from form to form, which draws them to a center, presses them outward, and beats against them as against a metal. Thereupon he follows that spirit alone; form is no longer more than a symbolic sign which he has not sufficiently studied and into which his desire is to precipitate the torrent of universal life rolling from his soul to his heart, and with this torrent, his love, which binds and cements the whole. In his vague arabesque, in the sinuous and continuing curves which make of his intertwined groups something like a single block of life, in which milk and blood, the carnal intoxication of the mothers, and the gluttonous

EUGÈNE CARRIÈRE. Sleep (*Private collection*).

avidity of the infants flow without interruption, to make round the breasts which are offered, to sculpture the skulls which press against them, and to unite the arms which seek each other, the great idea of transformism appears for the first time in painting, as something voluntary and conscious. It is too voluntary and too conscious, for it sees no more than itself, and tries to expose and impose itself; and it is only in the weakest manner that it kneads its clay around it, the material being but barely animated by reds and grays, in which the shadows are sometimes hollow, in which the projections are sometimes awkward, and the embraces are often swollen, as if wrought in some unknown matter from which the skeleton and the muscles were absent. Moreover, one divines in this whole art an irresistible need to subordinate to moral sentiment the plastic intoxication which, with the heroes of painting, subjugates, dominates, and sweeps along in its wake the highest moral sentiment. But a great idea broods over this work, and one sees it fumbling in the irregular movements of the new-born babes, rising with the growth of the children, lighting up as their astonished eyes open upon the world, and bursting forth with nobility in the images that he has given of the faces of certain men, and of himself. The thought is powerful, the work is uncertain, standing very high in sentiment, but disintegrated by irreconcilable forces and showing only the few distant summits which emerge from the mist accumulated in the backgrounds.

With Rodin, the last of the great romanticists, one who seems to assemble in himself, multiplied, the lyric power of the loftiest natures of romanticism and the structural impotence of the poorest men who were inspired by it, the preoccupation with expressing the spirit which circulates in all the elements of a group, diminishes, on the contrary, from work to work, in the measure that he accentuates the strength of the living detail, of the volume determined by the summit of the movement, and of the play of the lights and shadows on the vibrant surface over which rolls the wave of muscle. Often—too often, alas!—the gestures become contorted, the unhappy idea of going beyond plastics and of running after symbols creates groups in which the embracing figures are disjointed; the volumes fly out of their orbit, the attitudes are impossible, and, in the whole literary disorder, the energy of the workman melts like wax in the fire. Even in his best days, he lives and works by brief paroxysms, whose burning sensation runs through him in flashes. There is Impressionism in him. He is not slow in binding the center of his vision through sinuous lines and continuous passages with everything round about which prepares or propagates that vision. It is there, alone, tragic, like a cry in the silence. In order to express it, he does not even have to add a head or arms to a torso, or, under a face and a neck, to establish the torso which carries them. A quivering belly, a moving breast, or an agitated head, full of projections and hollows, imperiously alive and marked by the beat of the blood, the fluid of the nerves, and by thought, suffices him to create a work which makes everything around it seem neutral and dull. With an indication of movement, a spot of aquarelle on a drawing, or a colored vibration overlapping the lines or permitting them to overlap like a spatter of flame, twisting, sinking down, or launching forth, he renders the quiver of everything that is most furtive and most like the lightning in the very spirit of the form through which his mysterious life penetrates us incessantly.

The expression. Everything is sacrificed to that undefinable thing. Never did Rodin quite understand the French sculptors of the Middle Ages, whom he for a long time claimed to follow, and who, in their dominant preoccupation with saying what they felt, gave proof of so much balance and measure; and when, later, he turned to the philosophic sculpture of Greece, he did not, again, completely understand its meaning, and how it is prolonged beyond the passing moment, and what it is that causes its echoes to resound beyond the space in which it lives. And that is not necessary, and his desire to seek in the past for corroboration is perhaps that which is smallest and least pure in his nature, that which has too often led him to tricks of plastics which would swamp his work if a sensual and spiritual force did not almost always uplift it.

In reality, like all the romanticists, this sculptor is a painter above all, and, more than any other among the romanticists, unsuited to erecting a monumental en-

Eugène Carrière.   The kiss (*Private collection*).

semble wherein the architecture of the world should appear summarized.   All the palpitations and all the inner leaping of the life of expression produce a sonorous undulation which the light on the surface of the form gathers up, in order to set it vibrating, like a string under the fingers.   The dance sends into the life of expression the quiver of its muscle; the sobs of music convulse its depths.   Since Rembrandt, no one had so powerfully brought up, from within the living masses, the living spirit which stretches, or breaks, or relaxes the muscles, swells the breasts, and causes them to move, rolls and furrows bellies, marks out the bones of the face, and escapes from the open eyes.

It is thus that subterranean force gives to the ravaged face of the soil its irregular modeling. The sculpture of the whole century had labored sufficiently to bring to the point of culmination of the attitudes in action the inner fluid which determines their form. While Pradier, the "Athenian of the rue Bréda," is continuing Falconet, Clodion, and Chinard, by disrobing frail goddesses in his very Parisian apartment, Rude transports movement into stone. The great Barye who, near Rodin, seems as calm as an antique, because he conceives form in the ensemble, as an architect does, builds organically, spreads and distributes movement through the muscles and the skeleton, accumulates it in jaws and paws, and, under the vibrating planes, keeps his wealth of energy at high tension. The movement gathers itself together and bounds, cracks with the crushing bones, wrinkles at the muzzle of the wild beasts, shines at the level of their flat heads with the eyes like burning stones, and lays their ears straight back in anger or in fear. One would say that the artist courts with it all the scattered, hidden, or quivering sources of power in the world, to concentrate them into the active or reposeful mass, beating with palpitations and traversed by waves of force, as the Egyptians concentrate, in their composite monsters, the light and the spirit as they wander. Dalou, at first far too much vaunted, and then, for political reasons, a little too much forgotten, surprises it at times in the fold of a feminine torso, the gentle hollows, the dimples, and the fat curves of the flesh. Carpeaux sees it springing from all the surfaces, causes it to shine forth from teeth, mouths, glances, feet, hands, knees, hair—the whole nude skin calling forth dancing flames from the whirlwind which he whips to frenzy, with the movement of the nervous limbs, the fleshy torsos, and the round breasts, and to the sounds of festive music leading a brilliant, light, and cynical world to the ditch filled with blood. In his work, the movement turns

C. MEUNIER. Bas-relief, bronze.

in a circle, vivifying everything, but not knowing where it can come to rest. Rodin comes to this work to gather up its movement from its summits alone; as he animates them, and as he penetrates through them to its very center, to the burning focus whence the movement radiates, he attaches them to it directly, no longer perceiving on the whole husk of life anything but the living impulse which arises from its depth.

It is thus that he expresses, with dramatic lyricism,

Rodin. Eve, bronze (*Musée Rodin*).

that which is most unseizable in life, and that which
is most permanent also. Love haunts him, because it
is love which brings about in the forms that seek
each other and unite at its call, the strongest expression
of forms given over to the tragedy of their fate and
sent rolling into indifference toward morality and toward
death by a power higher than morality and death. It
is in vain for "Eve" to hide her face in her arms; she
is victorious; behind her flesh, already sinking and losing its freshness, she drags men, beasts, the plants, the
oceans, the stars, and a whole troop of slaves following her scent, as the wave of dead leaves runs in the
wake of the wind. Here are pitiful couples united by
the cohesion of love. The man tries to flee the outstretched lips, to tear his devoured skin from the other
devouring skin, to lift his athletic torso above the
breasts which undulate and breathe like the sea. He
cannot. He is held there by his soul, whose merging lyricism and revolt boil up at each of those
contacts of mad couples who seek, in their fusion, forgetfulness of thought and of the void. When the embrace unlocks, there is clotted blood on the bodies and
the limbs, which have been laid open and bruised like
those that have been on the rack. The bodies,
rolling with every flux and reflux of the spasm, are
like the damned of Dante, at once drawn together
and repelled by the burning within them. It is impossible for the spirit to tear itself from the flesh and
from the soil, because there is, in the flesh and the soil,
a spirit more universal than itself; it is only a fragment
of that universal spirit, turning in space around its
motionless force and seeking to escape it. The "Hand
of God," in which sleeps the embryonic form, need
only close in order to crush the intelligent larva which
palpitates as it assumes its rudimentary form in the
primeval clay. The "Thinker," in his harsh tensity,

over the gate by which one enters hell, is animated by the same spark which, around him, convulses birth, youth, love, the death struggle, and death itself. The will, being less powerful than hunger, "Ugolino" crawls, like a filthy beast, on his hands and knees. The portraits cling to the earth, which rises in them from everywhere, with the soul and its majesty. The "Balzac" is like those menhirs which the elementary forces seem to erect on our roads. The "Claude Lorrain" has worn-out boots, a clumsy bearing, and awkward gestures, but its face is dazzled by the light. And if the "Apollo," whose every step causes sunlight to burst forth, has vanquished the hydra, his two arms remain fixed to the stone of a pedestal.

RODIN. Woman's torso, plaster.

One would say that Rodin rose from the soil and from the flesh in order to reach the tragic spot to which Michael Angelo descended from the summits of the intelligence, and in order to utter the cry of the earth as he meets him who brought us the cry of heaven. Whether their starting point be the senses or the mind, materialistic pessimism and Christian pessimism meet halfway, in order that, through orgy or through knowledge, they may teach despair. Incredible obstinacy of the greatest natures in accepting neither their senses nor their soul. Sublime also since, apparently, this conflict is necessary, every thousand or two thousand years, for the gaining of a higher equilibrium between senses and souls, and of resignation to the intoxication of living, whose intensity is multiplied by their agreement.

RODIN

RODIN

AIX-EN-PROVENCE

Chapter VIII. THE CONTEMPORARY GENESIS[1]

I

F the work of Cézanne did not interpret with singular power a thoroughly general desire that was willed by our character, it would not have suddenly gained that ascendancy which has gone beyond the borders of France and has brought Europe flowing back to it, in quest of a new intellectual order. While the fugitive impression and the fact without commentary were establishing around him the endless and yet so quickly exhausted motif

[1] PUBLISHER'S NOTE.—This chapter was revised since the publication of the original French edition of the *History of Art*, and will appear only in the definitive edition in French. We thank M. Elie Faure and M. Georges Crès, his publisher, for having authorized us to reproduce the new version from the manuscript.

of literature and of painting, his work suddenly appeared like a refuge, coarsely but solidly built, and glowing with its somber harmony, in which the artist could find the elements of new generalizations, and through which he was constrained to pass. It presented so radical a type of opposition to Impressionism that it was but natural that men should try to condemn, in the name of Cézanne, that movement of purification and of research which was so necessary for us. This is the usual rise and fall of the balance between action and reaction. In reality, the work of the master of Aix continued, completed, and terminated Impressionism, and reassembled, in view of a new construction, the materials which it had selected and contributed.

The work of Paul Cézanne was even confused for a long time with that of the masters of Impressionism. He occupied a secondary place in the group, standing a little in the background, between Guillaumin and the charming Berthe Morizot. That was quite natural. He was of their age. He had become their companion during their trying times. He exhibited with them. The public linked him with them in its censure, although he was already in advance of them, and although the Philistines of 1875, who condemned Claude Monet in the name of Delacroix or of Courbet, could not foresee that the Philistines of 1900 would condemn Paul Cézanne in the name of Claude Monet. He had made the acquaintance of the founders of the group about 1862, when he met, at the atelier Suisse, the fiery Pissarro, who initiated him into Courbet's painting. Zola, his companion from childhood, took him to Manet's studio. His tense and fierce sensibility loved the independent nature of his new friends, their passionate ardor, and the power of enthusiasm revealed by their words. He followed them to Auvers-

CÉZANNE. Woman sewing (*Private collection*).

sur-Oise, where they revealed to him the play of reflections on surfaces, where he watched with them the passage of the wind over the water, the eternal undulation of the leaves, and the shadow which the clouds carry over the soil and over the red roofs of the houses, and through the tremble of the flowering apple trees and cherry trees. To them, in spite of his education and habit, he was indebted for the clean eye, the probity of intelligence, and the original and unknown power of his blood. With their aid he shook off the influences which had been tyrannizing over him for fifteen years: Courbet, then Daumier, then Delacroix, then, though less had been seen of his work, Corot; then, working backward over the traces of their souls, Rubens, Veronese, and Michael Angelo. To his friends he was indebted for the laboriously and slowly gained freedom from the despotic seduction of the great works, the freedom to consider the heroes of painting not as guides whom one is in duty bound to follow, but as witnesses whom one has the right to invoke. When he returned to Aix-en-Provence in 1879, he was still far from perceiving in himself the regular and powerful beat of the unknown rhythms which he brought to us later. But he had at least a pure, high-keyed palette, and the moving face of the world impressed upon his sensibility its most fleeting and living images, those freest from literary or sentimental interpretation. That was what he owed to Claude Monet and to Pissarro. And he never forgot it.

It was at Aix itself that he was born, forty years before. It was at Aix that he had lived a studious and wild childhood, that he had learned from Vergil the love of the classic soil and of measure in art; there, with the young Zola, he had spent the days of his vacations, like a little faun drunk with sunlight and cool water, spending nights in the depths of the woods, and the burning hours in the rivers, drying his sunburnt skin in the eternal wind which, through the corridor of the Rhone, whirls the dust of the roads and the pulverized marble of the circuses and the aqueducts. When he returned there, he was alone. No more pagan illusions, no more friends. His art at the time was a weapon which shone, certainly, but which he

CÉZANNE.   Still-life (*Private collection*).

handles unskillfully. Around him was indifference, slander, folly, prejudice, and a total lack of comprehension of what he was, of what he desired, and of the torturing sensibility which drove him to take refuge in himself, to avoid unknown faces, and to flee the obligatory conversations and visits which make up three quarters of the provincial adventure. This wild, badly dressed man, who lived on his income and who painted, was certainly a lunatic. People spoke of him with severity. He was ridiculous, besides, clean, to be sure, but with spots on his coat; and his red nose, his watery eyes, his small twisted beard, and the impression he gave of being hunted set the whole pack of street boys upon him. The poor loved him, for he had an open hand. But no one took him seriously. Certain people exploited him. And moreover, as he did not wish anyone to "get his hooks" into him, he drew back into himself, like life when it is so sensitive that every hostile or rough shock from without wounds to its depths.

He suffered. No one knew that. He held out until the end. He could have lived in Paris, and found friends and admirers, and their encouragement. He did not wish to. He shut himself up in his strength, fixed his inner images, and around him, sought that which confirmed them. Sometimes he returned to Paris, where he passed three quarters of his time in the Louvre of Veronese, of Courbet, and of Rubens. He made two or three short sojourns in Flanders and Holland. He desired to know nothing of Italy, as if he had feared that contact with the great works which attracted him above all others, would corrupt his growing resolve to reach his own ideas. And that is all. When he regained his native soil, the history of his life was ended. That of his mind was opening.

Those landscapes of Provence, bare and rigid, those red lands sown with thin trees and rising toward the rocky hills whose profile against the dark sky is so pure, and that reddening gold which bathes them at twilight without veiling their fixed lines, were very soon to furnish him with the elements of a plastic vision which he would perhaps never have discovered in the heavily watered luxuriance of the valleys of the north. In Provence the houses pile up like stones, the leaves do

CÉZANNE. Landscape (*Private collection*).

not conceal them, the angles of the roofs and the walls
cut from the light geometrical figures which bring the
mind naturally to simplifications for which it finds
reason in the dry, hard bareness of the rocks which bar
the horizon, of the sky which is generally without
clouds, and of the trunks stripped of leaves which shoot
up straight and clean, cutting through space at regular
intervals. From no other place could he have drawn
more naturally the desire for a sober form, shorn of
ornaments, of puffery, and of incident, a form firmly
based upon the soil, heavy, deep rooted, and reduced
to those masses alone and those lines alone which define
its relationships. Each time that he found himself in
the presence of a bare wall, of a road, of a motionless
pond surrounded by stone bluffs, or a vast space described by the granite chain of the mountains of the
country—something straight, rigorous, and categorical
—he held the central motive of the poem of color
which floated in his inner vision, and which he was
ceaselessly seeking to confront with the nature of the
senses, in order to justify it and to build it. The
houses, the roads, and the hills of Provence brought to
the massive lyricism of the painter the monotonous,
but compact, sonorous and full rhythm in which his summary phrase voluntarily inclosed itself in order to express the ordered conception which he had of the
world. It was as if great verses were unrolling with
force, laden with mind, hard with condensed matter,
and moving with a powerful swing to strike the rhyme,
as if to cause the image to penetrate more profoundly
by keeping it at the summits of memory and sensation
alone.

The unfinished appearance of Cézanne's canvases
gives to those who have not a rounded understanding
of his thought, the impression of an incomplete nature,
limiting itself to taking notes of the world, which are

essential, doubtless, but summary, and instinctively seized on the wing. Each one, in reality, represents enormous work, and a spiritualization, progressively and laboriously obtained, of exactly those sensuous elements which constitute the origin of all his painting. He was wont to say that all the forms in nature may be reduced to the cone, to the cylinder, and to the sphere, and this saying has had its victims. At bot-

CÉZANNE.   Sainte-Victoire (*Private collection*).

tom, it was only a symbolic manner of expressing the final appearance which the forms *tended* to assume in an abstract universe, whose imaginary limits he took good care not to overstep, when he had the palette in his left hand and the brush in his right. His imagination, quite unsuited to extend itself over surface, however weakly, developed its power when he treated the question of depth. Never has there been an artist less capable than he of inventing and combining figures,

of finding in the myth, the event of daily life, or the
personal dream, a pretext for exalting and transforming the images. The Spaniards themselves, Velasquez,
Zurbarán and Greco—not to speak of Goya, a satanic
poet of lust and of death—and perhaps the Hollanders,
knew less badly than he how to transport the immediate, outer world into an imaginary world. He seemed
to copy what he saw, he tried to recover that innocence
of the first ages of life during which curiosity awakens
—it is that innocence which, with the man who knows
much, having thought much and suffered much, borrows the language of the most self-conscious will in
order to assume the majesty and the power of the law,
stripped of all commentary. His candor was a victory.
His impotence to imagine assumed singular appearances, which would awaken doubt of his power of creation if the plastic quality of his work, comparable with
that of the greatest, were not there to reassure us. In
illustrated books, in the History of Charles Blanc, in
the *Magasin pittoresque*, and even in fashion journals,
he hunted up external silhouettes which he enlarged
and colored like a child, incapable of inventing a gesture or an attitude which should combine harmoniously
with the attitudes and the gestures round about. He
did not invent, he could not invent. It was only
"from the motif" that he knew how to abstract and
to simplify—to the ultimate limit of abstraction and
simplification, remaining uniquely, and despite everything, a painter and nothing but a painter, perhaps, in
truth, the most intense, and the most completely
bound up with the matter of which things are made,
that ever existed.

The universe, in fact, is for him only a pretext for
holding, within an architecture reduced to its soberest,
but also solidest, expression, a matter magnificent and
dense, in which the rocks which pierce the crust of the

Cézanne. L'Estaque (*Luxembourg*).

earth seem to have been pulverized in order to harden, unite, and condense the red soil, the dark foliage, the thick azure, and the lusterless seas of the Mediterranean countries. He took as his pretext the great denuded landscapes, the figures encountered at random on the road, among the people around him, and at the inns of the country—peasants, children, card players around a rough table, women in old-fashioned house dresses, or else those round, heavy fruits which he would throw down on the table amid the unwashed glasses and the half-filled wine bottles. Whatever he painted, he knew well that in starting out from the sumptuous materials with their dark splendor which he drew from one aspect of life as well as another, and in never losing sight of the great, summary lines between which he perceived them, he would gradually succeed in giving to his form the most powerful volume, and in making it turn in space like those geometrical figures which expressed in spiritualized language the directions of his glance. "When color attains its richness," he used to say, "form attains its plenitude." [1] The one met the other halfway, sought it out, and defined it little by little, in the measure that it gained in opulence, in somber light, and in heavy maturity. The tone appeared to him like an actual secretion of the form, which itself appeared to him like a gradation of the tone. . . . I imagine that in the depths of the silent hearts of the old sculptors of the Middle Empire of Egypt, those who erected the statues, dense, and defined by receding planes, and who saturated the compact grain of their granite with indigo, red ochre, and with emerald, there must have trembled something of the brief fervor followed by the restlessness of despair which beat in Cézanne's heart when, after weeks of exhausting effort, he had been able to wrest from mystery one of those

[1] Cited by Emile Bernard.

somber harmonies, as much a thing of architecture as
a temple, which have revealed painting to those worthy
of loving it.

In nature, there is for him no other "subject" than
the plane. It is but of little importance that the object be exactly followed in all its contours and finished
in all its details. That which is necessary is, that it be

CÉZANNE.   Landscape (*Private collection*).

in its place in the depth of space as regards the other
objects, that, at the same time, the gradations of its
edges give it its own existence, and that the object,
in relation to the world, and the world in relation to
the object, possess complete solidarity. He leaves to
those who will come after him the care of polishing the
phrase, of rounding the period, and of animating the
recital. He put the straight or curved surfaces in their

place, like a mason, whose hands are rough, but whose mind is made up of the sense of balance he has acquired, of the calm of his will, and of subtlety. His landscapes have the appearance of a section of the planet seen from a far distance, stripped of its local life, and reduced simply to the essential masses which define its construction. His personages are placed like living statues, frequently awkward and ill squared, but forcefully defined by sustained planes and by profiles whose clearness is uninterrupted by any useless accidental. His still-lifes have the splendor of the heaps of fruit which concentrate into themselves the whole of surrounding life, and which seem to send forth their full and spherical form and their color in its saturation, from the innermost center of their matter. The most immediate and the most material sensation, which is always present with him, is ever carried by the mind of the painter to its maximum of severity, of purity, and of comprehension.

"I remain," wrote Cézanne at the decline of his career, "I remain the primitive of the road which I have discovered." [1] "The archaic," he might have said. There is in the work of this master an impersonal and general character very different from the spirit of minutiæ manifested by the primitives, and this quality of Cézanne's gives to his work a sense whose importance he himself never suspected. As primitivism announces the advent in history of the individual, archaism is at the beginning of the great collective rhythms. . . . Whenever one of his pictures of former years was presented to Cézanne, he did not wish to see it and, in his own mind, judged very severely those who liked such things. He forgot his canvases as soon as they had left him. They lay about everywhere, under cupboards and behind furniture; they were used to wipe

[1] Emile Benard.

CÉZANNE. Card-players (*Private collection*).

the stove and the floor. A childhood game of his son's was cutting out the windows and the doors in them. He sometimes abandoned them in the open fields. He rarely signed them. Like all the great anonymous men, he expressed a kind of social need, going beyond the individual in order to erect one of those grand essays of rudimentary architecture which announce in society a unanimous movement of concentration in depth. He went regularly to church. A sincere Catholic, fleeing the priest and the bigot, he was evidently seeking in the past the shelter of one of those imposing social structures which he did not find in the present and did not suspect in the future. There is nothing less sentimental and less moral than his work. There is no anecdote; no thought of pleasing or of interesting. It is a pure metaphysical monument, and the materials with which it is built and which make it perceptible to the senses are the most thoroughly tested and chosen, but also the most summarily cut, in the world. Even when he tries to compose, as in those extraordinary gatherings of nude personages where, visibly haunted by the memory of Poussin, he makes an awkward attempt, amid the great choir of the trees, of the vast sky, and the running waters, to build up a broad sensual melody, even then he is absolutely free of any kind of psychological or literary intention. And even then, his classicism, that need for order and for measure which had been pursuing him since childhood, is unaware of its own significance. He, the provincial, the Catholic, is in accord with the secret rhythm of his century; he is urged on toward the unknown organism hesitating on the threshold, by profound forces of which he is no more conscious than were the masons of the last Romanesque churches whose nave was suddenly to leap, lighten, elongate, and hover like a wing, with the generation which was arising. A lofty and lucid intelligence, as long as there is question of building with the incomparable material which the generosity of his nature permitted him to discover and to isolate in the world, he is, even so, surpassed by the grandeur of his influence. And it is

RENOIR. Woman at a table (*Private collection*).

for that reason that this influence cannot be exhausted save by the realization of the organism awaited.

The end of this great man is well known. He took sick one day when he was working in the country to arrest upon a canvas the inexhaustible movement which was revealing to him, by its perpetuity and its constancy, certain concordant directions and certain eternal aspects. He expired two days afterward, and no one, outside of a few dozen artists, knew of it. And this was well. He had always disdained homage and despised those who abase themselves in order to surprise it or to force it. He had desired that solitary life which, to the end, he protected, against the assaults of fools, by outbursts of noble and savage modesty, for which no one understood the necessity and the reason. The shadow which hovers around us from the time when we are forty years old, did not, even if it grazed his heart, turn him away from a mission whose importance he felt, and neither did his tardy and restricted, but so lofty, renown turn him away from it. He knew himself to be the greatest painter in Europe. When one has that power within one, one may go forward alone.

II

Indeed, one is in oneself a multitude. One is the center of a whirlwind of scattered forces, ignorant of one another, and the testimony to which must be sought in social phenomena. When the artist wishes to compose, it is certain that his desire responds to those general desires which were formerly called religious or metaphysical, and of which, most of the time, he is ignorant himself, because they do not interest him. Composition, the subordination of all the parts of a work of art to some idea of rhythm and order, is not an external thing, dependent on an individual caprice or a passing fashion for its rejection or adoption. The mystic sentiment of a work to be undertaken in common goes beyond the individual. And painting, the most individual, and the most intellectual of the arts, either remains uncertain on all its frontiers, or else concentrates itself in some anonymous and summary form in which the archaic outline of an unknown architecture appears. The love of an ancient order, classical or religious, is only the most puerile manifestation

RENOIR. Woman dressing her hair, pastel (*Private collection*).

of this universal need. It is the rôle and the destiny of the most innocent of men—he who labors or he who thinks—to gratify this need.

Thus, while Courbet's and Manet's materialism of form was, through the Impressionists and the Neo-Impressionists, approaching the end of its investigation, while the moral current born of its pitiless decisions was introducing acid and vitriol into painting, through Degas, through Toulouse-Lautrec, and through the ferocious Forain, at the heart of the movement itself, an unknown force was organizing itself and attempting, through Cézanne, to give architecture to the universe, outside of all sentimentalism, and, through Renoir, to recreate a sentiment indifferent to moral purposes, by seeking, in the play of the reflections and of the lines revealed by matter itself, a harmony without object.

For let us make no mistake. There are no works more distant from each other in aspect, or nearer in essence and in direction, than the one created by that man of the will, bringing nature to obey the systems he built up in order to react against the disorder of the time, and that of the man of instinct, finding in nature, without apparent effort, forms which wed each other, and colors which penetrate each other, in order to react against the despair of the time. Anarchy is pessimistic, and what is more, sad. Those who have traversed its hell find no repose save in the power to create order and health for themselves, or else in death.

The powerful man, in order to recover joy, has no need to flee the cities, and to go, with Gauguin, to live among the primitives of to-day—as the pre-Raphaelites, victims of the same sickness, lived among the primitives of former times—and to build up, in distant islands, the burning landscapes whose tense and confused sensuality does not dissimulate either their slightness or their softness, and which halt at the façade

of the Cézannian edifices.   He does not permit himself
to be vanquished before his hour, in the manner of van
Gogh, the Hollander, a great heart burned by the
flaming earth he paints, by his electric waters, by his
trees and grasses crackling like tongues of fire, his
roads, his houses, his harvests, his figures, and all the

Renoir.   The Opera-box (*Private collection*).

faces of man, convulsed, warped, and battered as if they
were expressing some conflagration, subterranean or of
sentiment, with this painting of precious stones and of
yellow gold, these drawings whose swarming life over-
powers one, this rain of gnawing acids in which the
soul and the senses are corroded, and this desire
for wild joy, of an apostate ascetic.   The powerful man is not mad.   And he is simple.   He hums a

tune while he paints, and is bored when he is not painting. It is certain that he suffers, in his heart, like anyone in misfortune; and his bones are twisted with pain. But he never complains. He says he is only too happy to have kept the sight of his eyes, those miraculous eyes, mirrors of the world, gray and gentle and sad, sometimes sparkling with the mischief of the young painter, in his withered face, bent, lengthened by his white beard, and so noble—recalling that of Titian when he was almost a hundred years old. "It is he," he says, "who looks like me. He has stolen my tricks from me." He does suffer, as a matter of fact. But in his nature dwells the mysterious joy which he recovers instantly at the depths of his wasted organs and his twisted joints, the moment that he seizes his brush; and it is immense, pure, full of movement, undulating, and renewing itself from the depths, like the source of a great river, overflowing with sinuous forms and with waves of changing tones, which penetrate one another, obedient to the fecund rhythms of a sensualism grown more rich, more moving, and more complex in the measure that sickness and age dry him up and weaken him a little more. How long ago it is—the time when, a little astonished, a little respectful, and a little inclined to jest, he listened to the passionate demonstrations of Pissarro, and, standing beside Claude Monet on the banks of the Seine or of the Marne, watched the mottling of the water and the mottling of the leaves under the wind, the round spots of the sun on flesh and on the earth, and the vibration of the air in the silence of the summer! In those days he had muscular hands, which caressed the surface of the world. Now with his feeble hands he twists the world in depth.

The history of Renoir—born at Limoges, the country of masons, potters, and enamelers—is even of less im-

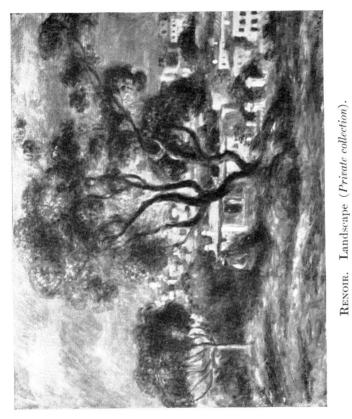

RENOIR. Landscape (*Private collection*).

portance than that of Cézanne, for he does not seem to
have struggled to discover his innocence. He had
perhaps nothing factitious, or almost nothing, to elim-
inate. He did not continually prune off, like Cézanne,
but rather added constantly. He belonged, like Cézanne, to the Impressionist group and shared its un-
popularity; later on its success. He continued, like
Cézanne, to receive the collective hatred or admiration
vowed to those who composed it, by a public enamored
of classifications as definitive as they were unprecise.
For the public he must, again like Cézanne, still belong
to the group, although both of them departed from it
to such a point that one and the other may pass as the
prophets of the movement in the opposite direction
which has followed it. It was, indeed, by watching
the reflections on the bark of the poplars and the oaks,
on the rippling banks of clouds, on the skin of his nude
women, and on the full-blown petals of the anemones
and the roses, by pursuing them in the flight of the
planes, and the sinking of the luminous shadows, that
he turned around the forms with those reflections and
those shadows, and bound up the mass of the universe
with the lyrical movement of his mind. He necessarily
underwent the evolving influence of the greatest among
the greatest painters, Masaccio, Titian, Tintoretto,
Velasquez, Rembrandt, Watteau, and Delacroix; and,
starting out from Claude Monet, he rejoins Rubens by
crossing the world of the flesh with its movement and
its sensations, and he will subject it to his increasing
strength, and constrain it to burst forth again from him
with the regularity, the simplicity, and the constancy
of the harvests issuing from the soil. Whereas Claude
Monet started out from the immediate form realized by
Courbet and Manet, while he pursued the moving
tremors made by the light on the changing husk of the
form and rendered them more and more subtle, Renoir,

taking as his point of departure that husk itself, followed the opposite path, and swept with him the tremors of the air and of the waters, the tremors of the blood in the blue veins, and the tremors of the flowers under the sun and the dew, and carried them into the very substance of the air, of the water, of the blood, and of the flowers.   And whereas Impressionism refused more

RENOIR.   Woman at her toilette (*Private collection*).

and more to recompose the world in the mind and to transpose it into painting, Renoir, whose imagination, by the way, was almost as rudimentary as that of his friends, recomposed it and transposed it in his very instinct, seeing life, harmony, and coherent, solid, and continuous form born where, for other men, there is only appearance, discord, the hollow surface, and chaos.

Imagine a whole room hung with pictures by Renoir. It seems to stream with red, from the fruits, the blood, and the flowers pressed against the walls. From a little nearer, there is an Oriental confusion, like a miraculous carpet; several studies are on the same bit of canvas— a nude woman, a little girl with a pink or red hat, a bouquet of roses, of poppies, of pinks, of geraniums, or of sage, and a landscape the size of one's hand with the circle of the sea and of space. But from this red mass emerges something like those currents of sap which rise from the center of fruits to color their skin, and infinite ashen grays in which silver and mother-of-pearl tremble, in which the emerald, the turquoise, the pearl, and the black diamond penetrate the opal, where the slightest colored palpitation of the slightest touch of paint resounds gently through the ones farthest from it by subtle waves impossible to follow with the eye. And nearer still one sees the beach and the ocean, the trees twisting their flame, the rivers rolling into the reflection of the sky, the ribbons, the hats, the dresses, and the unbound hair of the women—all the dews of the earth mingled with all the prisms of the air, converted into trunks and branches bursting with sap, flesh swelling with blood, young breasts, round arms, firm bellies, glistening hips, and heavy translucent waters filled with the scintillation of the ruby.

It is a lyric transposition, ingenuous and spontaneous, into a form which seems born and reborn incessantly from an inexhaustible focus of the senses, a transposition of everything in the world that has radiance and splendor, the downy pulp of peaches, the cherries, the pomegranates, the rind of lemons and of oranges, the roses of amber color, the blood-colored roses, and the fields of crimson clover, of cornflowers, and of buttercups, and the mouths, and the laughs, and the glances, and the fire of glowing stones in the

RENOIR. The toilette (*Private collection*).

ripples of the brooks, and the sun setting over the
clouds, and its iridescence around the leaves. There
really is in that spring, with its tremble of silver, a little
of the blood of those bare breasts, a little of the blood
of those pinks, and there is some of the silver of that
spring in those pinks and in those bare breasts whose

RENOIR. Women bathing (*Private collection*).

red reflections it passes on to the air while taking from
it some of its fire. Those massive forms turning in
transparent space define painting itself, and the least
of them expresses the glory of life and the power of
summer.

When a painter has this ability, everything encountered by his eye is instantly transfigured. A hand on
some gauze, a necklace around a neck, or a rose set in

the hair causes us to think vaguely of a butterfly wing on the pollen of some giant flower, of a fruit laid on some blond marble, or of some unknown gem gleaming in the darkness. Everything is tremor, everything is a caress; the silks are like flesh and retain their lightness, the flesh is like silk and retains its weight. An arm emerging from satin and resting on velvet borrows from the satin and the velvet their pearl and their purple, and in exchange transmits to them its warmth; faces in the glowing penumbra of an opera box continue the penumbra and illuminate it, the life of the flowers and of the lights circulates in festival halls to mingle with glances, to wander over bare bosoms, and to quiver upon bodices, ornaments, and ribbons. Before the earlier Renoir, one thinks of Velasquez as he might be after the passing of three centuries, when his soul, joined by a hundred tributaries, had borrowed more of maturity and also more of freshness from the light mists of France.

And before the later Renoir, one thinks of a Rubens who had descended to the Latin sea and had become more saturated in its sunlight. Especially when this painting, with its quality of flowers and mother-of-pearl, spontaneously mingling the pulp of the fruits and the sap of the corollas, goes down to the burning beaches, whence the trees seem to spring forth like subterranean flames, and where the gulfs and the sky unite in the expanse of gold. Above the blue and pink villas perceived through the branches of the pines and the olive trees, and above the russet walls of the old castles on the heights, the distant mountains arise, and their glaciers send forth fires and, between the waves and the clouds, pile up flames of mauve from the diamonds cut from the azure by the twilight or the morning. Then all the waters sing, the apples are about to fall from the tree, the anemones swoon, and the

RENOIR. Child writing (*Private collection*).

resplendent orgy of the colors, of the odors, and of the murmurs turns around the broad nude flesh spread forth in the heat. The form of the arms and of the breasts, of the torsos and of the legs, becomes concise and circular, like those vegetable organisms teeming with the blood of the heavy seasons. The carnal poem is spiritualized upon contact with an admirable love which embraces it in its ensemble, which no longer sees a detail, an accidental, an isolated or rare gesture, but only full masses whose inner force models the movement. It is a summarized and heroic movement, with a voluntary and profoundly expressive use of projections and hollows, of lengthenings, deformations, and foreshortenings of arms and of legs. As the first evolution of Renoir calls to mind Velasquez, and the second recalls Rubens, the third, I do not know why, makes me think of Michael Angelo. He is quite unaware of this, he paints in absolute freedom, and the direct sensation still passes into the crippled hand, which interprets it ingenuously, after having tempered it in the flame of the pure mind. The natural forms all meet and marry with curves suited to them, with volumes swelling with the same inner forces, and with a movement discovered and created anew by the same heart.

Those legs and those arms undulate like that stream, this torso is round like that tree, these breasts weigh and swell like those ripening fruits. The song of joy shouted in the burning shadows, in the curling of the waves and the streaming of the flowers, creates a kind of swooning silence around those women, recumbent or seated, or at play in the living water, and their wavelike forms continue and balance one another with an ease superior to that of Raphael and a plenitude superior to that of Jean Goujon. It is a plenitude full of movement, which beats to its very depths and trembles in the light, where the air, the reflections, and the dew of perspiration marry with it in order to sculpture it summarily. It is a plenitude in which blood quivers and milk germinates, and where, in the cloudy faces, in the fleshy lips, and under the whole tense and vibrant skin, animal life abounds, and all the mind evolving in it. Never, perhaps, had the profoundest and simplest instinct for living passed from flesh and from eyes into the soul of a great painter, to be sent back into flesh and eyes by that soul. Those babes clinging to the heavy breasts, those vibrant arms which support them, those little beings whose form still hesitates and who lean over a page of writing or over a toy, those little girls with red hair whose astonished eyes open so wide as they marvel at the world, and those young mothers who have grown heavy, express with such intensity the peaceful majesty and the inner, mechanical circulation of life that they seem to be on the plane of life, merged with it, and issuing from the same hearth. A grand animality breathes in them, in its peace and in its power. The gestures and faces of family life, the eternal attitudes of the dance, of the toilet, of distraught meditation, of abandon, of joy, and of repose, live innocently within them. Carrière saw those canvases and the great, red-chalk drawings like things of the antique awaking from a long sleep, and the profound charcoal studies in which the childish and maternal forms are fused, and despite his too didactic striving for spiritual transposition he never attained the expressive power of their structural form, independent, even, of the miraculous harmonies with which Renoir surrounds them and permeates them. Universal life inundates the most furtive gestures of the play of maternity, of love, and of childhood in the sun and in the grasses, and there is no metaphysical need to tell of this life. Here is the most secret mystery of the greatest painting, a pulpy, fruitlike substance un-

Van Gogh. Self-portrait (*Private collection*).

confined by the living lines, its boundaries marked out by turning masses and moving volumes, and brought, by an infinite circulation of colored particles, into its intimate relationship with the whole of space.

III

Igor Stravinsky [1] has crowned the spring. Already before him, the youthful painting of France bore witness to the decomposition of the old rhythms, and saw, coming to birth out of the chaos, troubled harmonies, relationships at once touching and uncertain, and lines, sounds, and forms groping to find one another. As it was barely beginning to suspect the power of the edifice raised by Cézanne, as it still felt but incompletely the influence of the lyric transposition imagined by Renoir, it was manifesting a singular freedom of intelligence and of impressions. One might have said that it was thus substituting for the reasoned Impressionism of the visual sensation transcribed with fidelity, a kind of impressionism of the total sensation transposed with innocence. Still insufficiently equipped for that task, it was thus returning to the tradition of the greatest painting by the path of schoolboys.

The rhythms revealed by Bonnard and Vuillard on one hand, and by Matisse and Marquet on the other— sometimes by Jean Puy and, on those days, with a lyricism of matter and of color as compact and pure as a flower or a gem—are, I certainly believe, among all the most significant ones, the former by their character of spontaneity, as if they were quivering and moving in the incessant and surprised germination of embryonic life at the edge of a furrow—the latter by the preoccupation with essential equilibrium and with fundamental organization which they reveal, with more

[1] (Translator's note: *Le Sacre du Printemps*, by Stravinsky.)

Van Gogh. Street in Arles (*Private collection*).

innocence in the one case and more science in the other than is generally believed. Already the reaction against these painters has begun, while they are still young, for it is their misfortune to live in a period when neither fashions nor systems last for long. Perhaps, moreover, it is not the fault of the period, for no other has been so rich, none, in so short a time, has become so rich in acquisitions of the senses, of poetry, and of sentiment, all cast one upon another in a marvelous disorder. People are forgetting that, at the very time when Cézanne and Renoir were finishing their task, these painters were continuing the effort of the Impressionists toward freedom of sensation, and were thus restoring to painting the rights of the imagination; people forget how their minds were prepared by these artists to receive, with an ardent impartiality, the unforeseen contribution of the schools and of the epochs which were in no way concerned with European tradition, and which thus broke down the last resistance of Greco-Latin academism.

With all the impassioned and confused decorators of that time of confused passion, Vuillard, Bonnard, Valtat, Roussel, d'Espagnat, and Albert André, we were witnessing, toward the end of the last century, something recalling a very brief period of blossom between a winter and a summer, a being emerging from slumber. There was an uncertain swaying in this art, doubtless, with Valtat, an obscurity due to the force of his brilliance, but there was also evoked the primitive organization of a world in which the purest essence of the most profound color might emanate from matter itself in order summarily to define it, red from the central fire, blue from the high sea, and rose from the peaks covered with sunlit snow. . . . It was too well-informed an art with Roussel, too much impregnated with culture; radiant, generous, lyrical, but perhaps a little too negligent, too abundant, with d'Espagnat; and, on the contrary, direct, measured, discreet, savory, but a little timid with Albert André.   And with Vuillard, a minute embroiderer of intimate symphonies—with his satin, his brocaded velvet, his feathers of changing color, and his silk threads powdered with pollen—an unprecise,

GAUGUIN.   The Wave (*Private collection*).

and often even an irresolute but tender poet of the moral atmosphere circulating around beings and things, this art is a little too careful to surround the houses of the intellectuals and of the people of fashion with discreet psychological harmonies in which the spirit of painting is at times too much subjected to the phantoms and the puppets which dwell in these houses for a day.   But this art is living, and it bursts forth and is symbolic in its innocence with Bonnard, the miraculous illustrator of ancient and modern life, the poet so unforeseen in his spontaneity, the astonished searcher, and the extravagant story-teller, who recounts the monotonous adventure in which our own intellectual incertitude unrolls among the fanciful lines of an instinct ever amused.

In those singular decorations, which appear shaken and commingled by some quaking of the earth, one has the sensation of a world decomposed into diffused tones, from which, here and there, there emerge embryonic forms which tend to group themselves and organize themselves along unknown lines. The glacial art of Odilon Redon, of a spirituality so rare—a mottled tremor on the surface of a transparent and suspected water in whose depths there may be mother-of-pearl and coral, and which, in the literary manner, symbolizes these obscure fermentations sufficiently well—is the antithesis of the work of these artists, for it tries to catch in the crystallized sheen of its jewels and its flowers that which is only hesitation, tremor, passage, and undetermined movement. But the Russian Ballet carries into the plastic rhythms the formidable orgy of Oriental colorations, and mingles impassioned gesture with the color of sounds, and the intoxication of the eyes with the transports of desire. And Debussy introduces the perfume of gardens into the sound of drops of rain, sways brilliant pollen to the murmur of the trees, and whispers with the confession on trembling lips, with memory and secrecy. The universe turns to a more and more precipitous rhythm. The dance and music are transposed into painting. And Bonnard is perhaps the central sensibility in which that confusion takes place.

I know nothing of his life. It effaces itself. If I were acquainted with it in all its gestures, I should know less who he is. I cannot resist an affection for it as it reaches me through the universal and continuous quiver of his painting. It is one of those lives which proceed without a halt from daily activity and the

ODILON REDON.   Flowers (*Private collection*).

inner world to the moving and multiple form which constitutes its physiognomy and its daily confession. Consider what he brings to you. Do you not find the man himself in those wooded masses cut by luminous alleys, and in those flowered lawns where children and animals run and frolic? It is the movement of his mind that is revealed in those trembling bouquets, those slender stalks, and that whole fragile splendor of flowers and pure water and in transparent glasses. Strewn flowers, light stuffs, and mirrors reflecting delightful apparitions—it is through you that I know him. Along that path which he has followed to reach that room where your harmonies penetrate one another, brush by one another, and enchant me with their tangled and furtive reflections, like a vague music, he has tarried everywhere. He has leaned on this bridge, to watch the river gathering up a sky of troubled silver through which run shudders of turquoise and of sapphire. I have surprised him at the corner of a lane of mauve, where, with the delight of a child, he was observing that a lantern all askew, a little shop window, a garbage can, the greasy pavement, the gutter, and the most humble animals and the poorest people participate in the glory of the mist and of the sunlight. With comic or tired gestures, the jewel, the faded rag, the mottled fur, or the downy plumage, the quivering ear, the wagging tail, and the leaping, snorting horse, all obey, and enter, without effort, into the whirlwind of his soul. Everything obeys joyously, as if to merit the enchanted tenderness which attaches him to everything that lives. The iridescence of opals, of emeralds, and of jet, and the limpidity of translucent stones into which the lightest down of the flowers and the pollen blown from their corollas penetrate and mingle, have, by their aërial voyages, made me appreciate his heart. That which is most spontaneous, most fugitive, most light and delicate on all moving surfaces is that which he gathers up and mixes, to model his fleeting form, to make his skies recede, and to embroider his diffused world into imponderable harmonies, in which the drop of water, the blade of grass, the butterfly's wing, and the elytron of the insect furnish, if he desires it, the

HENRI ROUSSEAU. Pastoral (*Private collection*).

central and colored motif around which his whole universe turns.

Has he perhaps been called an "intimist"? It is quite possible. And if it is true, the discovery is a comic one. He is in the intimacy of all life. He flows and flees like the secret force which circulates within things. I cannot halt his unseizable mind in the blowing hair of a little girl as she dances or runs, in the ball of wool that slips from the basket, in the brisk gallop of a colt, in the circle that widens on the water, and in the growth of little plants. He wanders through nature like that dull movement which manifests the spring and which reveals itself everywhere by the rising in everything alive of the liquids which nourish them. And, besides, he is the spring. Like the rarest artists, he gives the impression of having invented painting. And that is not only because, everything in the world being new for him each day, he expresses it in a new way, but also because he comes at the dawn of a new intellectual order, and because he is the first to arrange, according to a rhythm unknown to all before him, the good old harmonies which have made us what we are. I have been told that Bonnard was an expression of decadence. Decadences ferment, and the ferment of decadences builds the future monument.

I perceive all the less that irreducible opposition which is claimed to exist between Vuillard and Bonnard, and the young painters, who say that they are to-day building this monument in their reaction against Vuillard and Bonnard, because, while the latter, precisely, were doing their work, Matisse, less spontaneous, more reflective, and more doctrinary, but like them deriving from Impressionism, was attempting to draw from Impressionism itself the means of erecting a systematic construction of color. His activity is inseparable from theirs, as the activity of Cézanne and of Renoir is inseparable from Impressionism, which gave them their point of departure. In general, the future attends to the reconciliation of the contraries which are only faces of the same reality. The disciplined orgy in which the sumptuous still-lifes, and the flaming expanses of Morocco and of Spain saturate, with dark harmonies and with brilliant notes, the most rapid portrait, the most summary landscape, or the decoration most strongly inscribed in a few directing lines and a few dominant tones, would show a didactic power of will in Matisse, which is entirely lacking in Bonnard, if one did not ultimately discover in the former a second ingenuousness which is only a progressive gain of control over the personal elements of his equilibrium. In his case, to be sure, there seems to be a willful awkwardness. But that is because it expresses a desire at once lucid and impassioned, to reunite the material harmonies dispersed throughout our needs. All things, in this art, are reduced to the essential indication of the structure of their form and, more especially, of their color, which causes them to assume an unexpected splendor in the unbroken silence around them. Each one becomes the symbol, direct, concrete, and voluntary, of a central idea which presides over the choice and over the association of the tones, and over the disposition and the direction of the lines. Whether he paints a portrait, a still-life, a landscape, or nude women dancing, the arabesque is always there, dominating in order that it may direct, master, and give shades or subtlety to the harmony, whose rhythm comes from it, and with which it plays as a bow draws forth from the string sonorous waves which it swells and contracts. "Nature" is pretty far away. The artist imposes his system with such rigor, such exactitude and logic in the relationships of his sumptuous elements, that he creates a plastic universe of the richest accent.

I think, indeed, that, for this reason, this painter is the
one who, least of all since Cézanne, causes one to think
of the subject which his works represent.   They tend
untiringly to organize his universe from the angle of
painting alone, absolutely delivered from the attrac-

BOURDELLE.   Decorative Fragment (*Théâtre des Champs Elysées*).

tion of sentiment or of the picturesque in the object.
At bottom, they express no object.   At all events, the
object is, with him, no more than a pretext for the creation of new organisms, which a powerful love for
form is alone capable of imagining.   And thereby, the
recreated object attains a life infinitely more general,

in the first place, but also, unexpectedly enough, infinitely more direct, than that which it is supposed to represent. . . . See how, on a red background, the play of the blacks, of the grays, and of the yellows is concentrated, or the play of the grays, of the yellows, and of the reds, on a black background. In the one case, abstract space hovers like a liquid atmosphere; in the

SEURAT.   Drawing (*Private collection*).

other case, we see a mirror in which the light is absorbed. The uniformity of that background which, with a bad painter, would be the most banal of means for masking his indigence, becomes, in the hands of Matisse, the rarest instrument for manifesting the most voluntary and the highest distinction. One would imagine oneself *seeing* music. The most decisive paintings of Matisse make me think of Chinese porcelains, or of hard Japanese lacquers, immobilized, as it were, under some deep water, and in them Goya's power for surprising life seems mysteriously united with the silent and lofty soul of Velasquez. I am thinking of those mat surfaces, almost black or red, in which some solid apparition—flowers or a face—surges up from the silence, in the ardent solitude of its own reality. It is quite evident that this alone, perhaps—I

BOURDELLE.   Leda, fresco (*Théâtre des Champs-Elysées*).

mean the distant impression which he gives of a chromatic didacticism of the kind used by the Orientals—has not been willed by him. But the forms of sensibility expressed by the art of the Far East have entered so deep into the reason of the Occident that to-day they determine one of the most splendid aspects of its regenerated symbolism. Were I acquainted with the frontiers of the object and of the subject, curiosity as to the world would be extinguished in me. The grand style lies precisely in their secret meeting, and in our impotence to determine its place. And that, I certainly believe, is what gives to Matisse's painting a decorative majesty which it is practically alone in possessing, at a time when almost all painting tends to decoration. The picturesque and the anecdote draw away from it. Music rises from it, in absolute silence.

A great lesson, which begins with Cézanne, and which very few have been able to understand. The painting of Dunoyer de Segonzac, somber and dull, and less decorative, moreover, and above all that of Charles Pequin, more traditional in appearance, are the only ones to-day which give me that immediate musical impression; but with them it is less striking, it is veiled like some chamber-music, which the former sends winding about in sensual arabesques, and in which, with the latter, there arise the purities and the sonorities of the violoncello, against a harmonic mass as solid as a monument. With the former, a quality of heat in the paint, which seems mixed with mud and a little gold, twists the expression like a clay, while the india-ink draws it out into the long frail flames seen among the branches of winter. With this painter, a stirring quality, which seemed almost lost since Chardin, and which one finds to this degree only with Cézanne, reappears in painting: one would say that it was from within, that the color, in ripening, saturated the form, which, on its side, might be said to model the color. The light, the reflections, and the shadows play into the thickness of the paint itself in order to incorporate it with the movement of the masses as they seek their own depth. These inner exchanges are almost poignant in their unweakening intensity, and they maintain the rights of the sensual imagination in that "constructed" form which all are seeking in our day— the recent rôle of Cubism being to keep alive the need

for it in the intelligence. Charles Pequin, like Segonzac, represents French measure, whose future, in the
presence of the current invasion of foreign ideas and
sensibilities, we do not know. Thanks to these artists,
thanks to L. A. Moreau, less of a painter, but quite as
determined not to renounce the teachings of direct
emotion, thanks to
Despiau, the sculp-
tor, the purest of
the image-makers of
France, and to his
closely modeled
faces, in which the
expressive masses
alone survive the
original emotion,
French plastics will
perhaps regain its
path.

The art of Mar-
quet, on which Ma-
tisse leaned heavily,
at least during the
time when they
began together,
seems to me to have
been the first step
in that direction

SEURAT.   The Quay (*Private collection*).

which tends, by a revolutionary reversing of the dis-
abled ship, to a rejoining of the national tradition of
measure in lyricism, and of simplicity in expression,
which one finds in this country with the great and the
little masters, from Foucquet to Corot, passing through
Ingres sometimes, through Joseph Vernet, Chardin,
Louis Gabriel Moreau, Claude Lorrain, and Poussin
always. If one insisted absolutely upon discovering

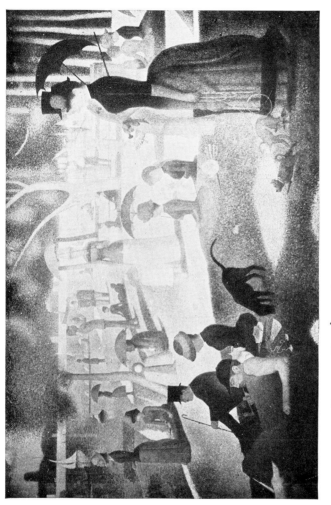

SEURAT. The Île de la Grand-Jatte (*Private collection*).

the origins of Marquet, it is there that one would have to seek them. But classic art resides in harmony between the faculty for feeling and the faculty for comprehending, and not in any particular manner of painting or of drawing. The origins of Marquet are the quays, the bridges, the river, the monotonous streets which open up, and their shop windows, their signs, their flags, and the pathway of sky between the embankments of the roofs. The ever similar construction of his canvases has in it something of an absolute necessity, like that of the streets themselves, of the rivers, of the quays, of the bridges, of the roofs, and of the sky. Is it ingenuousness, or is it skill? I know nothing about that, and no more does he. In his viewing of a landscape, of a city scene, or of the sea, the means is always so simple that it disappears. If he suppresses something that bothers him, or accentuates something that touches him, no one sees that he has done so.

It will be clearly seen that such an intelligence of things does not occur without a profound, intimate, and living culture. But he never parades it, any more than he does his taste for the picturesque. He seems more enamored of skies filled with mist and smoke, of snow, of sleeping water, and of the places where the adventure of modern man unrolls, between the door of the factory and that of the slaughter house. But he is at home in this Paris of the Cité, where Notre Dame and its pedestal, the quay, the bridges, and the river with its canals, seem to impose on the very sky, on the clouds, and on the airy and golden light diffusing everywhere, harmony, concrete clarity, logical distribution, and spontaneous measure. And he has penetrated with authority into the blond opal which incloses the seas of the north. And he is very much at ease in the flame trembling around the masts, the smokestacks,

Vuillard. The Copyist (*Private collection*).

and the pennants on the roadsteads of the sun. I know well that this ease is too often made up of a careless misunderstanding of architectonic foundations, excused, however, by the startling exactitude of the vision. The values stammer, but they are so sure that they transport into the painting the exact perspective of the city and of the planet, and the exact gradation of the sky. Sometimes the houses sway, and the roads are askew. A sudden change of tone on the same quay, the same bridge, or the same river would destroy the harmony of plane of the picture, if it were not exactly what brought life into the whole, and if the approximate construction and the impeccable values did not impose unity upon it. One would say that elements of nature are seeking one another, beginning to organize themselves, uniting awkwardly, and making an attempt at some evolving equilibrium, for which they are propped up and made fast by some inner force.

IV

Here, then, are certain authentic artists whom the new tendencies assume to dispossess from the direction of men's minds—I speak of those issuing most directly from Impressionism, for it seems to me that in the case of isolated men like Charles Pequin or Despiau, none of the criticisms addressed to these artists by the most uncompromising "constructors" can touch them, and leaves them on the road which goes from Cézanne to Derain. As a matter of fact, all painting and all sculpture have, for twenty years, turned around the indifference of Cézanne and of Renoir toward that which is not plastic expression, the first stage of a feeling for general subordination to some impersonal monument which we do not perceive, but which, with them and at their very time, during

the full tide of Impressionism, the full tide of naturalism, others, like Henri Rousseau, were sketching
roughly without knowing it or, like George Seurat, they
were already trying, with an acute consciousness of that
fact, to build it up consistently from all sides. The
unbroken candor of the one, and the sovereign intelligence which, with the other, never ceases organizing

HENRI MATISSE.   The Cliff (*Private collection*).

and spiritualizing its gifts, seem, in our day, to penetrate the influence which these two masters exert together, and in them is summarized the effort of the
nineteenth century in France to give, with that influence, a strong skeleton of plastics to that feeling: I
persist in believing that neither Bonnard, nor, above all,
Matisse, stands in any opposition to it, and that, on
the contrary, by giving the final freedom to poetic

sensation and to chromatic sensation, they have contributed to clear the way for the most singular innovators. Was it not only yesterday, in fact, that Seurat was considered a Neo-Impressionistic dissociator, and that a bare few—and I was not of the number—perceived the purity and the calm of his rhythms, free and cadenced like figures in a dance, and his masculine power of representing to himself the most picturesque, and even the most commonplace, universe under monumental aspects?

The feeling I speak of is new only in its unanimity. The renaissance of great decoration which has been going on for a century, announced it, unknown to all. And from the fact that the painters of to-day reject all decorative intention, one should not conclude that these two movements oppose each other. To speak of the setting, also, is to imply subordination. But the decorators of the last century had not understood, and would not have been able to understand, that contemporary edifices were not built for them, that they were survivals of an outworn period, and preceded another period whose style, even to-day, is not born: their ambition was a noble one even if misdirected, their attempt was an isolated one, not standing outside of painting—let it suffice to cite Delacroix and Chassériau—but foreign to the preoccupations and to the means of a majority of the painters of their time. However, painting was, even independent of its destination, to assume certain decorative tendencies. The object for its own sake was diminishing in importance, even when it remained the sole pretext for the sculpture or for the picture. And it was an essential part of the phenomenon that these tendencies were to be observed among the most unlearned and the most cultivated of the artists. One surprised them thirty or forty years ago already in Henri Rousseau himself, a contemporary,

without knowing it, of Puvis, of Redon, and of Cézanne; he was an old innocent, a real primitive, a Giotto
without training or culture, a customs officer certainly,
and doubtless as unqualified to perform that work well

HENRI MATISSE.   Flowers (*Private collection*).

as he would have been for the functions of an acade-
mician; but he was haunted by tropical landscapes so
luxuriant, so pure, so fresh, so full of brilliance and of
candor, so far from us, and so near to imaginary para-

dises and to miraculous gardens, that everything grows pale at times and effaces itself when hanging with these paintings which go beyond all bounds, like green plants, or like carpets of the Orient. The decorative tendencies burst forth in all the Neo-Impressionists, insistent or repentant, in Seurat first, with his tremendous faculty for impressing upon his naturalistic "subjects" an architectural aspect; in H. E. Cross, with his fervor so charming and poetic; in Signac, an enchanting tapestry-maker, weaving the skies, the atmospheres, the waves, and the masts out of solar light, and not fearing to see the division of the brush strokes as the very instrument for decoration. In J. P. Lafitte, it was as if a band of iron was stifling the new growth, which burned in him and which the war ended. One respected the tendencies in Maurice Denis, with whom they are didactic, dogmatic, intent on recreating a whole system of classicism, and obstinately turning toward culture at a time when restlessness and invention were bursting forth everywhere. In Pierre Fauconnet one saw the decorative resolved to go beyond the limits of the picture, to address itself to the accessories of the theater, to invade costume, and to spread over social and fashionable life, which Raoul Dufy, on his side, impresses with his lyricism at once profuse and precise, a thing of fantasy, whirling and ordered, like a dance. One finds the tendencies again among the young painters most eager for innovation, and thus Dufresne's paintings assume their aspect of shimmering and sumptuous carpets. One accepts the decorative, as it results, in some cases, in a conscious archaism or turning to obsession—an almost painful one, and insistent upon introducing romanticism into the new house, in the case of Bourdelle, the only artist of to-day to possess the instinct of the higher symbolism. His art is full of flame, but of smoke also, and it is expressed

MARQUET. Notre Dame (*Private collection*).

in a language which is not always his own, wandering, in its inner torment, from the Gothic men to Michael Angelo, from Ingres and from Carpeaux to Rodin, from the Assyrians to the Hindus, and from the Egyptians to the Greeks: however, in his art, whether fresco or

DESPIAU.   Portrait of Mme. D.

sculpture, there is a lyric force in which the thought, accustomed, in general, to use a different language, twists and stiffens in order to make itself understood, and gives to the whole work an ardent tension which ends by imposing itself.   One surprises the decorative tendencies in the heavy statues of Joseph Bernard,

BONNARD. Decorative panel (*Private collection*).

stones intoxicated by their power of sweeping upward the density and the awkwardness of stone, and sketching, with an archaic note, his images of games, of innocence, and of love. One admires the robust achievement of the decorative, as it comes forth from the earth with fruits in the hollow of its hands; here it has given us works hard and round, and modeled like a column, in the sculpture of Maillol, which would, with sufficient fidelity, symbolize the birth of a season, if the indeterminateness, the vague murmur, and the undefined and sensual love that lives in Oriental color, in music, and in the dance did not express the same thing in a manner at once more direct and more diffused.[1]

The imagination of the peoples, in their enervation, turns, indeed, around an invisible flame whose focus is in Paris, and into which each one feverishly casts the treasures and the refuse of its old soul. The most important contributions from abroad have been those of Holland and of Spain; the former country, already many years ago, brought forth Jongkind, and above all van Gogh; to-day it has the bestial and resplendent van Dongen, while Spain makes her voice heard, yesterday with the savage and solitary Regoyos, with Julio Antonio, a Roman of Saguntum, who died, almost a boy, overcome by the weight of his bronzes, to-day with the monotonous, candid, sharp, and perverse Iturrino, and with Picasso, now a genius, and now a man of skill. But aside from these, French painting alone persists in the dispute of the schools, and constitutes the nucleus of a world art impatient to burst forth. Germany, at the end of the last century, possessed certain interesting painters like Leibl, Liebermann, a kind of feudal retainer of French Impressionism, and Marées, but German art developed by itself, stiff and didactic, outside the symphonic movement of

[1] See Appendix, (b), p. 497.

which France was the center, and its present-day
"Expressionism"[1] denotes only a social movement, for
the moment, in which Kokoschka alone seems, with his
confused and muddy quality of paint, to be preparing
realizations which count; his character is exasperated,
his violence is chaotic, and his "expression" sways, to
be sure, but its fire and its life afford an art whose savor
is undeniable.   Hodler, the Swiss, was a vigorous pro-
fessor.   Belgian art since Meunier offers but little

BONNARD.   Going to School (*Private collection*).

more than one isolated figure, James Ensor, who, with
frail forms and pale harmonies, revives the marionette-
theater spirit of Breughel and of Jerome Bosch.   Italian art, before it flowers again, seems to await the full
effect of the new urge which Italy is feeling and which

[1] This "expressionism" is perhaps nothing else than a transposition of
the impressionistic state of mind passing, if I may be pardoned these barbarous terms, from French objectivism to German subjectivism, and from
the plastic plane to the musical plane.   Impressionism, at least at its beginnings, assumed to express itself with any means that came to hand,
provided the impression was exact.   Expressionism teaches that one must
express oneself with any means that comes to hand, provided the expression be personal.

is manifesting itself especially, up to the present, through the trenchant character of the forms of its industrial or naval architecture — forms such that only America has found any that are as decisive. Modigliani, the morbid and feverish poet of hands, of bodies, and of

faces of women, which he notes suddenly, with a light, eager, and flowing brush— the poet of distortion, of sensual deformation, of flesh, of hallucinating eyes, and of the energetic Italian grace which surges up, warped by the Semitic ferment, after two centuries of sleep—died too soon for us to be able to deduce a general principle from his furtive apparition.

BONNARD. The Cat
(*Private collection*).

Meanwhile, in France and outside of France, outside of the schools and in the schools, one comes upon parallel phenomena at every step.

With the most restless of the artists, form assumes a special instability which reminds one of that of the primitive organisms.[1] With those who are most guided by the will, one finds a rigidity corresponding with the fixed images of geometrical abstraction.[2] In the one

[1] See Appendix, (c), p. 503.   [2] *Ibid.*, (d), p. 503.

Maillol.   Woman Seated, plaster.

case, there is an attempt to force the expression of time into the plane of space, the only one at the disposal of painting. In the other case the attempt is to express in this one plane all the dimensions of space. . . . After Braque, a Frenchman of France, comes Picasso, a Spaniard of Andalusia, in whom the Arab dream is continued, and its impassioned pursuit of ideographic form through the natural forms reduced to their geometrical figures; Picasso tries, for the first time in Europe, to create a universe without contact with the real, with the pretext of placing in evidence a dimension of which, if I conceive the thing rightly, the "value" already expresses that which can be expressed on a flat surface. "Plastic equivalence" has existed for a long time. It is, first, architecture, then furniture or pottery, and then geometrical decoration, the arabesque, and the carpet. It can coexist with plastic "transposition," can frame it, complete it, and influence it. It cannot replace it.

Meanwhile, Picasso is not anchored to it, but turns around it, leaves it, returns to it, uses it as another instrument in his orchestra, and has been careful not to comment on it or even to baptize it—the word "Cubism," like "Impressionism," was at first a term of sarcasm—and with Picasso the movement has broken its narrow dikes and resounds from one place to another, over all the sensibility, all the thought, and all the energy of to-day. The restlessness of Picasso is one of the most ardent leavens in our contemporary fever. It is a nomadic but fruitful restlessness, which stirs up the springs, and the mud at the bottom of them, and the flowering plants that grow on them, a perilous dance of the intelligence as it seeks unheard-of equilibriums on the sharpest summits of sensation, suddenly giving up one game to fling itself into another, a work that is uncertain, and dramatic just through that fact, admirable in flashes, and quite frequently disappointing. But it is always impressive through its attention to character, its constant bent for style and for purity of the form, which is cleared of all incident, and through

Dunoyer de Segonzac.   The Drinkers (*Private collection*).

its disinterested desire to find in the undulations, the swellings, the taperings, and the contrasts of lines, the law of structure of the masses which they symbolize, and the law of continuity of the monumental ensembles which they, when taken together, make up for the dance, for play, for swimming, and for repose on the seashore. It is a work of singular importance, for by its play it demonstrates that what was formerly called "composition" is a system of equilibrium, a general form, which the undulating lines constantly bring back to turn, like tongues and crowns of flame issuing from one hearth, and moving around a central point which is the veritable "subject." It is a confident work, for it opens up hope to so many painters, by its free rehabilitation of fantasy, of invention, and of poetry in painting; confident in its intoxicated and lucid twists at the point of the pencil, and the edifices it builds, unforeseen, but logical as a dance. It has a quality of unexpectedness besides, not allowing one a second of respite in its unceasing evolution, its sudden leaps, its bizarre acts, its feats, its wild whims, and its inflexible reason. And yet it is essential, through its definite break with the Impressionism which Cézanne, Renoir, and Seurat had brought back into the great pictorial tradition, while preserving all its gains, but which,

OSCAR KOKOSCHKA. Self-portrait
(*Private collection*).

JAMES ENSOR. Masks (*Brussels Museum*).

again, was preventing all their descendants from manifesting architectonic invention and plastic imagination.
But this work of Picasso's is dangerous also, in its indefatigable wandering between museum painting and
magazine illustration, in which latter field he gives
scenes of the circus or of the life of Bohemia, lugubrious
visions which turn at times toward the laughable,
phantoms, boneless puppets, faces of fever and of
famine, and surprising but learned forms whose line,
through their constant attention to style and to cal-
ligraphy, very soon separated from that of the tradition
of the marionette theater, which we first find with
Daumier in France, which was lightly touched by
Manet and Cézanne, to be taken up again by Degas,
Toulouse-Lautrec, and Seurat, and in our day, carried
by Rouault, in the bloody mud of his paintings, to its
paroxysm of character, of somber and burlesque tragedy, and of sadness and of horror. And the work of
Picasso is dangerous for those who are fascinated by
the ability to do what is merely difficult, and dangerous
perhaps for the one who performs these feats and who
seems—I say only seems—sometimes to have re-
nounced being merely a great painter in order to watch
how others imitate him, and to note the surprise in the
faces of the public.

For now is the time when, around this work people
anathematize, preach, didacticize, and dogmatize.
They bring forth Revelations of the Truth. They
quarrel, as in the heyday of the School, over the pre-
eminence of form or of color. They lose their time in
cursing or in travestying "Impressionism," which,
meanwhile, is nothing but ashes. And as they say
that it is necessary "to construct," each one proposes
his plan. They resort to deformation systematically
as, in bygone days, they used to idealize systematically,
thereby, even while they curse romanticism, ingenu-

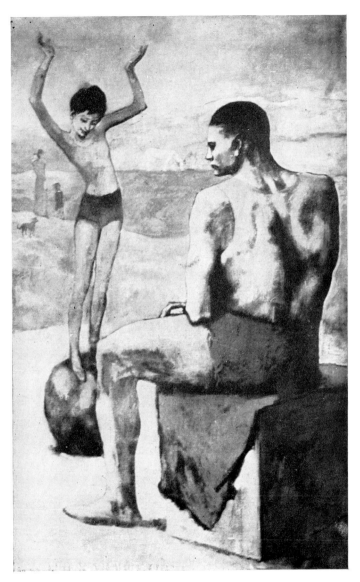

Picasso. The Girl on the Ball (*Private collection*).

ously substituting a romanticist academism for the classicist academism. In a few months they exhaust the teachings of one after another of the great dead things which took twenty centuries to evolve. The Negro replaces the Greek in the preoccupations of a new doctrinism. The noble Greco-Roman of the old studios disgustedly throws aside his heroics and his helmet in order gravely to seize the tom-tom. They declare themselves primitives as a reaction against the skill which is everywhere; they declare themselves archaic in order to obey the demands of a culture which is at once weary of its science and eager to draw from it synthesized conclusions. They forget that a system does not suffice to create a great art, and even less to create a great artist. When one seeks order, one expresses oneself, one does not demonstrate to others the manner of expressing order.

Of all these confused movements, all that one needs to retain are the collective desires of which they are the symptoms. The art of to-day, despite the artists themselves, still too much given to assuming a look of singularity at any cost, is, unknown to itself, protesting against that individualism uncontrolled by its own discipline, into which a part of modern Europe is sinking, after having reached thereby one of its most splendid flights. A new intellectual order announces itself. And the "constructive" effort of Cubism may be regarded, in this sense, as a stirring symptom. Decorative in itself, it ruins decoration to set up architecture.

Here is the real crux of the problem, which the architect will resolve, but which certain works of painting or of sculpture—after having assimilated, in a few redoubtable years, the immense contribution of the Oriental arts, which see things in great masses and with pure profiles—are already proposing to the evolving consciousness of European humanity, with a power

which constantly impresses one. "Nature" now retires to a secondary plane. It is, decidedly, no longer
anything but a "dictionary," as Delacroix said it should
be. Conceptualism is reborn. This is not the place
to say whether Europe is playing its true rôle, and
whether it is not too exhausted to take up once more
the enormous labor of Asia in constructing a monumental universe which shall elevate form in itself to a level
where it would sufficiently justify destiny and effort.

GEORGES BRAQUE.   Still life (*Private collection*).

In any case, Europe is attempting this, and attempting
it in Paris.

André Derain, who is at the center of this decisive
movement, seems to reconcile, in time and space, the
most distant and most antagonistic worlds: he shows
us hallucinating settings, saturated blacks, disturbed
oranges, massive nudes, profound and heavy portraits,[1] and vigorous landscapes in which there is a
meeting and the beginning of a fusion between the
tragic sense of space of Sesshiu and the Chinese, the

[1] See Appendix, (*e*), p. 503.

attentive lyricism of Lorenzetti the Sienese, the ingenuous imagination of Rousseau, the customs official, and the geological density which characterizes Corot—the whole seen as if through a layer of transparent water,

a polyp world, coral-like and crystallized.   It is in this powerful painter, I believe, that we find the result, in our day, not only of the example of Cézanne and Renoir, but of the whole decorative effort which followed it, and especially of the whole constructive effort, that feeling at once irresistible and vague, around which

Picasso unrolled his precise arabesques, but which, always and from everywhere and with Picasso himself, encountered the central, haunting, and invincible preoccupation of subordinating the whole of plastics to some monumental idea of form, in which the idea of imitating it gave way to the determination to comprehend its structure, its norm, and its meaning. Take notice, besides, of the fact that André Derain has had

PICASSO.   Reapers Resting, drawing (*Private collection*).

the exceptional strength, in the whirlwind of systems, of crossed influences, and of innumerable revelations, in which we have been living for twenty years, to bring this whole thing back, by a slow, broad effort, to the external and the spiritual aspects of his country, in which Corot, Delacroix, Barye, Renoir, Claude, Poussin, and Foucquet would recognize themselves without difficulty.

A majestic unity characterizes the painting of André Derain to-day.   Like the greatest among the painters

DUFRESNE. Decorative panel (*Private collection*).

—and like the greatest only—he resolves the incessant contradictions of appearances by intuitively reaching and by bringing into relief that which Baudelaire called the universal analogy. A skull; a stretch of country in which the skeleton of the soil marks its outlines; a tree, and a human torso, nude or draped—obey the same forces, whose direction, simplicity, and accent are revealed to us by the union of the light caressing, and of the color saturating the surface of their volumes. Now his pictures seem cast, as a block, in some unknown metal, colored from within by some deep force which appears to spread over the surface of this block its dull wave, in order to saturate with somber gold this shoulder, this neck, and this forehead, to illuminate this eye with a gleam as of stone, to pour some thick nocturnal wave into this heavy hair, and to run through these twisted branches, or this hilly plain, with the central fire which passes into the sap and into the rock. One would say that they had issued from some subterranean forge, where a hot lava mingled and fused with red bronze and silver would assume, under the blows of the hammer and the work of the file, the summary and compact form which no accidental, no incidental, is capable of disintegrating. There are still, with Matisse himself, preoccupations foreign to form, as might be expected from so enchanting a colorist, however pure and disinterested he is. Here the concentration has become almost tragic, and, although very French, through the measure, the sober harmony, and the spontaneous equilibrium, it is rude, brief, and massive like a primitive idol discovered in the soil.

v

Certainly, there is a new springtime for mankind. A tragic spring, like all springs when murder and rutting passion combine to increase and multiply the energy which makes for fecundity. In these rebounding values, in this jumble of painting where the forms drag the backgrounds with them confusedly, and

ANDRÉ DERAIN. The Road to Castel-Gandolfo (*Private collection*).

where the blackgrounds reunite with space only after having brushed against the forms in order to gather up their echo, I perceive a kind of artless genesis. Our memories of Hindu art, of the "Paradise" of Tintoretto, of the entire work of Rubens, of the myth of Evolution,

the love for the great music which has developed among
us, Dostoievski, Nietzsche, Whitman, the awkward
and essential architecture of Cézanne, and the painted
symphony gained by Renoir, everything signifies the
approach of some great agreement, unknown as to its
methods, but for which these dispersed forms which
seek to rejoin one another are a primitive appeal. The
universe is remaking itself. The floating character of
the values of plastic art corresponds to the indecision
of science, to the fundamental instability of life which
the biologists are revealing to us, to its attempt to fix
itself in an architectonic rhythm, and to a collective
defense against that instability. Whatever the opinions of an ephemeral school—and every self-respecting
school is ephemeral—painting retains space as its domain, and will not escape from it. But the gradually
increasing importance which we give to time has
stealthily introduced itself into our former idea of
space. The cinematograph causes it to be born and to
die there, to be reborn and to die again under our eyes,
precipitating into the counterpoint of universal and
continuous movement that which painting, in former
times, fixed upon canvas: volumes, passages, values,
associations, oppositions, and contrasts—which modify
one another, reply to one another, interpenetrate, and
become entangled, ceaselessly and in all the dimensions.
And now, everywhere and all the time, evolving and
vague relationships of an irresistible accent are being
established.

Exhausted by solitude, man, in a word, calls to man,
in order together to build the house, and the unem-
ployed decorators consent to immolation in order to
converge their spiritual forces in the erecting of a temple which they will not see. The new order, creating
the new architecture, simple and bare like every organism in its youth, will destroy decoration, or will

GEORGES ROUAULT. Nude (*Private collection*).

transform it in such a manner that its present attempts can teach us nothing as to the form which it will assume.[1] All the things which, for twenty years, we have been thinking of as realizations, are perhaps nothing more than symptoms; symptoms of a rebinding, symptoms of concentration.[2] The most visible one is the increase in the spirit of association from which the social framework will probably come forth.

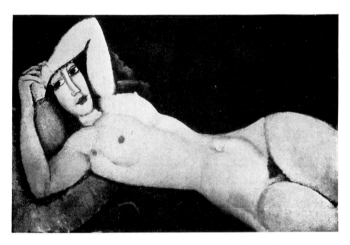

MODIGLIANI. Nude (*Private collection*).

The war is a most cruel one. But also it is perhaps the one which has had most influence in constraining us to look at ourselves, face to face, and to look within ourselves. In reality, it is of rather small importance that a great number of those who feel the universal need for communion should go to ask of dead political systems the secret of the new order. That is a symptom. It is a symptom also, and one of the most impressive, that we see in the insistent effort which Ger-

[1] See Appendix, (*f*), p. 507.   [2] *Ibid.*, (*g*), p. 507

many has been making, for a third of a century, to bring her triple hegemony, military, industrial, and intellectual, into the single frame of an architectural style determined by the will, a style whose simplicity is a pedagogical acquisition which has taken its elements from abstraction and from the past.[1] A symp-

RAOUL DUFY. Houses (*Private collection*).

tom again is that audacity of the Americans in erecting monstrous utilitarian constructions which shatter all known styles, in the brutal rush toward the sky of their metal framework, and in their continual effort to rise higher above the cities. And symptoms, above all, are those rational forms which have issued from applied science, and which gayly thrust into the ruins

[1]*Ibid.*, (*h*), p. 508

all the disordered habits, even though they call themselves the traditional habits, of the art of building.   A

André Derain.   Portrait of Mme. C. (*Private collection*).

great mystery is being wrought. No one knows
whither it is leading us.

Here are the tall chimneys like temple columns, the
living animals of steel, with a heart, intestines, nerves,

eyes, limbs, iron bones articulated like a skeleton, the turning, the sliding, the mathematical coming and going of belts, of pulleys, of connecting rods, and of pistons; here are the rigid roads, shining, and extending, and intersecting to infinity, and the silent round of astronomical cupolas following the movement of the skies; here are the giant halls, and the bare façades of the factories, cathedrals dedicated to the cruel god who knows no other law than that of unbounded production. Here we see the industries of war in agreement with the industries of peace, and, boiling with them in the bloody crucible of the future, the marine monsters of metal, the gigantic insects which fly with their harsh buzzing, the cannons which hurl their drama more than twenty leagues, the armored dragons which crawl like caterpillars, spitting flame and poison. . . . All of that is clear cut, without ornament, trenchant, categorical, and having the purity and the innocence of the function—indifferent to good, to evil, and to morality—of the function which is being born, endowed with an appetite which is fierce, insatiable, and joyous.

AMERICAN ARCHITECTURE

JOSEPH BERNARD. Pomona.

I have finished the History of Art, which is the history of man; I have listened with gratitude to all the voices which, for ten thousand years, man has used in order to speak to me. If the echo of those voices is sometimes heard in these pages, it is because I have loved him as he is and also as he desires to be. I shall die. Men live. I believe in them. Their adventure will come to an end only with the adventure of the earth, and, when the earth is dead, it will perphaps continue elsewhere. It is only a moment of it that I have recounted in this book. But every living moment contains the whole of life. Whoever participates with confidence in the adventure of men has his portion of immortality.

CLODION. Bas-relief.

APPENDIX

(*a*) We know the principle of Neo-Impressionism or Pointillism as it was sketched by Pissarro, developed by Seurat, expounded by Paul Signac in his book, *De Delacroix au Néo-Impressionnisme*, with masterly clearness, and carried to it highest point of decorative expression by Signac himself and by H. E. Cross. Here the question is no longer one of merely separating the tones, as did the Impressionists, who, moreover, often mix them on their palette in order to obtain the effects demanded by nature, but instead, of isolating the touches themselves on the canvas, in order, at a distance, to provoke optical mingling and, by this procedure, to obtain the maximum of purity in coloration and in luminous intensity. This is the final effort of the spirit of analysis, the final expression of political anarchy, a principle scientifically exact and æsthetically dangerous, like all æsthetic principles. The artist takes one of the *means* of painting for the *sole purpose* of painting, and remains the prisoner of a technique which can no longer undergo variations or make progress.

(*b*) I could multiply examples. The most anarchic period, seen in its ensemble and from a distance, is al-

ways a single thing, for it runs in the movement of
life for which the language of man is only a garment,
more or less severe or uniform, or, on the contrary,
shaded, overloaded, multicolored, and hesitating according to the diversity and the number of the needs,
the tastes, and the fashions which contribute to its
formation. No epoch has been richer in artists than
ours. And all are admirable decorators—or would be
if we knew how to utilize their passion. It is not more
difficult to find these tendencies in the fiery sensuality
of Dufrénoy than in the close and solid richness of
Manguin, not more so in the logical and dense construction of painted matter which defines Charles
Guérin, than in the patience of Lebasque when he embroiders his universe with a somewhat loose stitch; the
tendencies are as marked in Jean Puy's constant
striving toward purity of form as in the gift of sudden and complete evocation possessed by Laprade;
as marked in the broad vision of color, a little dull
and uncertain, with Camoin, as in the voluntary
juxtaposition of tones and forms which give to the
landscapes of Friesz both their intellectual and their
chaotic aspect; and as marked, once more, in the
concrete language and the sense of the intimate setting
in the work of Albert André as in the meeting, dear to
Francis Jourdain, of the most appropriate decorative
style with the love of family life. They show quite
as well in Flandrin, passing with a touch of melancholy
from the studied graces of the eclogue to the pampered
graces of the dance, as in Alfred Lombard, who is perhaps too much preoccupied with carrying his sumptuous gifts into the frame of a classicism, about which
opinions may differ, and which is too narrow for him.
The decorative tendencies are as manifest in certain
drawings of Bernard Naudin, trembling and melancholy
like leaves swept by the wind, as in many sketches

by Maxime Dethomas, silent, neutral, and hallucinating, like apparitions, or in all the illustrations of Delaw, large as frescoes, touching as legends, and deep
as the heart. With the productive, abundant, and indefatigable d'Espagnat, they cover earth and heaven
with flowers and would suffice to define the sensuous
optimism which, with Renoir, arose as a reaction from
the naturalistic and romanticist despair. One breathes
them also in the work of René Piot, surrounded by
poisonous perfumes, sumptuous certainly, but vitiated
by reminiscences of Florence, by literary intentions,
and by Byzantine Platonism. One discovers them in
the boldest efforts of the neo-constructors who react
against them, Lhote, Bissière, and Lotiron. With
some of those who claim descent from Cubism or who
have been influenced by it, men like L. A. Moreau,
Le Fauconnier, and Lurçat, they assume a grand aspect, a monumental one, so to speak, which can furnish painting with the most fecund resources. Cor-
neau, Gabriel Fournier, Riou, and Portal hesitate to
give them up. One surprises these tendencies again
among the women painters, in an incipient stage, as
they see things with a certain confusion in which the
form and the backgrounds merge as if in a dark matrix
swelling with heavy heat; thus the decorative appears
in S. van Parys, Charmy, and especially in Louise Hervieu, in whose work it seems so astonished at being
alive and so incredibly innocent, after our ten thousand
years of rottenness and knowledge, and we see it in
Marval, Blanchard, and especially in Marie Laurencin.
One notices that foreign artists escape from it no more
than Frenchmen, if one interrogates the work of van
Dongen, the Hollander, the bestial poet of jewels and
of rouge, and of the profound voice of the flesh where
death and cruelty keep watch in the warm shadows of
the arms and the mouths like carmine wounds; or the

work of Iturrino, the Spaniard, monotonous and subtle, and arid as a dry earth where a few blood-red flowers grow among the stones; or the work of Vlaminck, the Belgian, which seems like burning mud; or that of Paresce, the Italian, sharp, acid, trenchant, pointed, and Florentine, without being aware of it, through the power of atavism; and the essays, at once convulsive and lucid, of the disconcerted Picasso, and the gigantic, ill-formed, and geometrical illuminations which grow out of the earth of Russia, whose images come to us in the confused, driving uproar composed of the sobs of famine and of despair, of the cries from murdered men, of the crackling of machine-guns, and also, doubtless, with the wailing of a new-born world. The Poles— Kisling, Mondzain, and Wittig—would seem, on the contrary, to be in reaction against the decorative tendencies. As to the sculptors, to whom Rodin had opened the way with his "Gate of Hell," almost all are following the decorative tendency—Bourdelle, Maillol, and Joseph Bernard, as we have seen, Halou, Abbal, Marque, Sabouraud, Durio, Hoetger, and Duchamp-Villon who was carried away before his time by the war, were beginning their reaction. Lipchitz continues that effort.

This movement, moreover, is only attaining its critical period, from which will come its expansion if the soil of society is favorable, or else its end. From the beginning of the nineteenth century, indeed, the great decoration, so little understood in the seventeenth century and almost abandoned in the eighteenth to make way for the intimate ornamentation of the bedroom and the boudoir, has tempted all the great painters, beginning with Delacroix. But the true initiator, as Maurice Denis has shown in his book, *Théories*, is Ingres. Directly or indirectly, almost all proceed from him, first his mediocre pupils, Hippolyte

Flandrin, Jeanmot, the good Amaury-Duval, etc., and, at the other end of the movement, Anquetin, who promised so much, and Maurice Denis himself. Puvis de Chavannes, who first based his work on Delacroix, and then, very soon afterward, on Chassériau, certainly felt his influence, and also that of Corot. Mottez was a pupil of Ingres, and it was Ingres who had the younger man's fine portrait of a woman brought to Paris from the Villa Medici, where it was painted on a wall. Through this portrait, Mottez reintroduced into France the Italian fresco, which had been practically forgotten by the Italians themselves, and which, moreover, was perhaps but little suited to the climates of the north. Its resurrection is nevertheless a passionately interesting symptom of our return to architectural, impersonal, collective, and soon anonymous art. In our day, Paul Baudouin, who had not been able to convince his master, Puvis, has, one may say, theoretically and practically recreated fresco, after long years of ardent researches which were crowned by the resurrection, six or eight years ago, of the admirable book of Cennino Cennini. Following this, and sometimes with his advice Maurice Denis, René Piot, J. P. Lafitte (who afterward fell in the war), Dufrénoy, Alfred Lombard, Pierre Girieud, and Bourdelle have undertaken or finished great decorations in the Giottesque method. Once more, this is only a symptom, and perhaps destined to miscarry; but its significance is a moving one. It would be interesting to see what this admirable instrument would bring forth in the hands of decorators such as Bonnard or Vuillard, or Roussel, or Signac, or Valtat, or d'Espagnat, or Albert André, or Friesz, or Laprade, or Dufy, or Dufresne, or Lurçat, for whom, however, tapestry would seem better suited. Lurçat, moreover, has already made some impressive efforts in that direction.

(We may speak here only as a memory, of the innumerable official decorators from Louis Philippe to M. Poincaré. Their productions are no more concerned with painting than school books or works on archæology are with literature. Among them there are good illustrators of history, of whom the most honest appears to have been M. Jean Paul Laurens in France, the best documented being Menzel in Germany, the most picturesque, Verestchagin in Russia, and the most ingenious, Brangwyn in England. There are many illustrators, in painting and in sculpture, whom people take for painters and sculptors. It is a matter of definition. . . . The museum of Versailles is certainly worth a visit, and even several visits. . . . But that is upon condition that one goes there to seek not painting, but history, or rather historical anecdotes. The leading illustrator of history is Daniel Vierge, the Spaniard, who was sometimes incomparable in his fire, his horror, mystery, and evocative violence, and whose compositions have the advantage of not encumbering the walls. While English and American illustrators are so numerous and so intelligent, in France the illustrators have almost disappeared, since the delightful masters of the eighteenth century, Eisen, the Saint-Aubins, Moreau the younger, Gravelot, and Prud'hon. However, there were Raffet, sometimes Charlet and Tony Johannot, and the pompousness of Doré cannot make us forget the fantastic magic of some of his plates. The romanticist reign of history having come to an end, certain of our contemporaries have attempted to animate the margins of novels and of poems—Bonnard, who brings to the task his fanciful freedom and his insinuating poetry, Laprade, Maurice Denis, Louise Hervieu, Naudin, Segonzac, and the admirable Delaw, the entertainer of innocent little children and of cultivated grown persons. The resurrection of wood engraving tends, moreover, to renew illustration.)

(c) Italian *Futurism* is only a systematization of these tendencies, and an anti-plastic one, at that.

(d) *Cubism* is only an artificial stylization of form, basing itself on a wrong understanding of the saying of Cézanne to which I made allusion above, and which had no other pretension than that of symbolizing his thought. Independent of its pretensions to restore form in a block, in all its dimensions, and without taking account of the reflections, it is the extreme of synthesis following upon the extreme analysis of the Neo-Impressionists. Like all systems, it can afford discipline for the painters. Dunoyer de Segonzac, Ozenfant, Lhote, L. A. Moreau, de la Fresnaye, Boussingault, le Fauconnier, and Metzinger became painters by going through or by skirting Cubism. Braque, Léger, and Juan Gris remain painters in spite of it, and Picasso, who was a painter before founding it, becomes one again as he leaves it. And all, having come to it in order the better to obey Cézanne, will detach themselves from it, thanks to him.

(e) The art of the portrait has perhaps constituted the most permanent strength of the French School— and I say "School" for lack of a better word. This art has known scarcely any decline for seven centuries. All the Gothic image-makers were admirable observers of the human face. Through the sculptors of the tombs, they reach out their hand to the painters of the Renaissance, Froment d'Avignon, Foucquet, Jean Perréal, Malouel, the anonymous men of the fifteenth and sixteenth centuries, the Clouets, and Corneille de Lyon, so penetrating, so sober, so mischievously candid, pointed, and clear cut, like the intelligence which char-

acterizes and dissects, without thought of the social
station, of the function, and of the tastes of those
whom it examines, and who do not yet think of striking
attitudes before it.   In the seventeenth century, when
Lagneau and Demonstier introduced their science, the
psychological power of the old French masters enters
the architectural frame of method with Poussin, Claude
Lefebvre, Sébastien Bourdon, Le Brun, and Coyzevox.
Thenceforward, the portrait assumes a density and a
mass which, together with the whole spirit of the time,
constitute the imposing block of the classic period, in
which the resemblance and the savor of the object are
even more striking, for anyone who can appreciate
them, than the majestic order of the language which
describes it.   Rigaud, Largillière, and the Coustous
cause the structural science of the great century to
pass insensibly into those astonishing effigies of conversationalists, of artists, of philosophers, of abbés of
the bedroom and the court, of favorites, and of ladies
of fashion, through which La Tour, Drouais, Perronneau, Houdon, Greuze, Pajou, and Liotard of Geneva
smilingly place upon the slope of the abyss which is
opening, an aristocracy fatigued by its excess of mind.
David prevents the psychological acuteness of the artists from wrecking itself amid fashionable fluency,
and at the threshold of the nineteenth century, powerfully re-establishes, through his innumerable pupils,
the compromised solidity of the portrait.   After that,
Ingres will need only to confide to this framework the
plenitude of his sensual vision in order to transmit to
the naturalistic generation the tradition of the old
Frenchmen.

The nineteenth century, like all the great epochs—
and it is, beyond all doubt, the greatest epoch in our
painting—saw in the portrait only one of the multiple
aspects of the life to be expressed, and its masters,

Delacroix, Rude, Millet, Courbet, and especially Corot and Carpeaux, have done no more therein than follow, with a grand ease, the practice of the heroes, Raphael, Titian, Tintoretto, Rubens, Rembrandt, Velasquez, and Goya. From the fact that there are few "portrait-painters," although Ingres is one above all else, although a lesser but honorable painter, Fantin-Latour, is scarcely anything else, although certain startling medallions are all that save from oblivion the name of David d'Angers, although Rodin wrested from matter the most profound accents of the human face, although Cézanne discovered the firmest planes of its structure, and Degas the sharpest lines of its intellectual construction, one must not conclude that the nineteenth century is poorer in portraits than another. It has too many, and they are too close as "likenesses," which means, perhaps, that they might be closer. They swarm, from the gracious effigies of Baron Gérard to the honest photographs of M. Bonnat, from Winterhalter's puppets all dressed up in new clothes to the few pictures of bourgeois elegance painted by M. Carolus-Duran in his youth, and from the faces of Prud'hon, emerging from amorous shadow, to those of Ricard, which are a little bit lost in it, and to those of Carrière, which sometimes accumulate too much of it in their hollows in order thereby to make the projections stand out. In our day, it is doubtless Vuillard who represents the psychological tradition of the French portrait with the finest mind, and Mahn who represents it most faithfully. Moreover, the portrait, like the other plastic expressions, is undergoing the influence of the impressionistic and musical current and that of the architectural comment which, together, are destined to give to our epoch the accent which it will have for the future: Bonnard, like Vuillard, causes to circle around it his fugitive colorations, the shadows,

.the shadings, the reflections, and the murmurs; Vallotton works at it like a mason, with a morose obstinacy; Matisse brings it back, in its essentials, to decorative lines and tones; and Charles Pequin constructs it, like his landscapes and his still-lifes, with the purities and the sonorities of the violoncello, and with a feeling for the definitive significance of the face that is before him.

Outside of France, it appears to be especially in the art of the portrait that the English and the Americans have expended their superficial skill, with broad and creamy tones, in big, liquid brush-strokes, falsely robust and frank, of which Sargent is past master and which Whistler rebukes—happily for his memory—by causing to hover about his mysterious effigies the vague music of the half-tints and of the subtle arrangements of rare notes and shaded passages. The close resemblance of the faces, at once hollow and massive, of the Prussian Lenbach does not succeed in hiding his constant and meticulous padding out of his ostensible power. Zuloaga and La Gandara, the Spaniards, and Boldini, the Italian, vocalize and guitarrize—with their strength composed of theatrical make-up or with their grimacing impotence, and produce a fashionable art, which will leave strange psychological documents, less related to its models than to its authors. Evenepoel, the Belgian, who died too young, would doubtless have lived up to his promise. But we must wait for the profound effect of French painting in the nineteenth century, and of Cézanne and Renoir above all, on men of a strong and sincere nature. It is already manifest and salutary, as regards the art of the portrait, in the case of certain foreign artists among whom Rivera, the Mexican, seems to me the most interesting, at once because of his preoccupation with the architectural understructure and the turning volumes, wherein the double influence of the two French masters persists, and because of something unexpected, surprised, and phantomlike which makes clear his Spanish antecedents, manifested under the auspices of Goya and of Zurbarán.

(*f*) I fear that the multiplication of talents which we are witnessing to-day marks the end of the great French school of the nineteenth century. Painting and sculpture, moreover, are perhaps condemned to disappear in their present form and destination. The complexity of the soul and of the means of man increases from day to day. Who can foresee the destiny of an instrument like the cinematograph, for example? As symphonic painting succeeded melodic painting in flat tones, one may form an idea of a kind of cinematographic symphony succeeding the immobile symphony realized by the Venetians, the Hollanders, the Spaniards, and the French. Can one imagine the power of lyric exaltation which might be given to the mind by a succession of colored images painted by a Michael Angelo, or a Tintoretto, or a Rubens, or a Rembrandt, or a Goya, or a Delacroix, and precipitated into the drama of movement and of time by a registering apparatus?

(*g*) One of the most impressive testimonies to the disquietude of the artists, and to their need for drawing together and for understanding, is their disposition to write on their art and on the permanent or present tendencies of their art. This is common to all the artists of periods when systems change decisively—to the Italian universalists, the French, English, and German artists of the end of the eighteenth century, and to the passage from romanticism and materialism to the orientations of to-day. From Delacroix himself, and from Fromentin—even from Courbet!—to

Rodin, to Carrière, and to Redon, there are few who have not yielded to the need to expound their intentions or those of the others. Mention must be made, in our day, of Louise Hervieu, Maurice Denis, Emile Bernard, Bourdelle, Matisse, Signac, d'Espagnat, Albert André, Ozenfant, Jeanneret, Gleizes, Metzinger, Bissière, Lhote, and especially J. E. Blanche, as writers on art of great distinction.

(*h*) Notably the elements of the perpendicular style, borrowed in greater part from the palaces of the Achemenides and from the Gothic style of southern France, the Palace of the Popes at Avignon, for example.

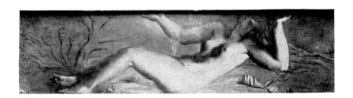

CHASSÉRIAU.

HENRI ROUSSEAU. The Bridge (*Private collection*).

ALPHABETICAL INDEX

OF THE NAMES MENTIONED IN THIS VOLUME[1]

[1] The names of the artists especially treated in the text are in italics.

SYNOPTIC TABLES